# IDEAS AND PLACES

To *L.L.*

# IDEAS

### AND

# PLACES

### BY

## CYRIL CONNOLLY

*. . . et nous errions, nourris du vin des Palermes et du biscuit de la route, moi pressé de trouver le lieu et la formule.*

RIMBAUD

*NEW YORK*

HARPER & BROTHERS

PUBLISHERS

*First published* 1953

ACKNOWLEDGEMENTS

My thanks are due to *Art News* and *World Review*, *Go*, *The Geographical Magazine*, *Partisan Review*, *The New Statesman*, *The Times Literary Supplement* and the *Listener* for permission to reprint the articles on Surrealism, Reputations, Bordeaux, the Dordogne, London Letter, Logan Pearsall Smith and Propertius. Everything else is from *Horizon* and I should like to express my gratitude to Mr. Peter Watson for permission to reprint from it and my great indebtedness to those who answered our questionnaire, 'The Cost of Letters', for material which is now in my opinion even more implosive than when it was written.

PRINTED AT THE CURWEN PRESS, PLAISTOW
MANUFACTURED IN GREAT BRITAIN

# CONTENTS

vi CONTENTS

# INTRODUCTION

'IT was a time of promise, a renewal of the world and of letters . . .' How many young critics have set off, like Hazlitt, to greet the dawn only to find themselves walking backwards into the sunset! Fortunate is the writer who, before he is fifty, discovers that his marvellous generation is the bull, not the matador; that it has nothing new to say and no new way of saying it. He has still a few years left in which to make a fresh start, to seek out his minute speck of originality, his *petit pan de mur jaune*. Ignorant, empty, liberated, he should excite envy rather than pity in his last quest for some unimaginable texture.

But the process of disillusion is painful, especially when the instrument of greeting has been nourished on youth and hope and when the end of a long war seemed to make 'a renewal of the world and of letters' a real possibility. 'A magazine should be the reflection of its time and when it ceases to reflect this, should come to an end' announced the first number of *Horizon* in 1939, and at first sight there might seem nothing more to be added. But since no successor has arrived in the last three years to take our place, even the ravings of the editorials in our last illness seem to be coming true. Are not the times themselves to blame? For *Horizon* was no ordinary failure, there were several years when solvency reared its ugly head and we sank, gracefully, by the stern with the band playing to a circulation of nearly nine thousand. Given the present vacuum, to reprint some of these old controversies may not prove irrelevant.

And there is another good reason. *Horizon* happened to live through some memorable days and, when these editorials are put together, they tell their sad story with coherence and clarity. The parish pump served no inconsiderable community, it bubbled up again in New York and the liberated St. Germain des Prés, while a great statesman, Count Sforza, mourned its last gurgle and *Pravda* rejoiced. The narrow obsessional nature of these policies seemed part of their strength, and even now may exercise a spell. To preserve continuity I have included material which may seem ephemeral and tedious on account of its minute historical significance in describing changes of opinion as they actually took place— from the first flush of victory to the growth of doubt—a monthly chronicle of literature under a losing peace.

We begin with D-Day and the optimism with which we hailed victory and greeted the bright, false dawn. A visit to liberated Paris in January 1945 leads to a joyous honeymoon with the Intellectuals of the French Resistance. 'Hommage to Switzerland' describes the first holiday abroad (summer 1945) and even at home there is a honeymoon with the new Labour government. Magazines pullulate, but all is not well, and so next year we begin to tackle the predicament of writers in 'The Cost of Letters' and to analyse the phenomenon which we christened 'Inflationary Decadence'. Our honeymoon with Russia is abruptly terminated by the publication of the treatment meted out to the Leningrad magazines. A few months later 'the Nizan case' describes a similar experience among the French writers who become embroiled with their Communist colleagues. It was a year of faint hand-clasps and darkling Utopias. The philistine attitude of the Labour government to culture and the continuing restrictions on the import of books provided another disappointment and by Christmas 1947 our position had become openly anti-bureaucratic and apolitical.

After a bracing interlude in America the editorials grow more and more preoccupied with the sickness of the Fisher King, the soul of contemporary literature. I must apologize for a certain monotony, a screeching note in these later comments.

Sometimes I wondered if I was imagining the predicament, if bile or teeth or liver were dictating their wishes or whether I was trying to externalize a guilty sterility on to the world and was painting a picture as plausible and unreal as a paranoiac's persecution fantasy—'Our unavailing championship of the living sheep against their dying slaughterers, of the artist against society and the people against the State'. Did such distinctions really exist outside my own mind? I seemed to be raising up dummies in order to transfix them with a toy sword which penetrated only myself. 'The wounded surgeon plies the steel . . .'

On looking back, I think that perhaps I was a little crazy and that the idea of decadence hugged and haunted me as if I were some Hebrew prophet; gangrene was spreading while I was powerless as a fly waving and buzzing among its silent comrades on the poisoned paper. And then at Christmas 1949 the magazine did stop. That much was not a cancer of the soul or a disease of the imagination. We closed the long windows over Bedford Square, the telephone was taken, the furniture stored, the back numbers went to their cellar, the files rotted in the dust. Only contributions continued inexorably to be delivered, like a suicide's milk, and keep on coming.

The true cause of the failure of private periodicals is the constriction of free trade and free thought generated by the Cold War—that is why such failures know no frontiers. But in our case London may have had something to do with it. Without doubt the most depressing capital of the post-war period, like Vienna after 1918, it is thoroughly toxic. In the country we have our ups and downs, but I no longer feel that I am behaving in some desperate way outside my control, like a reveller who suddenly catches sight of his face in a glass—haggard and stubbled under his tinsel hat. Of course, the 'cultural melancholia' of which I have been accused was somehow connected with editing; for the profession, though delightful, is in the long run unwholesome for an author. An editor, even one who writes, is not an artist; however numerous his friends, he feeds an enemy within.

I have reprinted a recent article on Surrealism because it is the kind of sustained constructive criticism for which I never could quite find the time or the energy when an editor—a hope for the future. It is only too clear that the 'places' have compensated me for the 'ideas', the glimpses of Paris, Switzerland, America, Bordeaux and the Dordogne show that Baedeker is still the antidote to Baudelaire. The pieces on Logan Pearsall Smith recall another dear ornament of the period, the oldest patron of *Horizon*, even as some of the contributors to 'The Cost of Letters' were the youngest. Auden's poem, 'The Fall of Rome' (which he dedicated to me) seemed to divine our illness and Dr. Zanotti Bianco's letter about Sybaris I still consider the most important suggestion *Horizon* ever published. The piece on 'Reputations' is an extension, in simpler language, of my obsession with *tout ce qui se résumait en ce mot: chute* and the final talk on Propertius a reminder of the permanence of all art that is both beautiful and intelligent.

When an *Horizon* anthology is published as a companion volume I hope it will produce an unexpected exhilaration and contain only what is profound, fresh, crisp, coloured and invigorating. Old Polycarp tearing his beard and bewailing the age from the iron balcony overlooking the plane-trees will find no place there. So bear with this corncrake music, reader; plunge into the immediate past; join the confabulation round the drying pump; try to follow these defunct and angry controversies of the day before yesterday, and if you cannot follow, skip. *Brevis hic est fructus homullis!*

CYRIL CONNOLLY

# IDEAS AND PLACES

## D-DAY

THIS number of *Horizon* appears during one of the decisive battles of the world's history, a battle which may remove for ever that scourge of Europe which has destroyed as much happiness as smallpox or syphilis, the German will to power. No people can sustain more than three or four attempts at world domination, and it is probable that in the next century the German menace to the world will seem to our grandchildren quite insubstantial. But for our world it has been terribly real; Bismarck, the Kaiser and Hitler have made three generations of Europeans miserable. That curse of the German temperament, their mass inferiority complex, the fear of freedom which leads them to welcome servitude for themselves that they may the better enforce it on others, has retarded all human progress, and three times in seventy years has thrown the world back into savagery. Now at last the stranglehold of all that is greedy, brutal, fearful and stupid in one country is about to be broken and its crimes against the human spirit to be avenged. It is a moment when every civilian forgets the past months of anxiety, impatience and boredom and can think only of the present operations and of the men who are risking their lives in them. Every word in fifty numbers of *Horizon* has gone uncensored, every idea and opinion unrebuked, because these men have fought for our liberties in what is still the freest country in Europe.

At the beginning of the war our relations with the armed forces were very close, gradually they have drifted. For as their new careers take hold we have received fewer and fewer contributions from them which are up to our standard, while in consequence we have ourselves become something of a back-water. Now in this crucial summer of the twentieth century our common hope has reunited us. At last the mists are going to lift, the ten-year nightmare perish; Himmler's fat handshake, Hitler's putty face 'like a dirty plate' will survive only in wax-works; once again, as at Salamis, the peoples who value liberty are about to bring down ruin on those who have despised it: we shall return to Europe to draw strength from the continent we have set free until the full tide of our Western civilization flows back over the scattered dried-up rockpools that every nation has become, to set them all breathing and moving again in the cool element of which they have so long been deprived.

*June* 1944

## LETTER FROM A CIVILIAN

DEAR VICTOR,

Yes, I got the Camemberts; they were not quite ripe, and inferior to the pre-war standard. I am not going to thank you for them. I am completely exhausted with thanking you and replying to your many letters, letters which always end 'It must be awful in London, but keep on with *Horizon*, it helps me to retain my sanity'. Well, it hasn't helped me to retain mine, so I am going to tell you exactly what I think of you. Even a civilian will turn, and, let me tell you, we civilians are ripe for mutiny.

I have first turned up some of your old letters.

1939–40. You were in France then if you remember—champagne—phoney war—Paris—Maurice Chevalier singing a funny song, Ironside and Gamelin firm on the Maginot Line. You managed to go to all my favourite restaurants in Paris, and then you fought your way back to Dunkirk. We lunched the day of your return; you were a bit shaken; the sniping, the

fifth-column, the bombing on the beach had upset you. 'I
almost thought the Party was over,' were your words—but you
were a far happier person than I, even then. That soft spotlight of History which was to hold you in its steady glow
through all the years to follow already illumined your cheerful,
sun-burnt features. Of course the Party wasn't over, and while
I had nightmares of the Gestapo and was arrested by some of
your friends for wearing a beard, you went off, fortunate as
usual, to the Middle East. There you raced through to Benghazi
and back, while we pushed our way through broken glass and
craters in the black-out, and lay awake through those nights of
the Blitz in our huge dentist's waiting-room. That was a nice
letter of yours about Syria, the quails and wild strawberries, the
bathing at Beirut, the ski-ing and the ruins—quite poetic—and
the descriptions of social life in Cairo during the 'Flap' were
unexpectedly satirical. You certainly can write, Victor, should
History ever condescend to release you for such a contemptible
occupation. Then came El Alamein; no letters for a bit, but a
Mention in Despatches, and then long accounts of Derna and
Tobruk, of 'sand-happy' delusions, of the configuration of
dunes, the flora of oases. You knew I would be interested to
hear how bananas grew in Derna, and how as always, 'the men
are wonderful'. Those wonderful men who seem, like you, to
have but one aim, to get out of History's spotlight and go back
to 1939. One cannot measure boredom in terms of time, but
the period while you were trekking from Cairo to Carthage
corresponded to the blackest phase in the dark night of what
was left of the civilian's soul. Sometime in that long year
Middle-age angrily flung youth's last belongings out of the
room that for the next fifteen years it was going to occupy.
Locks of hair, teeth, kisses, memories and hopes; all perished
during those slow months when the scurf thickened on our
collars and the bald patch shone like a rubber stamp, while
the daily walk from flat to office and back, past the second-hand

Oriental bookshops, and the bleak Ministry, insensibly became the dumb *rond des prisonniers*.

Just as it seemed that the desert had made you an ascetic and a mystic, your practical little girl-friend—for that is what your tank had become—picked you up and carried you out of harm's way to the flesh-pots of Tunis. Of course all this time you had to fight. Don't think I am unaware of all this fighting, it is just that which churns the guilt round and round till it curdles into a kind of rancorous despair. You are always fighting for me, in the favoured places of the world, and writing me your friendly unpatronizing letters which I have to answer. Oh, why can't I fight for myself?

Your next letter came from Sicily, whence you wrote to tell me of what was damaged—and what was not damaged—of Segesta and Girgenti, Palermo and Cefalu. Oh yes, and that week's leave you snatched at Capri—how very, very kind to describe that—and Anzio, where the men were more wonderful than ever. . . . That was the time of the winter-spring Blitz in London; fire-bombs fell everywhere. Some fell on the restaurant where I was dining and set fire to my good winter-overcoat. I was eleventh away from the blaze in the chain of bucket-passers! It was then that you got angry with me for the only time, when I wrote against the bombing of Cassino. 'There are just two things in the world I live for', you replied to me—from the beach-head, of course—'Literature and killing Germans, and I should have thought you with your anti-fascist record would understand how impossible the one is without the other.'

When you did return to London you were appalled by its shabbiness and expense, its dirt and vulgarity: and its carious houses, the contraceptives in the squares, the puddles of urine in the telephone boxes, the sulphurous wines and goat-stew in the restaurants, the bored, pale, ferrety people milling round the streets, fighting and rutting and crawling over the badly dressed prostitutes like bees round their queen. This was one of your rare glimpses, not of History, but of Reality; there was a puzzled look under the sunburn and the medals, but it was soon gone, for you went off to train in the Highlands of Scotland, and it was not until the eve of D-Day that you reappeared. It was at our last meal together that, after discussing my piles and my eczema and the horrors of the Museum Exchange, you said the most unforgivable thing of all. We had a bottle of champagne—we always celebrate in this way at your expense; besides it takes champagne to raise me to subnormal. Suddenly you leant your intelligent, modest face across the table: 'The one thing I am really grateful for is that in 1939 I was young enough, *just* young enough, mark you (with a look at me), to fight this bloody war with my body and not with my mind.' I could have slapped your face. I could have slapped so many people's faces and I never have. That's why I am a civilian. Well, we 'had' the champagne, and a week later your Camemberts started coming—and the Flying Bombs. I know one is not supposed to say so, but I don't care for flying bombs: to all guilty people (and by now all civilians are guilty), they are the final appointment in the dentist's chair, and, casualties apart, they have made London more dirty, more unsociable, more plague-stricken than ever. The civilians who remain grow more and more hunted and disagreeable, each sweating and palpitating like a toad under his particular stone. Social life is nonexistent, and those few and petty amenities which are the salt of civilian life—friendship, manners, conversation, mutual esteem—seem now extinct for ever. Never in the whole war has the lot of the civilian been more abject, or his status so low—he is the unpopular schoolboy in the keen, tough school whose fees are ten shillings in the pound, with no one who will take him in for the holidays.

Meanwhile, what about you, Victor? Fighting as usual, making history, drinking calvados—'you find France very little changed', 'you are billeted in a château whose salon contains a first collected edition of Voltaire', 'your tank goes faster than ever and now sprays flames in all directions'; 'you are delighted to see the French reviving in the liberated towns, and all the ugly marks of fear departing, but you are embarrassed by the head-shaving'—you have won a Mercedes-Benz and a D.S.O. on the field—and now you are back in all my favourite restaurants again. I die by inches: you live in a continuous exaltation, drunk with health and action, and rewarded for it by your grateful country. When the war is over you will be ten years younger than you were when it started, and I shall be twenty years older: past love, past lust, past exercise and past ambition—but not quite—for I still have one more which goes very deep—to possess enough moral courage, after the war, to be a bum.

So no more Camemberts please, and shroud your future movements on French soil in military secrecy. You may liberate Europe, but you cannot liberate me. And when the Party really is over and you come home and marry your Tank, don't send a wedding invitation, for he will have gone underground, to your bald, bitter, shabby old playmate.

—CIVILIAN.

*September* 1944

## HALF WAY

WITH this number *Horizon* completes its fifth year; it has survived five years of boredom and destruction—of the general deterioration of humanity—and seen the whole world move noisily into the Dehydra-headed Utility epoch. By now we should have a policy: we have. Accused of 'aestheticism', 'escapism', 'ivory-towerism', 'bourgeois formalism', 'frivolity' and 'preferring art to life' we plead on all these counts 'guilty and proud of it'. If *Horizon* regrets anything it is that we have published too much journalism and too many non-literary contributions in the past, but, believing that the end of life is art, we also believe that there is no art without life and that the artist must keep abreast with the scientific discoveries and political theories which may be of use to him and must undergo with a good grace experiences which he feels may prove constructive. *Horizon*'s first five years have witnessed a decline in all the arts, together with a belated recognition by the State of their importance. The State now sits by the bedside of literature like a policeman watching for a would-be suicide to recover consciousness, who will do anything for the patient except allow him the leisure, privacy and freedom from which art is produced. Books are becoming as bad as they are ugly; newspapers continue to be as dull with four pages as they were once with forty; reviewing has sunk to polite blurb-quoting; nothing original is produced; journalists grow sloppier, vainer, more ignorantly omniscient than ever; the B.B.C. pumps religion and patriotism into all its programmes; mediocrity triumphs, and ministries with their paste-and-scissor periodicals pour into Europe their selections from the few restricted magazines which are still able to dig up a little new material. 'Censorship of policy': 'cultural relations': 'no cultural relations without censorship of policy'! These are the slogans of the Nine Years' War.

It is apparent from Philip Toynbee's article in the November issue that a different state of affairs exists in France. In England writers have been exhausted by total war. Although it is Hitler who is responsible for this exhaustion, it is the State which appears as their enemy, for it is the State which continues to drain them by demanding new efforts. Consequently the attitude of our most valuable writers becomes one of anarchist passive resistance. In France there was no total war, but the Germans were directly in command. Instead of the State becoming the enemy (for Vichy was too weak for that) there was a military tyranny to be opposed. The attitude of writers therefore was not one of anarchic sulking but of fraternal conspiracy against the oppressor. And in the case of most writers their leisure and privacy were not interfered with. The French writers are still fighting an ideological war, they have retained the freshness found among English writers during the Spanish crisis, they have been hungry, but they have not been worn out by long hours, air-raids and propaganda work. We on the other hand who have neither starved nor been tortured, have never had our liberation, our moment of glory. As French politics become more externalized it may well turn out that the French writers will begin to suffer from the same ailments as our own and will come to understand why such a book as David Gascoyne's Poems remains for some of us one of the best since the war, why Edith Sitwell's *Poets' Note-book*, Bowra's *Post-Symbolists*, or the last novels of Maugham and Rosamund Lehmann appeal through being uncontemporary.

Every European war is a war lost by Europe; a war lost by Europe is a war lost by England; a war lost by England leaves the world poorer. This is the lesson we have to learn, and the only remedy is to strengthen Europe by action constructive in inverse proportion to the damage which has been done. Such action must lead to a European Federation—not a nominal federation, but a Europe without passports—a cultural entity where everyone is free to go where they like, say what they like, do what they like and pay how they like. If Europe cannot exchange economic nationalism for international regionalism it will perish as the Greek City States perished, in a fizzle of mutual hate and distrust under the heel of an invader. As Right Wing governments are always Nationalist this European federation can only be brought about by the Left—by a European Front Populaire which is determined to be strong and also to avoid a Third World War. *Horizon* will support with all the force of its rubber dagger any government which helps art and literature, but since all governments are equally philistine (for all Politicians worship power, and power excludes art) our role is much more likely to be in opposition to whatever government is in power in the interests of literature and art. We therefore celebrate the completion of our first lustre by wishing a merry Christmas to those in all countries who love literature for its own sake, to the secret members of the republic of letters, a republic without nationalism, without territory, without ambition. Most of its members are to be found in the United States, where such magazines as *Partisan Review*, now an admirable literary quarterly, represent it, and in France; but they must exist all over Europe, and also in Russia, and eventually we may reach a standard of civilization where they can all again communicate, and communicate through the enjoyment of masterpieces and not by the blowing of nationalist trumpets, by the improvement of cultural relations through the dissemination of bone-head attachés, the wiring of stuffed artists for sound, the blah and blare of broadcasting and journalism, or the murmurs of 'censorship of policy'.

*December* 1944

## ALMOND BLOSSOM

'Now that an element of fluidity has entered into the tactical situation, giving grounds'—writes the military critic—'for a reasoned optimism,' we press for an extension of this fluidity to the world of culture. Outside it is spring, and all over the world a host of 'little magazines' are putting forth their blooms, all deprived by their governments of any opportunity for cross-fertilization. In Italy there are *Aretusa* and *Mercurio*, in Switzerland *Formes et Couleurs* and *Labyrinthe*, in France *Poésies 45*, *Confluences*, *Esprit*, *L'Arbalète*, *L'Eternelle Revue*, *Le Spectateur des Arts*, *Messages*, *Cahiers du Sud*, not to mention the English number of *Fontaine*, which would do credit to any English publication. In North Africa there is *L'Arche*, in Sweden the admirable literary monthly *Nu*, in Cairo there is *Personal Landscape*, in the U.S.A. *Partisan Review*, *Accent*, *Chimaera*, *Kenyon Review*, *Sewanee Review*, *View*, *Triple V*, *The Vedanta of the West*, *Poetry*, *Hemispheres*, to name but a few; in Australia there is *Angry Penguins*, in the Argentine *Sur* and *Lettres Françaises*, and the world over there must be many hundreds more. Yet I doubt if any reader of *Horizon* can claim to have set eyes on more than half a dozen of these since the war, and many will not even have heard of them, and we are most grateful to anyone who can send a copy here.

The little magazine performs three very important functions. It helps to unite young writers into groups who discover common aims, and who can seek out their counterparts in other countries; it enables older writers to keep the public informed of their interim work (as by the publication of Joyce's 'Ulysses' in *Little Review* or his 'Work in Progress' in *Transition*); and it presents experimental or controversial work by writers who need encouragement and who are as yet incapable of producing a book. When one takes into account as well the time element, the reviews, obituaries and notes of the day, it is obvious that the number and variety of such magazines constitute a valuable indication of the cultural health of a country. They have five enemies, or wicked godmothers: Censorship, Paper Rationing, Currency Regulations, Shipping Space, and Labour Troubles. Censorship is not yet an oppressive feature to a writer in this country; he is not aware of it unless he is an anarchist, a Trotskyite, a book reviewer, a member of the Civil Service or the armed forces or a talker on the B.B.C. Paper rationing is particularly severe on little magazines, for the extra thousand copies which they are not allowed to print may make all the difference to their solvency and continued publication. Currency regulations explain why none of us has been able to read a single book review of Edmund Wilson's in the *New*

*Yorker* since he took the job, and shipping space why the French have not yet been able to read any of ours. Labour troubles account for enormous gaps between one number and the next, or for paper covers which come off. Nevertheless, miscellanies continue to be born. *Orion*, a constellation in which every star was lambent, burst from its swaddling clouds and zoomed across the sky, and now *Polemic* is stripping for the arena.

What we need is an immediate loosening up of the restrictions which affect the sale and interchange of magazines throughout the world, with the licence to import, export and distribute one another; and an incessant agitation from all the magazines involved, in all their languages against all their various authorities, with the help of all their numerous well-wishers to promote an orgy, a *sacre du printemps*, of exchange and insemination, and so make free for those who need it the penicillin of the Western Mind.

*April* 1945

# PARADISE REGAINED

'OR l'heure actuelle comporte cette question capitale : l'Europe va-t-elle garder sa prééminence dans tous les genres?

'L'Europe deviendra-t-elle ce qu'elle *est en réalité*, c'est-à-dire : un petit cap du continent asiatique? Ou bien l'Europe restera-t-elle *ce qu'elle parait*, c'est-à-dire : la partie précieuse de l'univers terrestre, la perle de la sphère, le cerveau d'un vaste corps?'

PAUL VALÉRY: *La Crise de l'Esprit*. 1919.

There have been three 'literatures' in France since the war. (1) The literature of collaboration (Giono, Céline, Montherlant, Drieu, etc.). (2) The literature of occupation—that is of those researches into the human spirit, the meaning of words,

myths and symbols, the fate of man at a level sufficiently deep
to evade the political censorship—such are the writings of
Sartre, Camus, Paulhan, Ponge, Valéry, Blanchot, Brice-
Parrain, Queneau, Michaux and most of the poetry of 1940–4,
and lastly the literature of resistance—literature of indignation
and revolt which can only be published clandestinely and
which has a political end in view—such are the brochures of
the *Editions de Minuit*, *Lettres Françaises*, *l'Eternelle Revue*
and the poems of Aragon, Emmanuel, Eluard.

In Paris now no one reads the collaborators. The literature
of the occupation, however, is widely commented on and
discussed, while the literature of the Resistance, which had of
necessity been unduly inflated, is now finding its proper level.
These distinctions are not absolute, for nearly all the 'occupation' writers were also in the resistance movement. One might
say that Aragon and Eluard remain 'Resistance' writers, and
continue to fight the battle (which for them has become the
policy of the Communist Party), so—but not as Communists—
do Camus, Vercors and Debû-Bridel.

When I went to Paris in January, these groups were just
beginning to confront each other. The heavy snow and the
emptiness made the city resemble Vienna or Petrograd, it was
so unlike the Paris of 1939, or the Paris of the Liberation, as
to awaken no nostalgic memories or civic exaltation, and yet
the visit made me indescribably happy. London seemed
utterly remote—a grey, sick wilderness on another planet, for
in Paris the civilian virtues triumph—personal relations, adult-
minded seriousness, aliveness, love of the arts. Literature is
enormously important there and one sees how pervasive,
though impalpable, have become the irritable lassitude, brain-
fatigue, apathy and humdrummery of English writers. At that
time the presence of the Germans could still be felt; in the café
chair where one sat they had sat not so long before. The three
familiar waiters of the Flore (the same as in 1939) had tales to

tell of them. There were even people who wanted them back. We were taken to see one of the worst of their torture chambers, the shooting gallery at Issy, a closed shed where not one survivor had been found to explain the meaning of the in- numerable impressions of hands on the asbestos walls, or the huge furnace for blowing in hot air—only the bullet-torn posts at the end with their blood-stained rags attached to them told a clear story. The sensation of utter evil and misery which emanates from these human abattoirs—as from the dungeons of the Montjuig in Barcelona—still impresses on the visitor something of the ghastly atmosphere of occupied Paris—and those sinister streets, the Rue des Saussaies, du Cherche-midi, de Lauriston, where the Gestapo had their late headquarters.

It is by bearing such an impression in mind that one can best appreciate the literature of the Resistance, and the wonderful courage and resource of those who wrote, printed, and distri- buted its flaming broadsheets. Some of these are outstanding. There is Jean Tardieu's beautiful lament on Oradour which begins:

> Oradour n'a plus de femmes
> Oradour n'a plus un homme
> Oradour n'a plus de feuilles
> Oradour n'a plus de pierres
> Oradour n'a plus d'église
> Oradour n'a plus d'enfants
> Plus de fumée plus de rires
> plus de toits plus de greniers
> plus de meules plus d'amour
> plus de vin plus de chansons . . .

Then there are Cassou's sonnets written in prison at Toulouse (where Malraux was also interned and where his resistance manuscripts were destroyed). There are accounts of the horrible effects of imprisonment (Cévennes, *Dans la prison*,

Minervois, *Le temps mort*, an account by Claude Aveline of a woman's life in prison), and *La vie des Martyrs*, the appalling document issued by the doctors in the Resistance movement, 'pathologie des prisons allemandes en France', which gives a bald and scientific account of the commonest illnesses, disabilities mental and physical, and grave disorders which follow on imprisonment, starvation, and the various kinds of torture inflicted by the Gestapo and Vichy police on their victims.

The finest words on the movement, apart from the poems of Eluard and Aragon, are perhaps the conclusion of Paulhan's little essay, *L'Abeille*. 'When I was a child,' he writes, 'I was surprised, like all children, to find so many more deaths than births chronicled in the newspapers. (The explanation—which comes to one later—is obviously that it is rare, except for kings, to be very well known at birth, while for a famous man there is nothing left but to die.) I had also the feeling that all that was going to change, the world was for the new-born, and we would all die much less.

'It was an absurd sentiment yet I think a common one, and it renders more bitter the tragedy of an age when we learn every month of the death of a friend. One was in the Maquis, his body, already swollen, has been found in a field. Another wrote pamphlets, another delivered messages. They were riddled with bullets while they sang. Others before their death underwent tortures more horrible than the sufferings of cancer or lock-jaw.

'And I know there are people who say they died for very little. A single piece of information (not always very accurate) wasn't worth that—nor a pamphlet, nor an underground newspaper even, not always very well edited. To those we must make reply: "It's because they were on the side of Life. It is because they loved things as insignificant as a song, a flip of the finger, a smile. You can squeeze a bee in your hand till it suffocates. You will be stung before it smothers." "It's not much," you may say. No, it isn't much. But if it didn't sting you, for a long time now there wouldn't have been any more bees.'

*        *        *

The triumph of the literary movement of the Resistance was in its refusal to hate. Of all anti-Fascist movements the French, I think, rose to the greatest height of humanism, as exemplified in the exquisite moderation of *Le Silence de la Mer*, or Eluard's *Liberté*. Never have such warm and poetical lovers of life been so thoughtfully willing to throw it away. It is difficult for us in a country which has fought the Germans but not been occupied by them to appreciate the intolerable conditions under which the Resistance laboured. One must first of all imagine every petty restriction under which we have chafed; rationing, call-ups, identity cards, black-out offences, form-filling, etc., as being imposed not by our own Government but by our conquerors, with a curfew and a continuous parade of enemy uniforms thrown in. One must then add on four years of propaganda, propaganda diabolically directed against our weaker spots, our masochism, our childhood father fears— 'you have all been bad, bad, bad, you have been intolerably insolent, and now God has punished you, Hitler has punished you, Pétain, Laval and Darlan have punished you. You have hurt them all terribly. They were all so proud of you. So punishment. No more jam, butter, no picnics. Work! Work! Work! Work, Fatherland and Family! And if you all work very very hard you will be forgiven—because God, Hitler, Pétain, etc., are not really hard-hearted. They are pretty decent really— only you've hurt them so. Look how nice they are to the good children, to Bergéry, Morand, to your policeman, your mayor, the good people in the big house. And they know what's best for you. In their will is your peace.' Frenchmen have told me how utterly demoralizing was this continuous propaganda. As Eluard wrote of the traitors who made it:

> Ils nous ont vanté nos bourreaux
> Ils nous ont détaillé le mal
> Ils n'ont rien dit innocemment.

Floods of anonymous denunciations kept pouring into the Gestapo, all that is vilest in smug bourgeois middle-aged opportunism, fearful of discomfort or distress, went veering round to the Marshal, all that was lowest in angry boorish youth dressed up in the black uniforms, copied from the S.S., of the *Milices Populaires*. A friend of mine, one of the most kind and charming people that I know, described to me his feelings on going out into the woods of Cap d'Antibes where he was staying and discovering '*mort aux juifs*' plastered up on every tree. He said that it was like suddenly finding that one had a loathsome disease, that he learnt to shun his friends, never to speak to one unless they first spoke to him, that he divided them into those who cut him and those whose welcome was over-effusive, as if they were determined to show they were not afraid of infection. One day he woke up to find every single newspaper in the country carrying in huge headlines a denunciation of his family, which was held responsible for the war and for every evil consequence which his country was undergoing!

And having imagined all this treachery and corruption we must then try to imagine the life of those who fought against it: the betrayals, the tortures, the separations, the executions and suicides, the denunciations of the resisters by their own people who resented the harsher conditions which German retaliation imposed on them, the terrible uncertainties and disappointments which befall the weak who rise against the stronger. I wonder, for instance, how many people know that Inspecteur Boni, the chief of the French Gestapo torturers of the Rue de Lauriston, who was recently executed, specialized in impersonating British airmen. He would call at a farm in R.A.F. uniform, beg for shelter, and if favourably received, ask if he could hide his pocket transmitter in the barn. Then he would go off and return with the Gestapo. Such is the background against which the Resistance worked, and it is to be wondered that once they had learnt to watch their friends die in agony and to carry their own death with them in a capsule as their most precious possession, any of them could even contemplate literature, as an end in itself and not merely a means for bringing people back to the truth.

Eluard expresses this conflict in a recent poem *Critique de la Poésie*, where the deaths of Lorca, the old symbolist Saint-Pol-Roux, and the young Decour, founder of the *Editions de Minuit*, and the clandestine *Lettres Françaises* peal like a funeral bell through the lovely golden sensuality of his image-glowing poetry.

## CRITIQUE DE LA POÉSIE

Le feu réveille la forêt
Les troncs les cœurs les mains les feuilles
Le bonheur en un seul bouquet
Confus léger fondant sucré
C'est toute une forêt d'amis
Qui s'assemble aux fontaines vertes
Du bon soleil du bois flambant

Garcia Lorca a été mis à mort

Maison d'une seule parole
Et des lèvres unies pour vivre
Un tout petit enfant sans larmes
Dans ses prunelles d'eau perdue
La lumière de l'avenir
Goutte à goutte elle comble l'homme
Jusqu'aux paupières transparentes

Saint-Pol-Roux a été mis à mort
Sa fille a été suppliciée

Ville glacée d'angles semblables
Où je rêve de fruits en fleur
Du ciel entier et de la terre
Comme à de vierges découvertes
Dans un jeu qui n'en finit pas
Pierres fanées murs sans écho
Je vous évite d'un sourire

Decour a été mis à mort.

The Resistance now belongs to the past, and is already becoming a legend. The Resisters are slowly losing their voice
in the Government, and may or may not lose their influence
with the people. The trials of collaborationist writers and
editors, however, have taken the place of the Resistance as the
second act in the public drama. They are No. 1 topic in Paris,
and when I was there came before food (No. 2), fuel (No. 3),
and Jean Genet's *Notre Dame des Fleurs* (a bad fourth). These
trials arouse the most violent controversy, which revolves
round the sentence passed and the culpability of the victims.
The Right tend to deplore the death sentences, the Left to
demand them. Mauriac, through his column in the *Figaro*, has
consistently pleaded for their remission. From the psychological point of view there is something ambivalent in all
discussions of collaborations, purges, etc., and however justified each individual sentence may be, one comes to feel that
the role of the English—to whom these provocations have not
applied—is to urge leniency. It is not that these writers are
guiltless, but that it is doubtful if they are as guilty as many
industrialists who have not been dealt with or as many
informers who have escaped. The world is full of hate, and in
France (a country which has had an undeclared civil war) it is

seething. Those who have the right to hate and do not choose to exercise it can do enormous good. In the words of Audisio, written in a German prison, 'J'ai haï les Allemands de toute la force de mon être. Je veux que le témoignage sincère en demeure, et malgré moi s'il le faut . . . et si je pleure, Allemands, sachez-le bien, c'est que vous m'ayez amené jusque là et que je *veuille* le dire; c'est que vous ayez, dans la haine stérile, enfoncé des milliers et des milliers d'hommes de bonne volonté.'

Justice will be done to those who have betrayed, tortured, and informed against their fellows. We must try to mitigate against the operation of envy, revenge, intolerance and spite causing the death of those who have merely held the wrong opinions.

\* \* \*

Leaving honey-tongued Eluard, splenetic Aragon, and the politico-literary staff of *Lettres Françaises*, *Action*, *Liberté*, *Carrefour*, *Combat*, *Front National* and many other bellicose and brilliant newspapers to take care of the Resistance, let us explore some of the quieter corners of the battlefield.

We might do worse than pay a visit to the Café de Flore. This pleasant haunt has now become a kind of literary bourse. The brokers are the editors who sit round with their *sommaires* or contents page of the new magazine they are going to bring out (when they can get the paper!), and these *sommaires*, which are handed round and discussed like a V-Day menu, are the kerb-prices of literary reputations. Each *sommaire* contains the same names, and many of the writers are in attendance. That excitable southern figure is Pierre Seghers, of Villeneuve-les-Avignon, whose magazine *Poésie* was the best of the Occupational monthlies, and famous for its equivocal anti-German and anti-Vichy contents. Seghers is the leader of a group of young poets, and one of the bravest of them. With him is André Freneaud, a solid young Burgundian whose French has almost an English accent, and who was a prisoner of war, before joining the Resistance, and Loys Masson, one of the youngest and most gifted of the group. They are joined by Bertelé of *Confluences*, a magazine edited at Lyons and suppressed by Vichy, which has also published some interesting books. His *sommaire* includes a new poem of Michaux and part of a long philosophical study of Baudelaire's dandyism which Sartre is preparing. Sartre is absent from his favourite table, though generally he remains there most of the day, but his friend Madame de Beauvoir (herself the author of a novel, *L'Invitée*, about the whole ambience of the Flore) will show you his *sommaire* for the new magazine which he is going to edit to be called *Les Temps Modernes* and which will have a sociological and political as well as a literary character, Koestler and Orwell are the writers about whom she asks for information. I have borrowed part of Sartre's opening article for *Horizon*. It is only the first few pages of his long introductory essay on the main theme of the day, *La Litterature Engagée*, but I have included it to show one of the clearest and most forceful defences of the attitude to literature which is held by the Resistant *Intellectuels*. Sartre occupies a dominating position in the world of French literature today. He is to its prose what Eluard is to its poetry. It is a position which is criticized, for his philosophy is most obscure and there is something Central European about his pessimistic thought which antagonizes. But taken as a philosopher, a novelist, a dramatist and a critic, his bulk is enormous, and tends to obscure perhaps the younger and equally gifted Camus, who is all of these four things and editor as well of the newspaper *Combat*. *Les Mouches* and *Huis-Clos* of Sartre, *L'Etranger* and *Caligula* of Camus (*Le Malentendu* is a little too much) are real literary achievements, fascinating to read, deeply original and stimulating.

At another table is Max-Pol Fouchet, the gay young inspirer of *Fontaine*, discussing his *sommaire* with Pierre Emmanuel.

Like Sartre, a professor of philosophy, Emmanuel, who is a non-stop talker and arguer, commands several media, but unlike Sartre, he is a strong Catholic and a great admirer of Jouve. They are joined by Jean Lescure, a saturnine and gifted poet who edits both the poetry on the French wireless and also an admirable magazine, *Messages*, which is the best of the poetry productions, though lacking the important *chronique* aspect of the monthly *Poésies*. At another table is Thierry Maulnier, whose quarterly *La Table Ronde* is a model of expensive printing, and rivals the magnificent *Arbalète*, which is edited, printed and published by one man, Marc Barbezat of Lyons. *La Table Ronde* includes some of the last writings and drawings of Max Jacob, whose terrible death in a concentration camp, wearing the Jew's yellow star, shocked the whole civilized world. It also includes a very long poem by Cocteau, *Léone*, whose verse the Master describes as 'marchant à pneu crêvé', like a car on three wheels. It is a strange limping somnambulant poem in which all the imagery from his other works parades past him in a waking dream, with Léone elusively personifying his muse. Cocteau you will not see at the Flore, but that smiling and somewhat rough-looking character is Jean Genet, whom Cocteau befriended, and who is the author of the extraordinary *Notre Dame des Fleurs*, part of which is published in the eighth number of the *Arbalète*. Jean Genet, who has been in and out of prison most of his life, has managed to produce a novel which makes *Voyage au bout de la nuit*, *Tropic of Cancer* and all stories of the *milieu* and the underworld read like *Peg's Paper*. It is a passionate, lyrical and criminal book, and reminds one of those photos of murderers with a huge *fatalitas* tattooed across their chest. It is the last word in the poetry of homosexual-anti-social outlaws, because the society against which Genet rebels is an unhealthy one, and because he happens to be born a poet.

But now it is time to leave the Flore, to pay for our *jus de*

*raisin*, *viandox*, or beer. There are still several *sommaires* we
haven't seen, that of the charming anthologist Parisot, with his
*Quatre Vents* and his *Vrilles*—and there are still several more
writers we would like to meet; the fantastical poet Prévert,
'ah, il est marron, lui', and the more sombre Georges Bataille,
the post-Nietzschean essayist and one-time editor of the extraordinary *Acéphale*. And it would not be a long walk to call on
Picasso in that high studio where the world's last great
alchemist turns our dross into gold, or to visit the apartment
where his friend Henri Michaux, a somewhat sadistic magician, applies his verbal technique to a general Chinese slicing
operation on the bourgeois personality. Or, to linger in the
sacred rue de l'Odeon, where those two bilingual sirens who
have so long enchanted us with all that is best in two literatures, Sylvia Beach and Adrienne Monnier, still decoy. But
time is short, we have a last date with Gallimard, in his magnificent new office, once Talleyrand's hotel. Here is one more
group of non-political literary explorers, who have come to
visit Paulhan (he has a *sommaire*, too, for he is soon to get back
the *N.R.F.*). Paulhan, like Eluard, Sartre and Michaux, is
another prince in the world of letters, an impassioned critic of
poetry and painting whose quiet high voice, like Lytton
Strachey's, can strike terror, especially when it strikes at
terrorists. (His *Fleur de Tarbes, ou la Terreur dans les Lettres*,
is a brilliant attack on the Puritans and anti-literary philosophical pedants who would banish from literature the graces
which they neither possess nor comprehend.) Paulhan, a pillar
of the Resistance Movement, is deploring the bad effects on
literature of coming into the open again. 'Art benefits by being
clandestine and subversive,' he is saying, 'all writers write best
under another name.' With him is Francis Ponge, the creator
of an extraordinary kind of prose poem, both lyrical and
scientific in its approach, which results in a three-dimensional
picture of his usually very tangible subject. Pebbles, insects,

bits of bread are his specialities. He is, in fact, a word painter of verbal still lives who has gone through cubism, a prose Braque. They are joined by Raymond Queneau, also of the *N.R.F.*, a vigorous and many-sided satirist, novelist, poet who, besides editing a new edition of *Bouvard et Pécuchet* and thus lighting the only candle in Paris to the greatest of provincials, contributes poems of a strange verbal dexterity to *Messages*. His *Trains dans la Banlieue Ouest* is a *tour de force* like Mac-Neice's *Bagpipes*:

> Nanterre et Rueil qui donc arrueille
> Qui donc arrueille les roseaux
> qui donc enterre qui donc anteille
> larmes mucus odeurs et os
>
> Suresne' Asnière' on va-t-et-vient
> le long du fleuve aux bois méandres
> trainent les pierres trissent les chiens
> sur des sentiers à la chair tendre . . .

It is a pleasure to talk to the husky Queneau and to discuss his fascinating and destructive *Exercices de style*—for he speaks English well and the others merely read it. But we are now quite tired out and must trudge through the blue snow to the Métro, laden with the presentation copies which have helped to produce this Number and which the English customs officers at Newhaven will thumb and snivel over like dogs growling round a stale herring. 'This is a *funny* kind of a book—Pie-kasso—do you mind just coming with me?' and then in an awestruck whisper to his superior: 'It's his book, sir, kind of *funny* if you see'.

\* \* \*

And still I have mentioned only a fraction of the literary world of Paris. I would like to be able to analyse the exhilaration which for eight weeks after leaving Paris I continued to feel,

and the absence of which I now deplore. It was partly a sense
of liberation, of getting out of the exhausted London atmosphere into a country where the war was felt to be over, and
where individuals were their natural size, neither inflated with
office nor shrunken with worry. It was partly returning to a
world of ideas. For the English literary world is not a world of
ideas but of personalities, a world of clubs and honours and
ancestor-worship and engagement-books, where a writer one
wants to meet has to be hunted for several weeks until he is
finally corralled at bay under some formidable marble mantel.
But French writers are not pompous, in everything but ideas
they travel light; intelligence flows through them like a fast
river and is not always being silted up by accretions of the
personality, by sales, honours, habits, social and official positions. And they have no B.B.C. On the whole the present
literary world of Paris is young and poor, and its experiences
in the Resistance have made it both generous and brave. I
think if I were to sum up its message in the way in which
nearly every English visitor has felt it, it would be something
like this: 'Don't worry. It's all all right. Everything you love
is still here. The ideas, buildings, books, and pictures, the
wine, the people, the trees. And they won't run away. Art and
life are beginning again. The European orchestra is tuning up,
and its members are as pleased to see us as we are to be with
them; the freemasonry of the intellect is at work and a new
humanism is being born. For what our world now most needs
is a positive and adult humanism. America could give it, but
she is too money-bound and machine-dry, Russia lacks the
sentiment of individual liberty, England is too bureaucratized
and war-weary. We have added the adjective "bloody-minded"
to our language, and must rest our laurels on that. But France
has known the tyrant, and been set free before the knowledge
destroyed her. France alone, if she can survive an acute
attack of nationalism, is capable of a bloodless 1789, of a new

proclamation to the world of the old truths that life is meant
to be lived and that liberty is its natural temperature, that
brains are to be used and beauty to be worshipped, and that
human beings (the only animals who can laugh) are intended
to be happy.'

*Spring* 1945

# FALSE DAWN

HORIZON is a war-baby: this is our first number to be produced in a Europe at peace. For sixty-six months we have been
waiting for this moment. *Horizon* has always hated war; but it
is not pacifist, for it has hated fascism more and therefore
recognized the value of that patriotism which derives from the
healthy human desire to protect our liberties and to fight for
our country against an invader. This patriotism is a biological
instinct. But when such patriotism becomes an aggressive
nationalism and the threatened becomes the threatener, the
enslaved the enslaver, it must be combated with all the weapons
of emotion and reason, and this nationalism is now the universal
danger. Peace on earth, ill-will to all men. How different from
the peace we have all longed for and dreamt of during these six
years of hate and boredom, of fear and suffering! I remember
being haunted by a line of La Fontaine, in his poem celebrat-
ing the Treaty of the Pyrenees:

> que les plus grands de nos maux
> soient les rigueurs de nos belles!

Faint hope. *Homo homini lupus.* What do we see? In place of
that United States of Europe of which we dreamed we watch
a new Great Wall of China being erected across its centre. In
place of those liberal or socialist democracies in which we put
our faith, we see kings and generals disputing tottering thrones
on one side of the wall, iron totalitarian regimes coming into
being on the other. Where Europe ceases and Islam begins the

Great Powers squat angrily on Arabs and oil-fields, the Indian gaols are full, and beyond them the Chinese fight and starve, while the Japanese pay the deserved and terrible penalty for the use they have made of the industrialism which once was forced upon them. At the same time in one or two countries men struggle towards peace and begin to recover a sanity which we hope is infectious. For the first time for ten years we have a vote; we are free in the next few days to decide on what kind of chains we shall wear. I hold a proxy for a friend in Italy and am going to use it for Labour. If I really thought that the situation were desperate, and that—carried on by the general gadarene impetus of nationalism, suspicion, greed and new explosives—we would be at war again in a few years, I should vote Conservative, for they can best protect us, and if there is one man to whom I owe it that I am not in a concentration camp, his name is Winston Churchill. But is the situation so desperate? Can those of us in England, America, France, Russia, China and the rest of Europe who believe in love, life and freedom communicate our sanity, our happiness and our liberty to the incredulous, to the under-privileged of head and heart? Now is the time for those of us who are natural pacifists, yet compelled by a hatred of tyranny and by biological necessity to support the war, once again to proclaim our principles—that human life is sacred, that killing is no remedy for killing nor hatred for hatred, that happiness is indivisible and consists in the liberty to grow, that all human beings are sentenced to death and that as the sentence will never be commuted, we are all entitled to the courtesies of the condemned cell, just as being all members of that most exclusive institution, the *club des vivants*, we are all privileged to enjoy the amenities of the spherical reading-room which is our world. Life is sweet and may we never forget it!

It is because I believe this that I shall give my proxy to Labour. I think many Tories believe it too. Yet to make

England a happy country, there must be a levelling up which socialism alone will provide; we cannot continue to maintain two utterly different standards of living. Then to make us really free there must be governments who don't like secret police or 'glasshouses' or uniforms or telephone-tapping or dossier-making—as at the anarchist's trial—from visitors' identity cards; we must be administered by people who will root out, like lumps of dry rot, the foci of fascism by which in our struggle against it we have become infected. I do not agree with the Prime Minister that socialism leads to the Gestapo. It was a Conservative government which condoned Hitler, Franco and Mussolini and their horrible methods. And when it comes to foreign policy I think that Bevin and Morrison are just as able to negotiate as Eden and Beaverbrook, and, judging from Bevin's speech with its emphasis on free trade and inter-nationalism, they are more likely to create the kind of Europe in which I believe, a Europe without passports, tariffs, cops and armies, without kings and dictators, without barracks full of Senegalese and dungeons full of artists, and to which England belongs by inheritance, for it is half the privilege of being English to have access to other men's weather, to the civiliza-tion of France, Greece or Italy, the mountains of Switzerland and Austria, and not least—and this is where Labour can help me—to the sunshine of Spain.

There is one more question which all voters who love the human spirit should ask themselves: Who will do most for the arts in England? I find for example that nearly all of our sub-scribers who are Members of Parliament are Conservatives, and important ones; they swallow our pink pills with stoic grace! Labour's record of assistance to the artist is lamentable. It seems to regard Art as a complicated secret weapon of the rich. In our greatest difficulties we were most helped by men like Harold Nicolson (National Labour) and Duff Cooper. The Liberal contribution to *Horizon* is also honourable, and I

would certainly use my proxy for that Party if I thought their
candidate had the best chance of being elected. One thing is
certain. England is now part of Europe: in Europe two instincts
have long been at work, a desire for unity, and an urge to the
Left. If we do not guide these instincts to fruition (and only a
liberal or socialist England will give the lead) the United
States of Europe will be created without us.

Meanwhile, time will show: if as usual the pin-stripe pants,
city faces and rolled umbrellas are returned, we shall scold them;
if the men of Blackpool about whom we know so much less are
for once elected, we shall lecture them as well—for though the
war in Europe is over, *Horizon's* battle is hardly begun. And
here it is right to recall the names of some of those who have
been killed in this war and who were on our side; on the side
of life, beauty, art and intelligence, and against all littleness
and bloody-mindedness. Robert Byron, drowned on his way
to Egypt; Antony Goldsmith, killed in Tunisia; Rollo Woolley,
shot down in the air above it; Alun Lewis, who died in India,
all four contributors; and those three young fighter pilots who
were such friends to each other and to us, Gully Mason,
Michael Jones and Bill Siprell.

> A florecer las rosas madrugaron
> y para envejecerse florecieron—
> cuna y sepulcro en un botón hallaron.
> Tales los hombres sus fortunas vieron ...

*June* 1945

## AFTER THE ELECTION

'REVOLUTIONS do not happen in this country, but every now
and then the public gives a great heave of boredom and impatience and something is done with for ever.' These words from
this column in April 1940 sum up the General Election. It was

not a vote about queues or housing, but a vote of censure on Munich and Spain and Abyssinia, on the shrewd, glib, boisterous city-gent *faux bonhommes*, 'all the old beaming second-rate faces' of the Baldwin-Chamberlain era. The Election result is a blow struck against the religion of money. It has given us a Government of reasonable people, people like ourselves who are 'we', not 'they', and who are unlikely to become over-excited by power or to use the word 'intellectual' as an insult, like some of the millionaire hoodlums whom we have just put out.

The new Parliament is one of the few good things to have come out of the war, a proof of the wisdom and vitality of the people, and of its desire to be more integrated with its rulers. It immensely strengthens our position on the Continent and gives England a chance to implement the anti-Fascist propaganda which we have poured out for the last five years and so to become that unique thing—a great power which is not greatly hated.

Morally and economically Europe has lost the war. The great marquee of European civilization in whose yellow light we all grew up and read or wrote or loved or travelled has fallen down; the side-ropes are frayed, the centre-pole is broken, the chairs and tables are all in pieces, the tea-urns empty, the roses are withered on their stands, and the prize marrows; the grass is dead. France, Italy, Germany, Austria are now but names to many of the Americans and Russians who are their custodians: never have occupying armies had less use for the countries they invest. The gulf between the civilizations has grown too wide. Each European country is struggling in silence against its particular disease; famine, bombed cities, blasted communications, black markets, corrupt minorities, jealous neighbours—or the insidious legacies of German occupation. While the sickness of Germany fills those who observe it with despair the condition of France is for her

visitors almost as alarming. Something is badly wrong, and all
the ills which in January were put down to the war, the occupation, the German armies in the Ardennes or the rigours of
winter, I found by July to have been aggravated. While those
who come back from Germany are astounded and yet somehow shocked by the beaver-like industry, servility and desire
to co-operate of the conquered, those who go to France are
appalled by the moral apathy, the physical slowness of recovery of the less-damaged nation. The French are immensely
mistrustful of each other; they all accuse each other of not
working, and of being dishonest. They still talk of nothing but
collaboration and seem to think that the interminable (and not
very dignified) trial of Pétain was a kind of positive reconstruc-
tive effort. But you can break a great many eggs without making
an omelette and you can shoot a great many collaborators
without getting an administration. Probably few Frenchmen
are more perturbed about conditions there than those round
de Gaulle, especially his younger collaborators, yet the remedies
they propose, derived from their military education and ideas
of *La Gloire*, are hopelessly inadequate for the symptoms.
France is much too sick to get up and march with a banner in
the procession. The gap between rich and poor is grotesquely
wide, nobody trusts anyone, hundreds of tiny newspapers
appear, each jealously guarding their right to have nothing to
say; the cost of living is prohibitive. The shops have nothing
to sell, the trains are among the slowest and dirtiest in the world,
yet to get a seat in them is almost impossible, everything looks
more beautiful and otherwise quite unchanged since before the
war, yet the whole atmosphere is subtly Balkanized. The black
market flourishes like a giant fungus, the Resistance is bitter
and disillusioned, edged out of its commanding position by
the Central Government; the Government, conscious of its
anomalous position and the impending elections, is bitter too.
The Socialist Party has been slow in recovering its organization

and its fighting spirit, and the Communists have improved their position at their expense. But the real trouble lies deeper —the soul of France is sick—the country has had a nervous breakdown—there is confusion about what France is and ought to be. As before, it is only with the groups of Resistance writers and artists, those who centre round Fontaine, *Poèsies*, *Lettres Françaises*, or Paulhan, Malraux, Queneau, Sartre or Camus, that one has the sensation of vital movement, of the mind in flower.

I spent the 14th of July wandering about the bleached tropical city rejoicing with accordions and fireworks (a proletarian city, like all capitals today) and trying to decide what was missing. For one thing, about ten thousand American girls, with their satchels and sketch-books, their exotic looks and wholesome voices to animate all the small hotels on the Left Bank, now miserably functionless and sombre; then a quantity of genuine artists and writers from other countries, lovers of Paris and serious ease, to argue in cafés and crouch in the book-shops, and sit too long over lunch. Then a horde of rich tourists and Latin Americans to pour money into every tattered court-yard and shabby street, and last a French Government which would welcome all this money and food and appreciation with dignity while continuing to experiment in the new possibilities of living and thinking and painting that have made this most beautiful of all northern cities pre-eminent. For it is no good if France becomes another Venice, a garden and museum with forty million people going bad in it—only federation, a federation of the Western European democracies—with Africa as the model farm—and American good will—can put up the marquee again. Or so I hoped—but by then I was walking along the quays by the Seine, it was after midnight, the opaque green river slid by the immense poplars, and I knew that my reflections on these political nostrums were a kind of middle-aged mumbling over the grave of youth, for even were this young

man's Paris to be resurrected, who can give back the eyes and
heart which first explored it?

> Weh mir, wo nehm' ich, wenn
> Es Winter ist, die Blumen, und wo
> Den Sonnenschein
> Und Schatten der Erde?[1]

And London? What can the new Government do about
that? I flew over from Le Bourget the other day. In France
there was a small heat-wave, and the sunshine extended over
the sand-dumplings of Le Touquet, over the Channel, like a
clean blue blotter, and the scarred elephant-hide of Dungeness.
Suddenly we saw from the plane a vast thick cloud of sooty
mucus, and below it ring-worm circles of brick villas, grey and
gloomy factories and towers; the Thames, an industrial river,
just too far to the south of everything to matter, and the complacent phallus of the Ministry of Information! A tiny oval of
grey-green was Regent's Park—another break in the brick was
Hampstead Heath—then the ring-worm of new suburbs erupts
again, with buses playing in the roundabouts, and we land at
Hendon. This iron cloud of August phlegm has never moved
since, and still lowers over forty miles of London. What can be
done to bring the weather above the clouds to the people
beneath it? And to clean up the great mess which the last
hundred years of unplanned development has made?

Londoners are perhaps luckiest who have never seen the
light and colour or the planned architectural compactness
which is to be found abroad. But for those who know what
urban life can be like—in Munich or Zürich or Barcelona—
the ordeal is becoming unendurable. It is not enough to patch

---

[1] Ah, grief, where do I take, when
Winter comes, the flowers, and where
The sunshine
And shadows of the Earth?

[HÖLDERLIN. *Translated by* VERNON WATKINS]

up the wartime shabbiness, to improve the dirt and dust, the queues, the stuffy restaurants and pubs, or to rebuild the ruined buildings—a vast deal more has to be pulled down before anything can be put up. There are admirable signs that the Abercrombie plan will be followed, and that London will be made smaller, not bigger, as a result—but what a winter this is going to be in this most favoured of European countries—no coal, though the earth is stiff with it; no wine, though the cellars of Bordeaux are full; no servants, though there are millions of displaced personages who would be only too glad to find places; no trips abroad, no access to snow or sun; only art and a little politics to keep warm by. After the surfeit of victory celebrations I should like to see one of the gloomiest winter days set apart as a day of global mourning, when all Europe mourns its dead—and also its folly—and resolves never to make the same mistakes again. And I should also like to see, as a global war-memorial, the abolition of the death-penalty, for until the State sets us the example of holding life sacred, it can hardly expect its members to—and such a credo is the unique reply to the Atomic Bomb.

*September* 1945

# LES GRANDS HOMMES

THE death of Valéry has removed one of the elixirs of western civilization. While our full tribute and estimate is being prepared, it is worth while recalling a last interview with him in January of this year. Valéry then seemed somewhat old and tired but mentally entirely alive. He talked very fast and in the back of his throat with a kind of raucous purring which I found very difficult to follow. He was immensely distinguished, inevitably the *cher maître*. He talked to me about England and

described a visit to Meredith at Box Hill which had been
arranged for him by Henry Harland. Wearing a top hat he
advanced along the platform to greet Meredith, also wearing a
top hat, who fell forward flat on his face, picked himself up
and came forward without a word, as if such a prostration was
the most natural thing in the world. He went on to talk of that
London of the Yellow Book, of the introductions to it which
Mallarmé gave him, of the reproaches he used to receive for
his idleness, 'for I was at that time very idle though I hope I
have made up a little for it since'—he then moved on immediately to his present English friends, Mr. T. S. Eliot and
Mr. John Hayward. I was able to give him news of them and
also to tell him about Day Lewis's magnificent translation of
the *Cimetière Marin*. Here he related, with feline savagery, an
incident at one of his last lectures at the Collège de France. A
young man had come up to him and said that he had once
greatly admired that poem, but that now since he realized that
it was not *la littérature engagée*, he could not enjoy it any
more. *La littérature engagée*—the phrase seemed to rattle
from the back of his palate—'what rubbish! There were always
moments in the history of civilizations when literature seemed
to have responsibilities—perhaps this was one of them—but
they soon blew over,' and as he spoke one felt that all the
authority of the nineteenth century was behind the remark. As
always when meeting these great writers whom for years one
has loved and admired there was a sense of inadequacy, for
how can one communicate to a small mocking figure across a
tea-table the glory of the wake which the passage of the great
vessel of his work has left for over twenty years across the
ocean of European thought. A friend of his told me that he
seemed now to make fun of everything—except perhaps
woman—for his tone would sometimes hold a certain reverence
when he spoke of her. *Tout est magie dans les rapports entre
homme et femme*. Certainly his *Mauvaises Pensées* (the most

original of his last books) is a devastating and ferocious panorama of human wisdom—a nihilist's breviary. It is nice to know that he lived to appreciate John Hayward's translation of *Mon Faust* in *Horizon* (the fragment seems to me to hold the quintessence of the serene exaltation of pagan old age) and that his fears about the rendering of *tu* and *vous*—a transition which he felt was very important in the text and which he was afraid would not easily be conveyed in English—were groundless—yes, it is nice, it is reassuring to know such things, yet in the light of that dazzling intelligence which is now for ever extinguished—except in his books—it is completely unimportant. It is the living presence of such giants for which Europe, bewildered and self-brutalizing, is now crying out.

\*      \*      \*

In England we still retain one or two of our luminaries of civilization. One is Mr. Logan Pearsall Smith who celebrated his eightieth birthday on 18 October. To my mind, quite apart from what he says, he writes English better than anyone now living, and it is to his collected essays, *Reperusals*, and to his autobiography that I turn, rather than to the almost over-fastuous *Trivia*, to be reminded of the modulations of which our vocabulary is capable. He has defined literature as 'the art of making people real to themselves by words', as 'that useless ornament and flower', as Ste.-Beuve described it. 'That delicate superfluity of life, which is the most precious and least perishable of all things on this perishable earth'—and that is a definition that will do to go on with. How prophetic is his description of the November ritual at Altamura, the secular monastery whose existence he imagined as long ago as 1898!

'Brief, however, as life may be, the pleasures of life are still more fleeting; and in November the Altamurans, following the course of human experience, turn from the poor earth and its joys, to those forces that make for the mockery and derision of human hopes, and the destruction of human existence—the decay of religions and civilizations, the prosperity of the wicked, and all the sinister aspects of creation—ill-boding stars, eclipses, wars, plagues, earthquakes and inundations.

'The Saints of this month are the great Pessimists, and Cynics and Suicides, the heathen Gods which were Devils, Moloch, Hammon, Chemosh, Typhon, Peor and the Baalim.'

*November* 1945

## THE FIRST CHRISTMAS

*Horizon* faces the New Year with a whole set of resolutions.

I. As it becomes easier for readers to obtain for themselves copies of French publications, to have fewer French articles. (It is still not very easy.)

II. To get out of the bad habit of enthroning a set of writers as 'the Best People' who can't be criticized because they are on the right side, and because to have criticized them during the war was to have played into the hands of anti-intellectuals, philistine journalists, and humble venomous Vichyite hair-shirters. It is time we tried clearly to assess where English literature stands and attempted to settle how much more Mr. E. M. Forster is than a promising novelist of before the last war; what one really thinks of Mr. Eliot's prose; why no one ever *quotes* a modern poet as we used to quote *The Waste Land*; why reviewing, between the zones of spirited ideological bigotry which we expect from the Marxist and the Papist press, has become so dull and mummified. And what is the matter with the young? And the B.B.C.? And America? Why are its serious writers so very pretentious and its popular writers so bad? All these problems must be tackled with wholesome blasphemy, and *Horizon* hopes to introduce a new series of critical articles on living Anglo-Saxon writers—'The Best and the Worst'.

What other resolutions have we taken? To continue to try to make the new Government for which we have voted do more to encourage culture; to try to get our prison systems cleaned up; to get rid of identity cards and restore our free-born privilege to use a false name once in a while; to facilitate foreign travel; to combat puritanism and nationalism and cruelty and injustice; to work for the abolition of the death penalty and for a new humanism which considers human life vulgar but sacred, and the happiness, even of other people, as our supreme aim. And to uphold the belief that Art is an end in itself, with a life of its own and rewards of its own: not a kind of rash on the body politic which can be explained by the economics of its digestion or the dogmas which the body has swallowed, but as something which 'happens', which, without knowing why, some people do better than others, which cannot, any more than life, be broken down in order to be mechanically created, and which is able to transcend time, even as the enjoyment of it transcends time.

# UBU COCU

LOOKING for some little Christmas masque or morality to gratify his readers, something with a taste of the time, the Editor of *Horizon* has hit on Acts I and II of Jarry's *Ubu Cocu*, reprinted from a newly found manuscript (a variation of *Ubu Enchainé*) by the Trois Collines Press of Geneva. The play was written for the 'Marionettes of the Théâtre de Phynances' in 1900, but—such progress has the new century made—there is no scene among those provided for his puppets which has not since been re-enacted many times over by real people in all countries. Poppa Ubu, with his mysticism, his fanatical belief in progress, in the essential goodness of human nature, in the responsibilities of friendship and—despite his unfortunate situation—in the sacredness of the family tie—is an epitome of the common man struggling for decency in the world we live in or (as some think) of a great power assuming

*The only genuine portrait of Père Ubu*

responsibility for a lesser; and he has every right (exclude me if I am long) to be known as the Santa Claus of the Atomic Age.

## ACT I

### Scene: Salon in the home of Professor Achras

ACHRAS: Oh but it's like this, look you, I've no reason to be discontented with my polyhedra; they bear their young every six weeks, it's worse than rabbits. And it's also quite true to say that the regular polyhedra are the most faithful and devoted to their master, except that this morning the Icosahedron was a little fractious, so that I was compelled, look you, to give it a slap on each one of its faces. And that's the sort of language they understand. And my thesis, look you, on the habits of polyhedra—it's getting along nicely, thanks, only another twenty-five volumes!

(*Enter flunkey.*)

FLUNKEY: Sir, there's a bloke out there who wants to have a word with you. He's pulled the bell off with ringing, he's broken three chairs trying to sit down.

(*He gives Achras a card.*)

ACHRAS: What's all this? Monsieur Ubu, sometime King of Poland and Aragon, Professor of Pataphysics? That makes no sense at all. What's all that about? Pataphysics! Well, never mind, he sounds a person of distinction. I should like to make a gesture of good will to this visitor by showing him my polyhedra. Have the gentleman come up.

(*Enter Poppa Ubu in travelling costume, with a suitcase.*)

UBU: Hornstrumpot, Sir! What a miserable kind of hang-out you've got here, we have been obliged to ring the bell for more than an hour, and when, finally, your servants made up their minds to let us in, we were presented only with an orifice so minute that we still don't understand how our strumpot was able to navigate it.

ACHRAS: Oh, but it's like this, excuse me. I wasn't at all expecting the visit of such a considerable personage ... otherwise, you can be sure I would have had the door enlarged. But you must forgive the absent-mindedness of an old collector, who is at the same time, I venture to say, a great savant.

UBU: Say that by all means if it gives you any pleasure, but remember that you are conversing with a famous pataphysician.

ACHRAS: Excuse me, Sir, you said?

UBU: Pataphysician. Pataphysics is a branch of science which we have invented and for which a crying need is generally experienced.

ACHRAS: Oh, but it's like this, if you're a famous inventor, we'll understand each other, look you, for between great men ...

UBU: A little more modesty, Sir! Besides, I see no great man here except myself. But, since you insist, I have condescended to do you a most signal honour. Let it be known to you, Sir, that your house is convenient for us and that we have decided to make ourselves at home here.

ACHRAS: Oh, but it's like this, look you ...

UBU: We will dispense with your expressions of gratitude. Ah, by the way, I nearly forgot. Since it is scarcely right that a father should be separated from his children, we shall be joined in the immediate future by our family—Madame Ubu, and by our dear sons and daughters Ubu. They are very quiet, decent, well-brought-up folk.

ACHRAS: Oh, but it's like this you see. I'm afraid of ...

UBU: We quite understand. You're afraid of boring us. All right then, we'll no longer tolerate your presence except by our kind permission. One thing more, while we are inspecting your kitchens, and your dining-room, you will go and look for our three packing-cases of luggage which we have deposited in the hall.

ACHRAS: Oh, but it's like this—that's not a good idea at all to install yourself like that with people. It's a manifest imposture.

UBU: A magnificent posture! Exactly, Sir, for once in your life you've spoken the truth.

(*Exit Achras.*)

UBU: Are we right to behave like this? Hornstrumpot, by our Green Candle, let us consult our conscience. There it is, in this suitcase, all covered with cobwebs. It is obvious that it's of no earthly use.

(*He opens the suitcase. Enter Conscience as a big fellow in a night-shirt.*)

CONSCIENCE: Sir, and so forth, be so good as to take a few notes.

UBU: Excuse me, Sir, we have no fondness for writing, though we have no doubt that anything you have to say would be most interesting. And while we're on the subject, I should like to know why you have the cheek to appear before us in your shirt?

CONSCIENCE: Sir and so forth, Conscience, like Truth, usually goes without a shirt. If I have donned one, it is out of respect for the distinguished audience.

UBU: As for that, Mr. or Mrs. Conscience, you're kicking up a great fuss about nothing. Answer this question rather.

Should I do well to kill Mr. Achras who has had the audacity to come and insult me in my own house?

CONSCIENCE: Sir and so forth, to return good with evil is unworthy of a civilized man. Mr. Achras has lodged you, Mr. Achras has received you with open arms, and made you free of his collection of polyhedra, Mr. Achras, and so forth, is a very fine fellow, quite harmless; it would be cowardly and so forth, to kill a poor old man incapable of defending himself.

UBU: Hornstrumpot, my good conscience, are you quite sure he can't defend himself?

CONSCIENCE: Absolutely, Sir, so it would be a coward's trick to make away with him.

UBU: Thank you, Sir, we shan't need you any more. Since there's no risk attached, we shall assassinate Mr. Achras, and we shall also make a point of consulting you more frequently, for you know how to give us better advice than we had anticipated. Now, into the suitcase with you!

(*He closes it again.*)

CONSCIENCE: In which case, Sir, I think we can leave it at that and so forth, for today.

(*Enter Achras, backwards, prostrating himself with terror before the three red packing-cases pushed by the flunkey.*)

UBU (*to flunkey*): Off with you, sloven—and you, Sir, I want a word with you. I wish you every kind of prosperity and I beg you, out of your great kindness, to perform a friendly service for me.

ACHRAS: Anything, look you, which you can demand from an old professor who has consecrated sixty years of his life, look you, to studying the habits of polyhedra.

UBU: Sir, we have learnt that our virtuous wife, Madame Ubu, is most abominably deceiving us with an Egyptian yclept Memnon, who performs the triple functions of a clock at dawn, at night a barrel scavenger, and in the daytime becomes the cornutator of our person. Hornstrumpot, we have decided to wreak on him the most terrible vengeance!

ACHRAS: As far as that goes, look you, Sir, as to being a cuckold I can sympathize with you.

UBU: We have resolved then to inflict a severe punishment. And we can think of nothing more appropriate in this case, to chastise the guilty, than the torture of Impaling.

ACHRAS: Excuse me, I still don't see very clearly, look you, how I can be of any use.

UBU: By our green candle, Sir, since we have no wish for our scheme of justice to go astray, we should be delighted that a person of your standing should make a preliminary trial of the Stake, to discover how it performs its function.

ACHRAS: Oh, but it's like this, look you, not on your life— that's too much. I regret, look you, that I can't perform this little service for you, but it just doesn't make sense at all. You've stolen my house from me, look you. You've told me to bugger off and now you want to put me to death, oh no, that's going too far.

UBU: Don't distress yourself, good my friend. It was just our little joke. We shall return when you have quite recovered your composure.

(*Exit*)

(*The Three Palcontents come out of the chests.*)

(*Song*)

THE THREE P's: We are the Palcontents
We are the Palcontents
With a face like a rabbit
Which seldom prevents

Our bloody good habit
Of croaking the bloke wot lives on his rents.
We are the Pals
We are the Cons
We are the Palcontents.

CRAPENTAKE: In a great box of stainless steel
Imprisoned all the week we feel
That Sunday is the only day
When we're allowed our getaway.
Ears to the wind, without surprise
We march along with vigorous step
And all the passers-by cry 'Hep'
Those must be bloody poor G.I.s.

THE THREE: We are the Palcontents, *etc.*

BINANJITTERS: Every morning we get called
With the Master's boot on our behind
And half-awake our backs are galled
By the bleeding kit we ave to mind
Then all day long with hammer greasy
We bash your skulls in good and easy
Till we restore to Pa Ubé
The dough from the stiffs we've croaked this day.

THE THREE: We are the Palcontents, *etc.*

(*They dance. Achras terrified sits down on a chair.*)

FOURZEARS: In our ridiculous loonyforms
We wander through the streets so pansy
Till we can plug the bockle-an-jug
Of any guy whom we don't fancy.
We get our eats through platinum teats
We pee through a tap without a handle
And we inhale the atmostale
Through a tube as bent as a Dutchman's candle.

THE THREE: We are the Palcontents, *etc.*

(*They dance round Achras.*)

ACHRAS: O but it's like this, look you, it's ridiculous, it doesn't make sense at all.

(*The stake rises under his chair.*)

Oh dear, I don't understand it, if you were only my poly-hedra, oh dear, look you, have mercy on a poor old professor. Look—look you—There's no sense in it, you see.

(*He is impaled and raised in the air despite his cries. It grows pitch dark.*)

THE PALCONTENTS (*ransacking the furniture and pulling out money bags from it*):

Give the finances to Pa Ubu. Give all the finances—to Pa Ubu—let nothing remain, not one sou, to go down the drain for the Revenue. Give *all* the finance to Pa Ubu!

(*Going back into their chests.*)

We are the Pals, we are the Cons, we are the Palcontents.

(*Achras loses consciousness.*)

*       *       *

(*Achras (impaled), Pa Ubu, Ma Ubu.*)

UBU: By my green candle, my sweet child, how happy we shall be in this house!

MRS. UBU: There is only one thing lacking to my happiness, my friend, and that is to meet the worthy host who has placed such entertainment within our grasp.

UBU: Don't let that upset you, my dear, to forestall your every wish I have had him set up here in the place of honour!

(*He points to the stake. Screams and hysterics from Madame Ubu.*)

CURTAIN

## ACT II. *The same.*

(*Achras impaled. Conscience, half coming out of the suitcase.*)

CONSCIENCE: Sir.

ACHRAS: Hron.

CONSCIENCE: And so forth.

ACHRAS: What's beyond this 'Rhon' I wonder. It's like this —I ought to be dead, leave me in peace.

CONSCIENCE: Sir, although my philosophy condemns outright any form of action, what Mr. Ubu did was too unworthy, I am going to disimpale you.

(*He lengthens himself to the height of Achras.*)

ACHRAS (*disimpaled*): I'm not the one to say no, Sir.

CONSCIENCE: Sir and so forth, I should like to have a brief interview with you. Please sit down.

ACHRAS: Oh, but it's like this, look you, don't talk of that. I should never be so rude as to sit down in the presence of an ethereal spirit to whom I owe my life, and besides, I just don't feel like it.

CONSCIENCE: My conscientious inner consciousness and sense of justice tell me it's my duty to punish Mr. Ubu. What revenge would you suggest?

ACHRAS: Hey, but it's like this, look you, I've thought about it for a long time. I shall simply unfasten the trap-door into the cellar . . . hey—put the arm-chair behind it, look you, and when the good chap, look you, comes in from his dinner, he'll bust the whole thing in. Hey and that'll make some sense! Goodie-goodie!

CONSCIENCE: Justice will be done and so forth.

(*He gets back into the suitcase.*)

(*Enter Père Ubu.*)

UBU: Hornstrumpot! You, sir, certainly haven't stayed put as

I arranged you. Well, since you're still alive to be of use to us, don't you forget to tell your cook that she's in the habit of serving the soup with too much salt in it, and that the joint was overdone. That's not at all the way we like them. It's not that we aren't able, by our skill in pataphysics, to make the most exquisite dishes rise from the earth, but that doesn't prevent your methods, Sir, from provoking our indignation.

ACHRAS: Oh, but it's like this, that shan't happen again.

(*Père Ubu is engulfed in the trap.*)—If you see what I mean.

UBU: Hornstrumpot, Sir! What is the meaning of this farce? Your floor-boards are in a rotten state. We shall be obliged to inflict a heavy penalty.

ACHRAS: It's only a trap-door, look you.

CONSCIENCE: Mr. Ubu is too fat, he'll never get through it.

UBU: By my green candle, a trap-door must be either open or shut. All the beauty of the Phynance Theatre lies in the smooth functioning of its trap-doors. This one is choking us, it's flaying our transverse colon and our great epiploon. Unless you get me out I shall be a dead man.

ACHRAS: All that's in my power, look you, is to charm your last moments by the reading of some of the most characteristic passages, look you, of my Treatise on the habits of Polyhedra, and of the Thesis which I have taken sixty years to compose on the tissues of the Conic Section. You'd rather not? Oh, very well, I'm going—I couldn't bear to watch your end, it's too sad.

(*Exit.*)

UBU: My conscience, where are you? Hornstrumpot, you give me good advice, don't you! We shall do penitence and perhaps restore into your hands some small fraction of what we have taken. We shall desist from the use of our debraining machine.

CONSCIENCE: Sir, I've never wished for the death of a sinner, and so forth. I offer you the customary helping hand.

UBU: Hurry up, Sir, we're dying—Hurry up and pull us out of this trap-door and we shall accord you a day's leave of absence from your suitcase.

(*Conscience, after releasing Ubu, throws the suitcase in the hole.*)

CONSCIENCE (*gesticulating*): Thank you, Sir. Sir, there's no better exercise than gymnastics! Ask any hygienist.

UBU: Hornstrumpot Sir! You indulge in a great deal of horse-play. To show you our superiority in this, as in everything else, we are going to perform the prestidigious leap, which might surprise you, when you take into account the enormity of our strumpot! (*He begins to run and jump.*)

CONSCIENCE: Sir, I entreat you, don't do anything of the sort, you'll only stove in the floor completely, and disappear down another hole. Observe our own light touch. (*He remains hanging by his feet.*) Oh! Help, help—I'm going to wrench my kidneys, come and help me, Monsieur Ubu.

UBU (*sitting down*): Oh no. We shall do nothing of the kind, Sir. We are performing our digestive functions at this moment, and the slightest dilatation of our drum-pot will make us instantly perish. In two or three hours at the most, our digestion will be finished and we'll fly to your aid. And besides, we are by no means in the habit of unhooking such tatters off the peg.

(*Conscience shakes itself, and falls on Ubu's stomach.*)

UBU: Ah, that's too much, Sir. We don't tolerate anyone try-ing horseplay on us, and you won't be one to get away with it.

(*Not finding the suitcase, he takes Conscience by the feet, opens the door of the lavatory at the end of the room, and shoves it head first down the drain.*)

## Scene II

*(Pa Ubu, the Three Palcontents, upright in their packing-cases.)*

THE THREE: Those who despise his beady eyes are all of them fools, and flunk-at-schools who'll get a surprise ere the day is out and learn what his machine is all about. For he doan wan' his royal person to be joked about by a son-of-a-gun. Yeh, he doan like his little Mary to be passed remarks on by Dick or by Harry. This barrel that rolls, arrel that rolls, arrel that rolls is Poppa Ubu.

*(Meanwhile Pa Ubu lights his green candle, a flame of hydrogen in a steam of sulphur, and which, constructed after the principle of the Philosopher's Organ, gives out a perpetual flute-note. And he hangs two notices up on the wall.)*

'Machine-pricking done here'

*and*

'Get your nears cut'.

CRAPENTAKE: Hey, Mister! Some folks gets all the trouble. Mr. Presscock, he's been eleven times this morning to your office in Bleed-pig Square. Hey!

BINANJITTERS: Mister, as you told me to I've carried a case of combustible clenched fists to Mr. Borwell and a full Crappy Box to Mr. Chas. Borgan. Hey!

FOURZEARS: I've been in Egypt, Mister, and I've brought back that there singing Memnon. By reason of which matter, as I don't know if he roightlee has to be put up before he sings every morning, I've set him up in the room underneath. Hey!

UBU: Silence, my eager beavers. We are moved to meditation. The sphere is the perfect form. The sun is the perfect planet, and in us nothing is more perfect than our head, always upturned towards that star, and stretching towards its form

—what else but our eye, mirror of this orb and cast in its likeness!

The sphere is the form of the angels. To man it is given to be only an incomplete angel. And yet, more perfect than the Cylinder, less perfect than the Sphere, from the Barrel radiates the hyper-physical body. We, its isomorph, are passing fair . . .

THE THREE PALCONTENTS: Those who aren't skeered of his Joadstool beard are all of them fools and flunk-at-schools who'll find themselves ere the day is done with his knacking-machine to start their fun.

(*Father Ubu, who was sitting at his table, gets up and walks.*)

THE THREE PALCONTENTS: This barrel that rolls, arrel that rolls, arrel that rolls is Poppa Ubu, and his strumpot huge, his trumpot huge, his rumpot huge is like a . . .

UBU: *Non cum vacaveris, pataphysicandum est*, as Seneca has said. It would seem a matter of urgency that we get a patch inserted in our suit of woolly philosophy. *Omnia alia negligenda sunt*, it is certainly irreverent, *ut huic assideamus* to employ the infamous usage as of emptying casks and barrels, which is deeply to insult our Master of Finance here present. *Cui nullum tempus vitae satis magnum est* and that's the reason why we have invented this instrument which we have no hesitation whatsoever in designating by the title of Shittapump. (*He takes it from his pocket and puts it on the table.*)

THE THREE PALCONTENTS: Hey Mister! Yas suh!

UBU: And now as it's getting late, we shall go to bed. Ah, I forget: coming back from Egypt you will bring us some mummy-grease for our machine, although apparently it runs away very fast, hornstrumpot! and is extremely difficult to get hold of.

(*He takes his green candle and his pump and goes out.*)

## Scene III

*(The Palcontents sing, without moving, while the statue of Memnon is erected in the middle of the stage, on its base of a wine-barrel.)*

THE THREE PALCONTENTS:
  Tremble and quake at the Lord of Finance
  little bourgeois who's getting too big for his pants!
  It's too late to scream when we're skinning your arses
  for the Palcontent's knock means he'll chip off your block
  with that sideaways look through the top of his glasses ...

  Meanwhile at dawn Pa Ubu leaves his couch
  No sooner awake than he's a hundred rounds to make,
  With a bang he is out and about on the floor
  where the verminous Palcontents snozzle and snore.
  He pricks up his ear, lets it down with a whistle,
  with a kick on the bum they fall in to the drum
  till the courtyard's a mass of unmilitary gristle.
  Then he reads his marauders their bloodthirsty orders
  throws them a crust, betimes an onion raw
  and with his boot conducts them through the door.
  With ponderous tread he quits his retinue
  enquires the hour, consults his clockatoo
  'Great God, 'tis six! but we are late today.
  Bestir yourself, my lady wife Ubé!
  Give me my shittaboard and money-tweezers.'
  'Oh, Sir,' says she, 'permit a wife's suggestion
  of washing your dear face is there no question?'
  Such topics displease the Lord of Finance
  (Sometime King of Aragon, of Poland and of France;)
  through his foul breeks he infiltrates his braces,
  and, come rain or snow or hail, slanting to the morning gale
  bends his broad back towards the lonely places.

*Translated by C. C., December* 1945.

148027

## 'CANNON TO LEFT OF THEM'

'HORIZON—oh no zir!' The only anagram which the word can produce (collect me if I am light) sums up the comment of our many thousand enemies. For we have enemies, and it is fitting to start a new year by squaring up to them. Here is what Edmund Wilson says in the *New Yorker* about these creatures.

'*Horizon* has been a remarkable magazine and Mr. Connolly an exceptional editor. It seemed to me a proof of his merit, when I was in London at the end of the war, that, in the political and literary worlds, everybody complained about him and it but that everybody, at the same time, seemed to some degree dependent on them.'

'Everybody complained'—but that means *you*, '*hypocrite lecteur*', ungrateful swine! So that is how you talk when our back is turned!

'People in London used to complain,' he continues, 'that Cyril Connolly was out of key with the wartime state of mind' —complain of the author of 'Letter from a Civilian' which reflected the wartime state of mind more closely than a thousand Gallups! Then they will complain of anything.

I put it to you, miserable readers, that complaining has become your second nature, off with your nears! and that the over-indulgence of that dismal faculty has reduced you to a peevish back-biting state in which you are incapable of reacting to any aesthetic or intellectual stimuli, in which you have forfeited your right to happiness and sunk beneath the pleasure principle into a morose and carping esurience.

We will now deal with some particular complaints. '*Horizon* has gone off'—'And left you behind, I fear'—'It's above my head'—Ah! your head, reader? What recent gains in sensibility have you to register? Do you read or think as much as you used to? You are aware no doubt that your consumption of tobacco and alcohol has practically doubled, you will pay two hundred

and fifty pounds for a hideous leather armchair which Ribben-
trop may have sat in, you will plank down three quid for a
bottle of Scotch, you can't be trusted with a railway towel or
a piece of hotel soap, the club nail-scissors have to be kept on
a chain, you'll queue a mile for a black-market lipstick, you
talk about 'putting the vedge in the fridge', and smoke all
through meals, your manners are dreadful, you're full of hate
against other countries, you talk of Frogs, and Yanks and
Wogs, and write to *The Times* against Picasso; you're more
anti-Semitic, even, than before. You think you are a cultivated
person yet you don't know who built the house you live in, and
can you honestly say that you would rather have your child
turn into Baudelaire than Lord Nuffield? You've probably had
a manuscript sent back to you recently. I thought so. It might
interest you to know that the psychosomatic branch of this
paper is making a study of 'Rejectee mentality', and is finding
out some interesting things about you. Anything more to say?

Ah, here we have our most fee-rocious critic, Mr. Julian
Symons, the fox without a tail.

'*Horizon* was born in January 1940. It printed all sorts of
work, by writers with all sorts of beliefs: but it avoided con-
spicuously the two most interesting literary movements of our
time—the movement towards methodological criticism represented by Yvor Winters, John Crowe Ransom, Allen Tate and
some other American writers, and the movement towards the
*literary* left, of those who experimented in the twenties and
early thirties in the dangerous medium of *words*. The most
notable thing about this bland and cultured magazine, indeed,
was the maintenance of its editions at a standard of gentlemanli-
ness hardly approached by any editor of a serious literary paper
in the last twenty years. *Horizon* was a neo-Georgian literary
paper with modernist overtones: its sire may have been the
*Criterion*, but its dam was certainly the *London Mercury*.' (In
*Now*, 5.)

'*Horizon*, it may be said, is in England and in wartime the head and shoulders of this movement to keep art going: a movement which to some of us seems today merely banal and disgusting.' (In *Focus one*.)

In *Partisan Review* he tells the Americans even more plainly what he thinks. 'The Editor of the quite frankly belles-lettrist *Horizon*, who prints odd fag-ends of the Twenties . . . bound together by no organized view of Life or Society, no stronger thread than his own erratic intelligence and whimsical Barryesque good taste.'

Mr. Julian Symons, brother of the author, and formerly the ardent admirer of Wyndham Lewis, to whom he sacrificed a whole number of his short-lived *Contemporary Poetry and Prose*, is a critic of considerable acumen, driven forward like his master by the spur of envious animosity. I call him a fox without a tail because he is the leader of the art-hating school of Left-wing writers, and always at his best when prophesying the ruin of art, literature, and the 'virtuoso trapeze artists' who practise them. 'The arts are disintegrating,' he exclaims in *Now*. 'The objective of art today is to divert attention from the class struggle,' 'The intelligentsia who try to nurture the coy bloom of art as we know it are tending a dying flower.' In 'Crisis and Dismay', his article in *Focus one*, he attacks the writers of the thirties for failing in their task.

'It was symbolically much, no doubt, that Auden and Isherwood should become ambulance drivers in Spain during the Civil War, that Spender should work at Barcelona radio-station and Day Lewis write a sonnet beginning " Why do we all, seeing a Communist feel small ". But practically it was not very much.'

Isherwood never went to Spain, Auden was never an ambulance driver, nor Spender an announcer—even the line of Day Lewis is misquoted—so perhaps the attack on them is not worth very much either. Or am I being methodological?

'The highest kind of creative work likely to be written today,' insinuates the fox, 'will be satiric: taking as a base the visible world and commenting on it with violence and hatred.' There is time for one more quotation before plunging back into the class struggle: a fox's prayer. 'If we stand on the side of "progress" we may find it necessary as William Morris suspected, to resign art altogether. . . . A transition might take place, more or less gradually in individual cases, to a situation in which the writing of creative literature in any way satisfactory to the artist seemed increasingly difficult and even unimportant; that will be the point at which the creative artist who is also an honest man will lay down his pen. This consummation would grieve all artists, and be death to some: but the transition from the bourgeois art of the last three hundred years to any possible socialist art of the future will not be made without such sacrifices.'

May I suggest that Mr. Symons, who is, I feel sure, as honest as he is creative, sets us an example, like a good Socialist, and makes that great sacrifice here and now?

*January* 1946

## HOMMAGE TO SWITZERLAND

THE journey from Paris, in the July heat-wave, was a nightmare of discomfort. The train, leaving at nine in the evening, did not reach the Swiss frontier till noon the next day; foodless, waterless, seatless, the occupants stood in all the carriages as well as the corridors while the train passed the long hours of tropical night panting and blowing beside some dried-up water-hole. Old, wild-eyed, and orange with grime, those who persisted into the Jura, reached the Swiss escarpment, stretching their legs by the buffetless frontier station. Then suddenly Canaan, a land flowing with milk and honey, the Val de Travers! After trout and ham and two kinds of white wine at the first Swiss station, Les Verrières, we became tourists—no longer those mean suspect civilian figures, shady and shadowed, which anyone not in uniform on a European train invariably appears—but tourists with guide-books, hotel-folders, packages of cigarettes and the *Journal de Genève* under our arms, while the neat bright electric train rattles over the torrents, brushes the spruce trees, cascades from bright sun into black pine-shadow and back again, coasting along the mountain shoulder of the Val de Travers, whose chalets and trout-streams and widening pastures, unfurl far below.

Such was our intoxication, Alp-starved since 1939, that every sleeper on the track, every cable and pylon, every newly born aroma of mountain sunlight and fir-forest and the name of every station appeared the last unbearable saturation-point in the rebirth of feeling—and then when this saturation seemed reached came the spectacle, quivering in the noontide haze, blue as the Aegean, green as Cumberland, shot by the copper sulphate and the azure of the sky, of the blue-green iridescence of the vineyards tumbling down, between their limestone walls with the name of the grower painted on them in bright black letters, into the lake of Neuchâtel. This dazzling lake, first reminder that fresh water can be coloured, we follow through the afternoon heat, until we can truly no longer feel anything. The names become German, the vines vanish and suddenly we are on the hotel balcony in Berne. I had almost forgotten that hotels had balconies. This one surely overlooks one of the most lovely views in the world; a near vista of pleasant hill suburbs gives way to mountain and forest, beyond these ranges are the perpetually white peaks of the Oberland with their creamy glaciers, while directly underneath the hotel, uniting all the landscape and seeming to rush straight at the spectator like a giant sword-blade, flows the green arrowy torrent of the Aar. On these summer evenings, or in the morning for breakfast, one would sit out on this balcony, under the awning, with coffee and fruit and some immensely provincial Swiss newspaper, watching the lights come out or the extraordinary procession of heads in the water (for the Bernese method of bathing is to throw yourself into the Aar at one point and let the current carry you down for half a mile). The bodies shoot by like brown matches, occasionally followed by some shavings which turn into a riotous canoe. I know of no city of Berne's size where the country and the pleasures of the country are carried like this right up to the hotel door. The town of Berne is, after five years of England, sheer hallucination. The streets are all arcaded and interrupted only by baroque churches and palaces. The houses are all window-boxes, the squares all fountains, the lighting like a new ballet, the air dry oxygen. The shops are like our first Christmas tree; indeed the shops of Berne and of the Bahnhofstrasse in Zürich must rank at this time among the best in the world. Watch-makers have such dazzling exhibitions of gold and chronometry that one ends by annihilating desire through the multiplicities of choosing. Watches with old-fashioned Second-Empire lettering whose case is a flat twenty-dollar gold piece neutralize the angular affairs of cubist pin-points; white gold kills red; submersible, waterproof, anti-magnetic, altitude-proof creations cancel out the kind that wind themselves up by the motion of the wrist; fingernail-size creations in platinum and diamonds vie with monsters which bear on dials large as a florin, the days of the week, month, year, signs of the Zodiac and phases of the moon. Patek Philippe (*très chic*), Zenith, Longines, Omega (*très à la mode*), Universal end by reducing the purchaser, like a Pavlov dog, to a state of nervous breakdown and one turns gratefully to the clock department, where the mysterious Atmos clock by Jaeger Lecoultre (an experiment in perpetual motion working from the minute daily changes in the room's temperature), reigns in solitary splendour. And what is not a watchmaker's is a clothes shop, or a

Bally shoe window or a tobacconist, where every known make of cigarette and cigar can be supplied in hundreds. One comes to hate the tobacconists in the end almost as much as the jewellers—or the chemists with their innumerable layers of vitaminized tooth-pastes and hair-restorers, their nylon brushes and electric razors, with all these gadgets which exert an increasing tension on our newly born free will. This fantastic luxury, this high bloom of materialism, carried out also in wine-shops, pastry-cooks and hotels, where laundry comes back the next day and where waiters are never rude, is undoubtedly the supreme achievement of Switzerland today. There is no country in the Old World where the Craft of Living (I am not so sure about the Art) has reached such perfection, where, for those who have the money, the commonplace routine has been brought to such a peak of aesthetic efficiency and pleasure. Witness Swiss trains, paradises on wheels, clean, fast, silent, superbly windowed, wonderfully catered for; hotels like eighteenth-century engravings; cities where the old and new architecture is indistinguishable; towns which are solidly compact of beauty and tradition as a Renaissance woodcut, yet to which plastics and new light-metal alloys or experiments in street illumination have given a strange abstractionist grace and lightness, floodlit town halls, dust-free offices, suburbs worthy of great Corbusier, to whom in fact they gave birth. . . .

To fly from London to Zürich, as one could in the past in one hop, is to leave a city three-quarters of which is dirty, unhealthy, moribund and obsolete, and be transported to the most progressive industrial town in Europe, with the best-built workers' dwellings, the healthiest factories, to a city which is fighting a constant battle to keep itself from expanding, where the proportions kept between man, mountain and lake are regarded as the key to a general harmony and where the wonderful salubrity of the air, manifested in experimental thought, encourages in art a daring and rarefied curiosity—as witness Klee, Gideon, Dada, Joyce and Jung.

What has Switzerland had to pay for this bracing and ever-present material progress? A certain price in guilt and smugness —for guilt and smugness are the hall-mark of the Neutral; not to have been bombed, not to have been invaded, not to have been ruined in the cause of freedom, for a country whose love of freedom is hereditary, must occasion much subconscious uneasiness. And an internal price has been paid as well, for Switzerland is now a country surfeited with luxuries, choked by its own gold, yet where the necessities of life are still scarce and dear. The working-class cannot afford the tea-shops and the hotel-balconies, their housing conditions are often bad, they have suffered from the strict food rationing, for the luxuries to alleviate it have been outside their reach. The Swiss predicament is partly due to the country having no commodi-ties to sell but jewellery and precision instruments on the one hand, and sun, air, snow and lake-water on the other. The selling of these elements it has, through its hotel industry, raised to a fine art, but they must be sold only for textiles and foodstuffs, and few today are the countries which can supply them.

The Swiss townsman is still but at one or two removes from the peasant. The peasants have had to contend for centuries with the intractable Alps and consequently the character of Swiss industrialism is greedy and thrifty. The typical German Swiss, with their close-set eyes, thin lips and shrewdly stupid expressions, sometimes fanatically gangling and idiotic, are not among the most immediately appealing of men. Yet these philistine urban peasants of German Switzerland, through its great wealth, are now the rulers, potentially, of Central Europe, and this is another factor in the Swiss predicament. Formerly the German Swiss looked to Munich, or Vienna; the French Swiss to Paris; the Ticinese to Milan; they were

consciously provincial. Now the roles are reversed. The provinces of Switzerland have unexpectedly gained the economic
mastery over their moral and intellectual capitals.

But it's really too hot to listen to these arguments. Let's be
tourists again. First a practice run; the early train to Interlaken,
an open carriage to the lake; a swim in the cobalt water of the
Thünersee. Lying on one's back in the water, until forced to
submerge against a dive-bombing attack from horseflies, one
looks up at the icy pinnacles of the Jungfrau. The glaciers
tower above us, the water temperature is seventy degrees.
After lunch and some hours of sunbathing we return on the
lake steamer, sometimes hugging the cliffs and woodlands of
the shore, sometimes dashing across to a lake village with its
vineyards and bulbous yellow church, its ruined castle and its
café under the chestnut trees, while we exchange one group of
sunburnt summer visitors for another, and the swans glide
round the landing-stage. After this preparation the real circuit
begins; we invite you, reader, to Lausanne and Geneva. It's
too hot to get out at Fribourg, home of the catholic aristocracy,
with its convents and palaces, its admirable university publishers (L.U.F.) and its Maritainist intellectuals; too hot to
leave the train till the evening, when a new balcony looks over
the smooth-sliding Rhône at the Hôtel de l'Ecu. This little
corner of old Geneva is almost Venetian: the river, intensely
blue, looped and coiled in a swirling kaleidoscope of vanishing
eddies, washes the very walls of the old down-at-heels hotel,
where Stendhal, Dickens, Balzac, Ruskin, Byron, Chateau-
briand and an intolerably distinguished clientele of nineteenth-
century beards haunt the corridors. Here let us evoke for a
moment the vanished Geneva of Ruskin and Henry James a
century ago, the small provincial city which Beckford considered had been corrupted by Voltaire from its Calvinist
austerity. 'A little canton, four miles square, and which did not
wish to be six miles square! A little town, composed of a cluster

of water-mills, a street of penthouses, two wooden bridges, two dozen of stone houses on a little hill, and three or four perpendicular lanes up and down the hill . . . And this bird's nest of a place to be the centre of religious and social thought, and of physical beauty, to all living Europe . . . this inconceivable point of patience;' Ruskin describes in *Praeterita* the old town, 'the group of officially aristocratic houses round the cathedral and college presenting the same inaccessible sort of family dignity that they do today.' There is the inevitable visit to the jewellers (which Henry James has so well narrated in the 'Pension Beaurepas') and then Ruskin returns, fascinated, to the Rhône—'But the Rhône flows like one lambent jewel; its surface is nowhere, its ethereal self is everywhere, the iridescent rush and translucent strength of it, blue to the shore and radiant to the depth.

'Fifteen feet thick, of not flowing, but flying water; not water, neither—melted glacier, rather, one should call it; the force of the ice is with it, and the wreathing of the clouds, the gladness of the sky, and the continuance of Time.

'Waves of clear sea are, indeed, lovely to watch, but they are always coming or gone, never in any taken shape to be seen for a second. But here was one mighty wave that was always itself, and every fluted swirl of it, constant as the wreathing of a shell. No washing away of the fallen foam, no pause for gathering of power, no helpless ebb of discouraged recoil; but alive through bright day and lulling night, the never-pausing plunge, and never-fading flash, and never-hushing whisper, and, while the sun was up, the ever-answering glow of unearthly aquamarine, ultramarine, violet-blue, gentian-blue, peacock-blue, river-of-paradise blue, glass of a painted window melted in the sun, and the witch of the Alps flinging the spun tresses of it forever from her snow. . . . And in the midst of all the gay glittering and eddied lingering, the noble bearing by of the midmost depth, so mighty, yet so terrorless and harmless, with its swallows skimming instead of petrels, and the dear old decrepit town as safe in the embracing sweep of it as if it were set in a brooch of sapphire.'

When I used to visit Geneva between the wars, it seemed a dull, respectable, expensive and luxurious city, most conventionally Swiss. Then it was the capital of Savoy, and, through the League of Nations, of the world. Now, cut off from both, it has become a somewhat forgotten and undernourished corner, a 'dear old decrepit town' again. The life has receded from the boulevards and from the huge hotels along the lake and withdrawn itself into the older quarters. The whole place has become more French; packed with French refugees, it has become a little bit shabby and *louche*—if *louche*ness were imaginable in Switzerland—and taken on something of the atmosphere of forbidden Provence. There are 'cafés de la Marine', 'brasseries de la Navigation', the Place du Molard with its pollarded plane trees, its flower market, its kiosk and large cafés full of unobtainable French *apéritifs*, is like the Boulevard of Aix. Here congregate the open-shirted 'Montparnasse' of Geneva, the painters, sculptors and art critics who gravitate about Albert Skira, former editor of *Minotaure* and now publisher of the only *avant-garde* art magazine in the country, the monthly *Labyrinthe*. A more academic literary group, less surrealist or preoccupied with the visual arts, centres round Pierre Courthion and his review *Lettres*. These editors, like Skira and Courthion, all come up against the essential uncreative smallness of Switzerland, which is a country meant to publish and to propagate the arts, to produce fine books, to distribute European editions and live by exporting them, rather than to nourish its own song-birds by regularly drawing out its cheque-book. So let us thank heaven for the Place du Molard and for any other still existing pockets of indigenous European culture, before we wander back to bed through the French-smelling streets and watch the moon over the water from the haunted hotel. 'I am sitting in our old family *salon* in this place, and have sat here much of the time for the last fortnight in sociable converse with family ghosts. ... I have treated myself, as I say, to the apartments, or a portion of them, in which we spent the winter of '59–60, and in which nothing is changed save that the hotel seems to have gone down in the world a little, before the multiplication of rivals.' So wrote Henry James to his brother, with 'the shooting blue flood directly under his windows', and since October 1888, when he was at the Ecu, it has gone down, except for the food, a little bit more—bowed under, perhaps, by the ghostly impact of literary imaginations, all suffering from the terrible 'wear and tear of discrimination'. So come, reader, let's go to Lausanne—for you have guessed by now that this is to be a literary pilgrimage—where it lies on its high clean sunny ledge above the lake—embalmed in the prose of Gibbon.

'Of my situation here I have little new to say, except a very comfortable and singular truth, that my passion for my wife or mistress (Fanny Lausanne) is not palled by satiety and possession of two years. I have seen her in all seasons, and in all humours; and though she is not without faults, they are infinitely overbalanced by her good qualities. . . . In a word, my plan has most completely answered; and I solemnly pro-test, after two years' trial, that I have never in a single moment repented of my transmigration. The only disagreeable circum-stance is the increase of a race of animals with which this country has been long infested, and who are said to come from an island in the Northern Ocean.'

There are even times when Gibbon seems to sing with the same voice as Rousseau—can you distinguish between these two paeans?

'Ce paysage unique, le plus beau dont l'œil humain fût jamais frappé; ce séjour charmant auquel je n'avais rien trouvé d'égal dans le tour du monde.'

'Je perdrois de vue cette position unique sur la terre, ce lac, ces montagnes, ces riants côteaux; ce tableau charmant, qui paroit toujours nouveau aux yeux mêmes accoutumés dès leur enfance à le voir—sur tous les pays de l'Europe j'avais choisi pour ma retraite le pays de Vaud, et jamais je ne me suis repenté un seul instant de ce choix.' And yet Lausanne today is not what it was; it is with Lucerne the smuggest of Swiss cities, the most sport- and tourist-ridden; there is too much tennis and golf and exiled royalty, it's all too much of a *Musée Bourgeoise*; one wants, as in so many Swiss towns, to let loose some Senegalese, some French sailors or workmen, some drunken American women, some props and pillars of moral worthlessness, someone to walk on the grass or spit in the funicular. Now we leave Geneva and the Pays de Vaud, the stronghold of Gallic humanism, for the Catholic Valais, where nature is worshipped rather than man, and whose writers have an added mystical savagery in their attitude. St. Maurice, Martigny, Sion (the loveliest of all Swiss towns according to Cingria, and certainly the most romantic) and we enter the burnt-up white landscape of little African hills, like the homes of Spanish troglodytes, the rainless apricot country between Sion and Sierre. Here the cicada is found, and up each long lateral valley is some curiosity of wildness; women of Saracen descent, smugglers' headquarters, rare Arolla pines, or the archaic village-kingdom, with strange costumes and marriage laws, of Evolène. Above Sierre, pitiless in the sun, we struggle up through the vineyards and peach or walnut orchards, past the ragged tawny romanesque villages, with their untidy and sunny poverty which is so soul-refreshing, after the northern neatness, to our last literary pilgrimage, Rilke's tiny castle at Muzot.

'It lies some twenty minutes above Sierre, set steeply in a less arid, but happy countryside gushing with many springs —with views of the valley, of the mountain slopes and far into the most marvellous depths of sky . . . For the Valais (why is it not included when one counts earth's loveliest places?) is an incomparable country. At first I did not understand the truth of this because I *compared* it—with the most significant things in my memory, with Spain, with Provence (with which it is, indeed, via the Rhône, related by blood), but only since I admired it for its own sake has it revealed itself in all its grandeur and at the same time, as I gradually came to see, its sweet gracefulness and its strong, passionate traditions. . . . Shrines, crucifixes at every cross-road, uplands ribbed with vineyards and in late season all curly with their foliage; fruit trees, each with its tender shade and (oh, so rightly!) single fully grown poplars dotted about, exclamation marks of space crying "Here!" '

The Lötschberg is one of those tunnels which separate north and south; baroque Brigue and the Valais, the vines of the Rhône and the baked white earth with the Catholic villages, are left behind; ten minutes of darkness and we are back in the Oberland, among the heavy, broad-eaved, opulent chalets, the cows and the ski-lifts. At Spiez the lake of Thün reappears, and a branch line takes us to Gstaad, the last lap of the journey. Gstaad is an up and coming Kitzbühel, not too high, not too enclosed—a mountain village open to the sun, surrounded by fir-woods and fat pastures. A Mozart festival is on, directed by M. Kuriel. The whole ambience has that exquisite stimulation of a mountain resort assured of a future. In the evening I would usually dine with charming and hospitable friends, who own an ancient chalet. To reach them I had to cross a small ravine and would often pause half-way down, surrounded by dark firs, with the grey torrent below me, while the grass-hoppers subsided, their day's barracking over and the cold night air assumed and rarefied the scents of hay and clover. In those magic twilights I came to understand what Switzerland now was—no longer a place one rushed through on the way to

somewhere else, nor even a general playground whose inhabitants one ignored, but a fascinating and unexplored vital organ
of European civilization. I had not yet discovered the Tessin, nor
revisited the Engadine, I had seen none of the famous baroque
monuments, I had never been to Lucerne, Lugano, St. Gall,
or Winterthur, but I knew this was a stronghold of civilization,
a country which had new power thrust upon it, and whose
federal system was an object lesson to the miserable rivalries of
its battle-scarred neighbours. After the last war the Swiss
refused to adopt the Vorarlberg province of Austria; it was an
example which the four great powers have yet to follow. They
may seem prudent, cautious and unromantic, invincibly bourgeois, but they are also admirably unambitious, unconsciously
liberal, wholesomely sceptical of ideologies, and, although
perhaps too attached to money, independent, wise; tolerant,
humane and free.

I returned to Berne, to one last desperate act of indecision
in the shops, a last farewell to the Anglophil staff of the
Bellevue, and then the new through-carriage to Paris, a carriage
which returned to the Jura in full Swiss cleanliness, only to
become poorer and dirtier with each ham-strung league
through crisis-ridden France. I had said good-bye to a radiant
hospitable country, to which I hope now constantly to return,
a bower of bourgeois bliss with its pre-war standards of health
and courtesy, the complex land of Rousseau and Calvin where
all Nature cries 'Forgive yourself!' and Man, defiant, answers
'Never!'

*February* 1946

# MAGNA GRAECIA

FROM time to time in its long history *Horizon* has come
forward with a plea for something or made some plan or suggestion. As these plans usually involve the spending of money

for a cultural purpose, the preservation of beauty or the encouragement of art they have always met with complete failure. Nevertheless, though deeply conscious by now that we live in a philistine country at one of the most triumphantly philistine moments of world history, we must still go on making such plans; it is part of our function. Here is yet another.

Those of us who are fortunate enough to have been able to visit the Greek Exhibition at Burlington House will have been dazzled once more by the extreme beauty of almost all the objects in the archaic section. There was a period which culminated at the turn of the sixth century B.C. and which ended a year or two after the battle of Marathon, when art, religion, and life were all one, when the essential *magic* of the human personality had not yet faded into a more serene and rational classicism, and before the mutterings of Platonic duality had arisen to poison man's long love-affair with his surroundings. In this brief spring morning between Peisistratus and Pericles man was both master of his fate and exquisitely at ease in the universe. Everything depended on him except the state of grace in which he found himself, his destiny so tragically linked with that of the Gods above, so movingly entwined with the fate of the trees and animals below.

There are a very few examples of the art of this period—the age of Heraclitus, one might call it—in the Greek Exhibition. There are not very many in the whole world. Could we not find some more?

*     *     *

Perhaps because none of us really felt that the War is over, the question of Allied War Memorials has not yet received much attention—but if there is one place where a joint Anglo-American war memorial is indicated it lies on the battlefields of southern Italy. Here, while overthrowing a tyranny, a multitude of English and Americans perished, and here a considerable portion of the world's heritage of beautiful things was destroyed with them. Let the memorial then take the form of our two governments setting aside money, labour, and some of the wonderful machinery which the war has begotten to the uncovering of new treasures in replacement of the old; let England take one site, the United States another and let us excavate them as perfectly as science knows how to and then pool the results in a common treasury, a museum of wonders to be set up on some battlefield like Cassino.

Having originally conceived this idea with special reference to Herculaneum, where it is a question of first building a new suburb for the inhabitants who live above it, but where the possibilities of finding the lost manuscripts of Livy, Tacitus and Petronius—of anything between Sappho complete, to the Autobiography of Agrippina—more than justify the work and expense, we were fortunate to be put in touch with a very remarkable Italian, Doctor Zanotti-Bianco, who is now the head of the Italian Red Cross. Dr. Bianco, who was badly wounded fighting with us in the 1914–18 war, is both a musician, an archaeologist, and an anti-Fascist, and during his long spell of disgrace with the Mussolini Government he was able to go on with his excavations at his own expense, and to discover, in 1940, the sculptures from the archaic sanctuary of Hera, near Paestum. He has been able to add two more names to the list, Sybaris, where modern machinery can divert the river which, in 510 B.C., the enemies of that most intelligent city, with puritan relish, had compelled to flow over it, and his own sanctuary of Hera near Salerno. (The metopes of the temple escaped falling into German hands because, owing to the refusal of help from Mussolini's government, they had to be stacked in a peasant's hut.)

The great advantage of excavating the rest of Herculaneum and the untried Sybaris is that both these names are common property. The memorial would not be a recondite and archaeological undertaking but something which we could all look

forward to and understand. We have taken enough beauty out
of the world in our lifetime; for the sake of the generations who
have yet to judge us, let us try to put some back.

*       *       *

DEAR MR. CONNOLLY,

During our recent conversation in London you asked me
which of the excavations now possible in Italy would be of the
greatest general interest; and you mentioned the high hopes
which were raised long ago and are still in our day excited
everywhere by the idea of bringing to light again the city of
Herculaneum, buried as it was in the full flower of its life. It is
certainly difficult for anyone replying to your question to divest
himself of his own preferences and to neutralize the prejudices
of his personal taste and of his own field of study. For example,
a prehistorian would without hesitation direct you to the
excavation of the whole of the aeneolithic necropolis which
Allied troops stumbled on in preparing an aerodrome near
Paestum. This necropolis is at the moment being scientifically
explored, although only on a very small scale owing to shortage
of funds. An Etruscan archaeologist would emphasize to you
the importance of clearing the whole of that area of Veii, where
a spirited enterprise recently undertaken has brought to light
very considerable new fragments of the famous group of terra-
cotta statues, among them further pieces of the statue of
Apollo itself (the Apollo of Veii in the Etruscan Museum in
Valle Giulia in Rome)—or else he would propose to you the
search for new tombs in one of the famous cemeteries of
Tarquinia, Cerveteri (Caere) or another of the many cities of
ancient Etruria. These tombs with their wall paintings and
their rich furnishings have always excited not only the interest
of professional archaeologists, but also the admiration and
curiosity of your fellow-countrymen, from G. Dennis, British
Consul in Italy last century, to the novelist D. H. Lawrence,

who wrote pages of such insight and feeling in his *Etruscan Places*. Others would talk to you of the Italic peoples or of Rome and her civilization, and of the many topographical and historical problems still awaiting solution. I have always felt that among all the artistic achievements created on our soil of Italy the noblest is the art of Magna Graecia, as much for its antiquity as for the powerful influence it has exercised on the rest of our peninsula. So, naturally, I turn my eyes to the south of Italy, which still remains, by and large, shrouded in mystery. To pass over Sicily, which is better explored, what a number of buried cities there are to disinter in the extreme toe, alone, of the peninsula! Heraclea, the birthplace of Zeuxis, whose laws were revealed to us by the two famous bronze tablets discovered in 1752 in a torrent bed; Ionian Siris, of which a fragment of Archilochus speaks, but its remains have not yet tempted the archaeologist's pick; Thurii, near which were found the tombs with the famous orphic inscriptions on gold foil; Pythagorean Croton, the archaeological zone of which is still all to be explored, as is Skylletion likewise, where the memory of Cassiodorus, too, calls us; Mataurus, the probable birthplace of Stesichorus, Terina, with its magnificent coinage, Temesa, mentioned in Homer.

But the most acute and fascinating problem of all is undoubtedly that of Sybaris, that rich and powerful city destroyed and desolated as early as 510 B.C. Its remains still sleep untouched in the magnificent valley of the Crathis. You remember the chorus of Trojan women in Euripides (*Troades* 222), 'Nearby, as you voyage in the Ionian sea, is the city nourished by that fairest of rivers, the Crathis. Its marvellous waters burnish the hair to a glowing chestnut. It ripens and enriches a land that abounds in men of vigour'.

Years ago, tempted by the hope of identifying the site of this ancient city—its discovery would be of fundamental importance for the history of West Greek culture and art, providing at last an absolute date for our whole chronology like that of the so-called Persian deposit at Athens—I made a series of trial trenches in the waterlogged and malarial plain of the Crathis, whereas my predecessors had directed their search to the surrounding hills. I started from the idea that a city so closely linked by commerce with Miletus in Asia Minor must have stood on the sea coast and developed round its harbour there. In fact, on the left bank of the Crathis, not far from its old mouth, where to this day the peasants claim to be able to see, in the low water of summer, the old walls in its bed, I found the remains of a building of the Roman period. If this corresponds, as I maintain it does, to the Roman colony of Copia-Thurii, planted in 194 B.C. in the territory of the Greek Thurii, according to Strabo, it is very probable that I really hit on the site of the ancient city, since Pliny (*Natural History III*, 97) says that 'the colony lay between the two rivers Crathis and Sybaris, on which had stood the city of the same name'. One thing is certain: from the deepest level which I just reached, I extracted a carved head in tufa with traces of its original paint in various colours, datable to the second half of the sixth century. This can be accepted as the first evidence of the lost city to come to light.

At this point you will perhaps think that I mean to indicate the excavation of Sybaris as the one on which all our efforts should today be concentrated. Unfortunately, the state of the ground is such as to make the enterprise not only most difficult, but enormously costly. Owing to the deforestation of the mountains the Crathis has in the course of centuries swept down so much gravel and alluvium as considerably to raise the level of its bed and to push its mouth out seawards. Formerly the owners, and more recently the State, with its system of land improvement, have striven to embank its waters at a higher level than the surrounding plain. Obviously, as a result any excavation at once provokes a strong uprush of water. In fact, to achieve my very restricted excavation, I had to keep two motor pumps continuously at work. An excavation on a large scale would require either the diversion of the Crathis into the bed of one of the nearby torrents or a big electrical plant to keep enough pumps going. Both alternatives seem to me out of the question under present conditions.

In contrast to this, there is now no hindrance to continuing an excavation which has already been productive beyond all our hopes and still appears full of promise. I mean the excavation at the mouth of the Sele (Silaris), which I have directed in conjunction with Miss P. Zancarri Montuoro, D.Phil., not only without any help from the Government, but, in fact, continually being hampered for political reasons. We discovered there the sanctuary, famous in antiquity, of Argive Hera. The amazing harvest of some fifty archaic reliefs of different dates is unexampled in Italy and is hardly to be equalled even on the soil of Greece. These reliefs have restored to us almost complete the frieze of a small temple of early archaic date, probably of Sybarite dedication and workmanship. We have not only the ground plan of this building, but almost all its constructional and decorative parts. We have, however, among the reliefs only five of the metopes adorning the larger temple, real masterpieces of ripe archaic art, which appeal not only to connoisseurs but to anyone with a feeling for beauty, and keep us in a fever of expectation for the remainder still hidden in the plain of the Sele. This, then, is an excavation certain to give results and not very expensive, since the Greek stratum lies at no great depth and we have already identified the places where the remains are abundant.

Finally, I return to your question about Herculaneum. The dream of bringing to light the exceptionally well-preserved remains of this more educated and refined neighbour of Pompeii, whose disaster it shared, remains as tantalizing as ever—it is kept alive by the thought of the Villa of the Pisos, which of itself has yielded a whole museum of bronzes, and the incomparable collection of papyri, of such importance for the history of philosophy, and it is fired anew by the most recent finds which modern scientific method can interpret so fully and preserve so perfectly.

But in this tragic post-war period in which our greatest anxiety is to secure shelter for the many deprived of it, it would be more than ever unthinkable to demolish a great part of the densely populated town of Resina. This difficulty has even in the past hindered the realization of the plan to excavate Herculaneum in its entirety, although it has been so often projected.

In conclusion, my dear Mr. Connolly, I reply to your question by putting in the first place for possible and promising excavations the sanctuary of Argive Hera at the mouth of the Silaris. In doing so, I am not, I think, letting myself be influenced by too personal a prejudice in its favour.

Even the smallest fraction of the discoveries so far published will, I hope, be enough to justify my choice.

Yours very sincerely,

UMBERTO ZANOTTI-BIANCO

*Translated by Colin Hardie.*

\* \* \*

'. . . Your suggestion for excavating a Greek site in southern Italy is magnificent. Why not start a fund? But if Sybaris is too expensive—I have been there and agree it would be—what about Metaponton? It is more famous than the Sele site because it was the centre of Pythagoreanism, the most mysterious and tantalizing of Greek cults. Its cemetery might contain extraordinary finds such as the gold orphic tablets found—was it?—at Laeri. It would be quite easy to excavate if one chose the non-malarial season. I spent an afternoon walking over the site which is thick with potsherds, and picked up two sixth-century coins without making any particular search.

'At the only house within a mile—a filthy hovel where we spent the night—the only food they gave us to eat was beans! But if the excavations are to be a war memorial, then they should be combined with a drainage scheme for draining the marsh where a particularly deadly mosquito breeds. Then a rich stretch of soil would be restored to cultivation again and something done for the peasants as well as for art and archaeology. . . .'

GERALD BRENAN. Aldbourne. 23 March 1946.

# POST-WAR ENGLAND

IF there is one sentiment which we have tried to avoid in *Horizon* it is national pride. But returning after six weeks (about which I hope to report more fully) I felt from Dover to London what can only be described as a patriotic glow. First, because we have no black market with its consequent atmosphere of dishonesty and of an immense cleavage between rich and poor. Next, because the new cocktail bar on the Golden Arrow is a cheerful and ingenious affirmation of the right to pleasure, something which is post-war and not merely a return to pre-war, a lyric contribution to the poetry of motion. Then because, unlike the Americans, we do not aspire to the moral leadership of the world while yet unwilling to impose rationing in our own country or to resist demanding far-flung bases from our old allies; we send no goats to Bikini Atoll, nor, like the Russians, do we obstruct every suggestion which brings peace nearer while acting in such a hypnotized way as to induce a war which we will patently lose. On the contrary, by our plan to evacuate Egypt and India, we are performing one of the rare democratic actions of our time. For at last we admit that the right of the inhabitants of a country to liberty overrules the benefits, however well-intentioned, of occupation. In a short time no Englishman need feel that any fraction of the guilt for a lathi charge is his. (It is always surprising that we, who have fought hard for our liberty, are so quick to use the word 'rebel' about those who defend their own when we have taken it away.) Egypt and India, after another ten years of rabid nationalism, will become rich and fascinating countries, as they were in the days of Herodotus; we shall look forward to the visits of their wise men, and I hope they, in return, will not be too difficult over our visas. Occupied countries are like caged animals; who would not rather photograph a wild elephant than ride on a tame one?

Two more bills, looming in the distance, complete the happy picture. A new measure of prison reform and an education bill which eliminates 'school certificate'. Prison reform can come only from a party whose members have not passed through the great public schools and thereby grown accustomed since childhood to the deterrent of a barbarous severity. Flogging, or being flogged, for many Tories is the first real experience of their life—hence their rebellion against the proposed abolition of the 'cat'. As for examinations, they should be for rusting Middle-age, or for very backward groups, like newspaper proprietors. The object of education is to teach the young first to want to learn, then how to learn. They can be left to examine themselves.

To remove complacency I then made a list of some major indications of a civilized community (limited to ten)—I doubt if any country has more than two. Other versions welcome.

1. No death penalty. (The State doesn't fear its members.)
2. Model prisons. (Criminals can be rehabilitated.)
3. No slums. (The material conditions which produce crime need not exist.)

4. Light and heat supplied free, like water and air. Clothing, nourishment, privacy and medical attention almost free. Transport as near as possible within the reach of all.

5. Vocations for all, not just work.

6. Full toleration of opinion. No censorship of written or spoken words, no tapping of telephones, opening of letters, compiling of dossiers. Special clinics for those who do compile them. No passports, identity cards or money-visas. All travel encouraged.

7. No residue of harsh and antiquated religious prejudices in the law, e.g. laws which deal with homosexuality, divorce, bigamy, abortion, etc., to be based on intelligent humanism. This goes also for regulations which affect men bathing without tops, women wearing shorts, etc., and all licensing and Sunday entertainment.

8. The acquisition of property to be recognized as an instinct which is, like the wish to excel, beneficial in moderation, but no one to own more property than he can see, nor the lives of other people, including children—and no children to be rich, which means also that no one would be the poorer for having them.

9. A passionate curiosity about art, science and the purpose of existence, akin to the admiration felt in some countries for sport, and a desire to preserve architecture, natural beauty and wild life.

10. No discrimination against colour, race, class or creed.

*June* 1946

## 'INFLATIONARY DECADENCE'

THE *New Republic* is a tough homogeneous American weekly, more hot for Left-wing certainty than our own *New Statesman*, and considerably less warm for the humanities. I have just come across a recent number in which the leading literary article castigates a minor English writer, whose name, since he is notoriously touchy, for the moment escapes me. 'Mr. ——', the article concludes, 'seems well fitted, by precept and example, to preside as *arbiter elegantiarum* over the cultural disintegration of the Empire. His work serves more or less authoritative notice that England, long declining into a second-class power, has begun her decline into a second-class culture.'

And aren't you pleased, Mr. Levin! For as always when encountering anti-British feeling one is struck by the short-sighted complacency of those who create it, as of a son getting drunk to celebrate his father having lost all his money. If, for example, we substitute France for England in Mr. Levin's sentence (which remains neither more nor less true), a considerable amount of self-satisfaction seems to ebb from it, for we all perceive that a second-rate France would be a disaster; and even substituting Germany for England is not reassuring. For we know now that culture, like peace, is indivisible, that when the culture of a country becomes second-class, the culture of another does not at once jump up and become first-class. There is simply that much first-class culture the less. If Mr. Levin did not suffer from that particular form of inferiority complex which is the intellectual fear and jealousy of Britain (the same attitude towards France is its equivalent here), he would be wringing his hands at having to make such a statement. For, of course, he is right. We are 'declining into a second-class culture'—like the rest of the world. What else is to be expected after the Nine Years' War? We are entering an age of Inflationary Decadence, an age when rewards increase as standards decline. Sometimes the State provides the inflation (for example, Ehrenbourg), sometimes it comes through a political movement (Aragon), sometimes from a mass publishing house or Hollywood or the Press. Thus in Europe inflation takes the form of honouring the writer while neglecting his work. The writer becomes a public figure and his reputation as a public figure, his platform manner, his political views, coagulate into something more real than his literary reputation; he becomes a symbol, an expression of a certain attitude, and whenever that attitude is required he is in demand by people to whom his work may be quite unknown. Ultimately, the public figure devours the private one. In America the inflation is monetary—the author's work is filmed or pulped into gigantic cheap editions until he grows accustomed to writing with an eye only to the films or to these cheap editions, at which moment the writer is usually dropped for one whose reputation is fresher.

Mr. Levin gives a few facts to substantiate his attack:

1. 'The ebb and flow of political exile and artistic expatriation have lately indicated that the centre of Anglo-American gravity is shifting towards this country.' Granted, but with the recovery of Europe and the cost of living increasing in America, as in 1920, it may well shift back.

2. 'The spread of Basic English, far from presaging a revival of British imperialism, seems actually to threaten an encroachment of the East upon the West, modifying the language of Shakespeare to suit the convenience of Madame Chiang Kai-Shek'—or enriching for her, as likely as not, the language of Hemingway.

3. 'The fact that, after twenty years of Bernard Shaw's dotage, his birthday interview is still the event of the literary season, is something less than a sign of vitality.' This seems to me like questioning the vitality of Mr. Levin in writing a book on Joyce's *Finnegans Wake*, because the one is dead and the other never existed.

4. 'Some resourceful French critics, *faute de mieux*, have gone so far as to take Charles Morgan seriously.' And a million Americans have bought *Brideshead Revisited*. Is that our fault, too?

5. 'The accumulating recognition of so sincere, so sensitive

and so essentially a minor writer as E. M. Forster is a damaging admission that England has no major novelist.' Yes, we may perhaps have no major novelist, though the recognition of Forster is due rather to the fact that, writing in an age of major novelists, he happened to be thirty years ahead of his time.

Meanwhile, there are three writers whom we envy America: Hemingway as a novelist, Edmund Wilson as a critic, and E. E. Cummings as a poet. America possesses many more good writers, but those three have something which we are inclined to lack (perhaps because they are father's boys and our literature is apt to be made by those more influenced by their mothers); that is to say, they are illusion-free and unite a courageous heart-whole emotional drive to an adult and lively intellectual toughness. Many possess this union but few write so well.

Meanwhile, what's to be done to prevent our culture becoming even more second-class? *Horizon* takes the matter very seriously. The current number is for those who wish in summer to relax and enjoy a story as perfect as Mr. Waley's 'Mrs. White' or scenes of travel as rich as Mr. Mortimer's.

August for the people and their favourite islands.

But in September we intend to open a long-drawn-out campaign which will start by consideration of the basic factor in Inflationary Decadence: the ways in which contemporary writers are compelled to earn their livings.      *August* 1946

# THE COST OF LETTERS

THE questionnaire which follows was sent out to a selection of writers of various types and ages. As nearly all the replies were too long we had to eliminate several by drawing lots and we apologize to writers who have thus suffered. For one reason or another about half a dozen of the most successful novelists whom we circulated could not reply, so that this point of view, so rewarding to others, is insufficiently represented. Besides the well-established, we have tried also to include some young writers who are just beginning to tackle the problem in all its enormity.

Naturally, many other factors besides the economic are responsible, some of which we hope to investigate in future numbers, but out of these varied replies the following picture emerges clearly: (1) writers do not wish to live more simply than members of any other profession; (2) the rewards of literature (as opposed to those of journalism) have not been increased to cover the added expense of living. Writers are, therefore, forced into secondary occupations which soon tend to become primary; (3) with the decline of private incomes and private patrons, the State must do more to help writers, preferably by indirect subsidy. This will not come to pass without much persuasion from the writers themselves, many of whom disapprove of the State and show no inclination to influence it.

QUESTIONNAIRE:

1. How much do you think a writer needs to live on?

2. Do you think a serious writer can earn this sum by his writing, and if so, how?

3. If not, what do you think is the most suitable second occupation for him?

4. Do you think literature suffers from the diversion of a writer's energy into other employments or is enriched by it?

5. Do you think the State or any other institution should do more for writers?

6. Are you satisfied with your own solution of the problem and have you any specific advice to give to young people who wish to earn their living by writing?

## *John Betjeman*

1. As much as anyone else.

2. No person requiring intoxicating drinks, cigarettes, visits to cinemas and theatres and food above British Restaurant standard can afford to live by writing prose if he is not 'established'. Not even a *popular* poet, if there is one, can live by his poetry.

3. I can speak only for myself. I would like to be a station-master on a small country branch line (single track).

4. I do not know.

5. The State cannot possibly help a creative writer since, properly viewed, a writer is as much part of the State as a Civil Servant. You are therefore asking should a writer do more for *himself*? A Government Office certainly cannot help since it is concerned, or should be concerned, with making living conditions tolerable, with giving us enough to eat, proper roads and drains and heat and light and arranging wars for us when our existence is threatened from outside. A few writers find their inspiration in writing about politics—most of them write vilely—but I would have thought the subject-matter of a writer is irrelevant to this question. I do not see why writers, as much as school-teachers or manual workers, should not be entitled to a State pension when their powers are over. As it is, they are subject to the publicity and niggardliness of the Civil List. A decent pension should be the limit of help from a Government Office.

The Society of Authors might arrange that when the State approaches a writer to write something, the State should offer a fee commensurate with a generous periodical instead of apologizing for the lowness of the fee and excusing it on the grounds that it is Government work.

6. No. Who is? But if someone is born to be a writer nothing will prevent his writing. Perhaps the bitter tests of

today are a good thing. But you need great strength of character. At all costs avoid an advertising agency where you will either have to write lies or embellish facts in which you are not interested; such work is of the devil. Journalism is a better way out for weak characters, such as I am, who are slaves to nicotine and drink. It teaches you to write shortly and clearly. It allows you to say what you think—at least reputable journalism does. It forbids you to be a bore.

But because I believe that there is such a thing as a balance between mental work and manual work and because I believe that in Britain today people are subjected to too much of one or too much of the other, I would advise a young writer to equip himself for manual work which he thinks he will enjoy. It is pretty certain to be better paid than is writing in its initial stages. If I had my life over again, I think I would take up some handicraft—making stained glass or weaving or french polishing or woodcarving—and with this to fall back on and to content the manual side of me without destroying my soul, I would be refreshed and confident when I wrote. But I would have taken on such work with writing as my chief aim. I would have taken it on in self-defence because I knew I must write and that God had called me to be a writer, but demanded that I do my quota of work with my hands.

## *Elizabeth Bowen*

1. I should say that, as in the case of any other kind of person, this depends on his liabilities and his temperament. In my own case, I should like to have £3,500 a year net.

2. I should say that, with *all* past books in print and steady production still going on, a writer, if his or her name is still of value, should be able to command two-thirds of the sum I have named by the time he or she is sixty or sixty-five.

3. I should say in a man's case a suitable second occupation would be either medicine, architecture or law. Very few

women would have time to carry on two professions simultaneously as their personal life and domestic responsibilities take up a good deal of time in themselves.

4. I should think that a writer's writing would be improved by any activity that brought him into company other than that of his fellow writers. Literary sequestration, which seems to be increasing, is most unfortunate. On the other hand, the diversion of energy is a danger. If a writer is doing two things at the same time he is likely to have more to write *about*, but runs the risk of writing with less high concentration and singleness of mind.

5. I find this difficult to answer, as I am not clear how much the State does already. Writers who have worked hard and shown distinction (in any field, or of any kind) should certainly be entitled to some help, or even a degree of support, in the case of illness or old age. And, equally, some sense of responsibility should be felt by the public towards the dependants (young children, etc.) of such writers. As far as I know, an extension of the Literary Fund, and possibly a contribution to this from the State, should meet the purpose.

6. I doubt if one ever does arrive at a specific solution of the problem—it is a matter of getting along from year to year. My advice to young people who wish to earn their living by writing would be to go at it slowly, with infinite trouble, not burn any boats in the way of other support behind them, and not either expect or play for quick returns.

## *Alex Comfort*

1. I cannot lay down an income scale for 'writers', as if they were a race apart from anyone else. I live on a combined income of about £500 per annum, with a wife, and one child expected.

2. In other words, can a writer who conscientiously produces work he considers artistically worth while live on the proceeds

of it? Yes, obviously he can, if he happens to write in one of the genres or styles which are commercially subsidized, but in the present world it seems to me highly inadvisable for him to do so. It means that one has to impose some sort of quota in order to live comfortably; it renders one dependent on the phases of an opinion which one ought to be forming, not obeying, and it continually dangles the temptation of subsidy-conditional-on-conforming under one's nose. I would not try to live entirely upon literary work myself, even though at the moment I probably could get paid for everything I write without being obliged to alter it. The writers who are working experimentally, or in forms such as lyrical poetry, would be quite unable to live out of their work, if only because of the relatively small volume which can be produced by one man. I have no sympathy with the Chatterton-Rimbaud fairy stories which lead writers to starve in garrets, or, the more modern equivalent, sponge on non-literary friends, because they are poets and find work too mundane. Artists are not privileged people—art is probably the human activity most deeply dependent on a responsible attitude to other people.

3. This depends upon the attitude which you adopt towards life. I believe that the most consistent and factually justifiable attitude towards life and art is Romanticism, by which I mean a philosophy based upon two postulates—that Man individually and collectively is engaged in continual conflict to assert the standards, beauty, justice, and so on, which are the product of his own consciousness, against an inert universe and a hostile environment, on the one hand, and power on the other: and that by reason of this conflict we have a definite, inescapable duty and responsibility towards all other human beings. We are afloat on a raft in a sea of mindlessness—our cargo includes all the things which consciousness regards as valuable, and there are one or two people on board who have lost their heads and are busier trying to assert their own

authority than working to keep the raft afloat. We have to
fight them with one hand and the elements with the other.
The two fights are part of one single conflict, and for me art is
the name we give to the struggle for spiritual survival and
science (the genuine article, not the kitsch variety), the fight
against death and our environment. One can add revolution,
the fight against the human allies of the dead environment.
That is why I regard scientific activity as fully continuous with
artistic activity—I don't know where one stops and the next
starts. I do not suggest that all artists should try to become
research workers, but I think that their second occupation
should be one which bears some relation to the general effort
of Man, which I call mutual aid.

4, 5, 6. My answers follow from what I have said. Non-
literary activity always enriches creation subject to my provisos.
As to the State, since one of the major battles of the sane man
in the present period is against obedience, an enemy second
only to death, I don't think the artist should touch the State or
its money with a barge-pole. The same applies to commercial
patronage, increasingly, from day to day. In a period of bar-
barism one has to be able to cut oneself off from all patronage
—put yourself in the place of the European underground
writers, and remember that the responsible human being is a
member of a permanent underground movement who must be
ready to carry on his work in the devastated landscape of the
next hundred years.

6. Yes, entirely satisfied. What I have written here and elsewhere about this question is the only advice I have to offer. It
boils down to this—be human, fight death and obedience, work
like anyone else, since that is part of humanness, despise kiss-
breeches and collaborators, and produce the work which you
feel compatible with these ideas.

For your information, my own non-literary posts at the
moment are M.O. in a Borough Children's Clinic and research

assistant at a hospital. I am paid for the first, but not the second.

## Cyril Connolly

1. If he is to enjoy leisure and privacy, marry, buy books, travel and entertain his friends, a writer needs upwards of five pounds a day net. If he is prepared to die young of syphilis for the sake of an adjective he can make do on under.

2. He can earn the larger sum only if he writes a novel, play, or short story, which is bought by Hollywood and/or chosen by one of the American book societies, but he can add considerably to his income if he tries to publish everything he writes simultaneously in American periodicals, which all pay most handsomely. This is the only dignified way of making more money without giving up more time.

3. A rich wife.

4. If you substitute 'painting' for 'literature', it becomes obvious that no art can be enriched by the diversion of an artist's energy. A good book is the end-product of an obsession; everything which impedes the growth and final exorcism of this obsession is harmful. All writers like to have hobbies and side interests to fill up the interval between obsessions, but this is not the same as having other employment. Compare Pope with Gray, Tennyson with Arnold, Baudelaire with Mérimée, Yeats with Housman. Pope and Yeats *grew*, the two dons, despite their long holidays, remained stationary.

5. The State, in so far as it supplants private enterprise, *must* supplant private patronage. But private patronage was not based on results, and the State should not count on them either. Free gifts of money should be made to those setting out on an artistic career, and at intervals of seven years, to those who persist in one. Most of our good writers need at the moment a year's holiday with pay. Furthermore, pensions to artists and their widows should be trebled, both in value and

quantity, and considered an honour, not a disgrace. All State-conferred honours to artists should be accompanied by a cash award. Furthermore, all writers and painters should be allowed a fairly large entertainment allowance, free of tax, and one annual tax-free trip abroad. Books and framed paintings (as opposed to articles, sketches, posters, etc.) should be regarded as capital and the income from them not taxed. This would encourage the production of books rather than the better-paid journalism by which most writers now make their living. Money spent on buying books and works of art by living artists should also be tax-free. Big Business, too, could do much more for writers and painters. Shell and London Transport before the war were setting the example. Even the general public can send fruit and eggs. The State's attitude towards the artist should be to provide *luxe, calme et volupté*, and when it receives *ordre et beauté* in return, to be sure to recognize it.

6. No, certainly not. What a question! As for the young, don't become writers unless you feel you must, and unless you can contemplate the happiness, security and cosiness of respectable State-employed people without loneliness or envy. Otherwise, like most of us, you will resemble the American 'who wanted to be a poet and ended up as a man with seven jobs'.

## C. Day Lewis

I could not generalize about any of these questions. Ideal thing, for most writers: a private income—small enough not to encourage laziness or dilettantism, large enough to relieve the worries, obsessions and grosser expedients of poverty, say £150 to £300 a year. Failing this, should a young writer make his basic income from (*a*) literary hack-work or (*b*) a second occupation? Depends so much upon the individual. Advantage of (*a*) is that it has (or can have) some relation to his serious work, something to do with words and ideas and even with the

imagination; and one only learns how to write by writing—
and 'hack' writing has its discipline, its opportunities to shirk,
to twist, or to be honest and careful, just as does 'serious'
writing: serious writing, in one sense, is any writing you take
seriously. Advantage of (b), for the beginner at any rate, is that
it is the best way for him to find out whether he is really meant
to be a writer: if he is not, the interest of the second occupation
will soon overshadow the interest of writing; and he will have
made a start with this other profession, instead of having to
start again from scratch. The most suitable second occupation
for a serious writer? A routine job, with regular hours, spare
time, and (particularly if he is a novelist) one which brings him
much into contact with people: for a novelist, who needs a
wide range and diversity of personal contacts, medicine, the
law, or commercial travelling might be recommended: for a
poet, in so far as he needs a deeper, narrower experience, the
instinctive kind of human relationship which comes from
working with other people is perhaps best—the relationship of
a Civil Servant, a schoolmaster, or for that matter a soldier or
a miner, with his colleagues. The poet is a special case, anyway: other serious writers can, with luck, and without loss of
integrity, make a living from their writing when established;
the poet cannot, by his poetry alone. Ideally, he should arrange
his life more regularly than the novelist; there is a systole and
diastole in his creative workings, and his life should be adapted
to these—a period of taking in followed by a period of giving
out. He, if any writer, should receive support from the State;
for, on the whole, his writing will be apt to suffer more than
others' from diversion of his energy either into hack writing
or a second employment: but State support should involve him
in no obligations except to his poetry; therefore it would best
come from some non-political organization such as the Arts
Council. On the other hand, since friction stimulates, no writer
should have things made too easy for him, materially, morally,

psychologically: a smooth, cosy life in the bosom of the State, or the intelligentsia, will not do: it is in his struggle with the ordinary business of living, even more than in his struggle with problems of technique, that the writer finds his own level of seriousness.

## *Robert Graves*

1, 2, 3. 'Serious writer' was, I think, a term invented by the young experimental writers of the twenties to distinguish themselves from the commercial, academic, and elder writers whom they lumped together as their common enemies. But if *Horizon* is using the word in a less provocative sense, it includes such different types as the modern novelist who writes for entertainment but not according to a commercially dictated formula, the literary historian, and the poet.

Novel writing is not an all-time job, and there is nothing against a novelist having a secondary profession if he does not happen to have inherited, or married, money. Fielding was a police magistrate, Trollope a post office official, and for contemporary instances consult *Who's Who*.

The literary historian requires whatever it needs to live in a University society with ready access to specialist libraries and specialist colleagues. The snag is the difficulty of getting a salaried post that does not involve so much routine teaching that he cannot get on with his real work.

To be a poet is a condition rather than a profession. He requires whatever it needs to be completely his own master. This need not involve great expense—W. H. Davies solved the problem by being a professional tramp.

4. This is too broad a question for me to attempt an answer here.

5. Those who pay the piper call the tune. The State (or any State-sponsored institution) is a dangerous patron of literature.

6. Everyone has to solve the problem in his own way. First by deciding to what category of writers he belongs. Many begin as poets or experimental writers, and end as journalistic hacks. On leaving the Army after the last war but one, I took a vow of poetic independence which I have kept ever since. The only job I took and held for a few months was that of Professor of English Literature at Cairo University, but I was my own master, had only one hour a week lecturing, and resigned as soon as difficulties arose with my French and Belgian colleagues. That was twenty years ago, and I have lived ever since by writing biography and historical novels: a profession which I find more easily reconcilable than most with being a poet. Shakespeare himself admitted the difficulty of a secondary profession in his sonnet about the dyer's hand; and to say that I am satisfied with my solution would be indecent—it would imply a greater satisfaction with my work than Shakespeare seems to have felt with his.

As for advice, if the young writer really wants it: never write anything that you do not really want to write for its own sake, whatever the fee is. And if you have made no critical discovery about life or literature that you feel so important that you must write it down, putting everything else aside, in the most direct and careful language of which you are capable, then you are not a serious writer. Apply for a job with a newspaper, an advertising agency or the B.B.C. But if you are a serious writer and have no money, then live on your friends, relations or wits, until you can collect a public large enough to support you. (That took me twelve years.) If you must take a job, find one wholly unconnected with writing, leave it as soon as you are proficient in it, and either live on your friends again or take another quite different one.

I cannot answer the question in terms of pounds, shillings and pence, because I live abroad and, anyhow, never keep accounts, and have a large family to support.

## Robin Ironside

As an aspiring critic, mainly of painting, I require, for the satisfaction of my aspirations and having due regard to the present cost of living, a net income of £15 a week, an amount I have never possessed and am never likely to possess. Because I am too poor, I have never been to Greece or to America; with £15 a week, I believe I could contrive to do so without great discomfort. The propriety, for a critic of fine art, of a visit to Greece, is obvious; nor is it possible to speak with any real authority on important aspects of French painting without some acquaintance with collections in the U.S. Such visits, even with the income I have proposed, would be exceptions to be paid for out of savings. But I should be able, without practising extreme thrift at home, to make brief annual excursions to France and Italy, and to visit any exhibitions, houses or museums, in the United Kingdom. Without these facilities, an aptitude for art criticism cannot adequately develop.

I regard £15 a week as a reasonable minimum, not as a bare minimum, and emphatically not as an optimum amount. Such qualities as my writings may already possess would improve as my income grew larger. I should be more diligent if I could work in a beautifully furnished room, if I could buy the books I wanted, if I could offer good food and wine to my friends, if I could be conveyed from place to place in a car, etc., etc. I am prepared to listen to people who tell me that there is a point at which money becomes a burden. But I do not really believe them. I could most profitably spend £10,000 in five minutes at Christie's; if I were excessively rich I would hand out the excess to others; if wealth is burden, it is a burden that is very easily removed.

Serious writers without private resources must necessarily make a living by some means or other. State patronage would be incompetent to deal with this difficulty. It is hard to imagine any scheme of Government support that would not, at some stage of its career, be exposed to the danger of passing a megaphone to the bad writers with one hand, while it silenced the good ones with the other. I believe that everyone interested in the prosperity of the arts should look to a general reduction of working hours. Humanity is only too conscious of its right to work; in fact, this 'right' is not a right at all, but a necessity; what we need is a recognition of our right to leisure. If the normal working day could be reduced say to four hours, the State could exercise its discretion in the matter of patronage with the certain knowledge that, however misjudged the distribution of its benefits, anyone wishing to write would at least have some time in which to prove his abilities; and time, of course, is even more necessary to a writer than a satisfactory income. I am aware that a general reduction of working hours is not immediately realizable. But it is an ideal that requires, like other ideals, to be acclaimed and pursued now, if it is ever to be achieved in the future; and I am led to suppose (perhaps mistakenly) by the pronouncements of scientists and economists that its achievement, in a world at peace, need not be regarded as a remote or Utopian eventuality.

I am not satisfied with my own solution of the problem. I have, for a writer on art, the apparent good fortune to be employed at the Tate Gallery. But the administrative needs of this very important but unhappy institution are such that, within its doors, I must largely renounce the pursuit of knowledge and that official occasions for enlarging my appreciations elsewhere hardly, if ever, occur. It is a situation that must frustrate more than it can assist any ambition to qualify fully as an art critic.[1] If I possessed a private income of even £5 a week or a capital sum of £1,000, I would resign in the brave but slender hope that additional sums earned by writing and

---

[1] Mr. Ironside subsequently resigned from the Tate Gallery to become a painter and freelance.

painting would provide a tolerable life for a substantial period of time.

Since I do not believe it is possible to make a living by writing criticism, I have no advice to offer to young people who wish to do so. I should be ashamed to dissuade and afraid to encourage them.

## *Robert Kee*[1]

There is something inside all artists which remains themselves whatever happens, and this has nothing to do with income unless income is so low that they have neither time nor energy to be themselves.

The trouble is that few writers can be certain of obtaining regularly from their writings even the £400 a year which I regard as necessary to supply the time and energy with which to write. They have to turn to bureaucracy or journalism or some other activity which demands allegiance to society and thereby castrates them as writers. However, if there is no other way for a writer to get his £400 a year, a part-time extra job is at least preferable to a full-time one. And as a writer's business is to do with words it is obviously more sensible for him to turn to some form of word-using rather than to glass-blowing or road-making. But let him be quite clear about what he is doing. There should be no attempt to compromise between money-earning and writing. There are already too many writers who, in the higher forms of intellectual and literary journalism, have lost sight of their real work. The principle should be: the easier the money, the more suitable the second occupation. If a writer cannot find enough to write about in what goes on all round him, without being 'enriched' by other employments, he might as well give up being a writer altogether.

But the idea of a writer having to descend to tricks to be able to follow his trade is unpleasant, and the society which tolerates

[1] Winner of one of the recent Atlantic Awards.

it is being short-sighted merely because it means that so much less serious writing will be done. How then is a writer to get his £400 a year? I suppose publishers could be made to surrender a great deal more of it than they do at the moment. The present relationship between writer and publisher seems as absurd as if a man were to be paid pocket-money by his butler. But this is really irrelevant because even if publishers did pay fairly it would not help the writer who produces little or who is not in sympathy with his time.

Therefore the State, as the instrument of society, should make £400 a year available to anyone who wants to be a writer. This would be renewable every year at the option of the writer. The only condition would be that no other employment could be taken during that year. There would be few abuses of this system. Four hundred pounds a year is not enough to tempt the crook. Moreover, any charlatan who had no intention of writing would get so bored with nothing to do on so little money that he would be eager to escape at the end of the year. Admittedly some appalling writers would be given a chance but, regarded as experimental waste, this would be a minor drawback. We are prepared to tolerate several million pounds-worth of experimental waste to produce a new atom bomb. Surely we could afford a few thousands to produce a new writer?

This £400 a year would in no way be an attempt to reward the writer for what he does. It would merely make it possible for him to write. The writer should be paid for what he is, not what he does. However, the State should also see that those writers who do produce something are more suitably rewarded than at present. No income tax should be payable on income derived from writing, though it would be payable on the basic £400. A considerable sum—say, the cost of about one afternoon at war—should be set aside every year to be distributed as prizes for poems, novels, criticism, editorship, etc. And if anyone thinks that this State interest in literature would lead to the same results as in the totalitarian countries, I would say that our literatures would resemble each other just about as much as our State legal systems do at present.

In answer to your last question I can only say that I now enjoy £250 tax-free for one year on similar conditions to those which I have suggested. In so far as this is not £6 a week and will not continue after the end of the year, I am dissatisfied. In so far as it does give me a chance to write, I realize that I am more lucky than many writers who have already produced distinguished work.

## Laurie Lee

The commodity most necessary to the writer is not money at all, but time. The writer needs guaranteed time, long avenues of it stretching far away before him, free from congestion, side-tracks or concealed entrances. For, ignoring the occasional lyric cartwheel, which covers no more than a moment of paper, serious writing is one of the most pedestrian occupations that exists.

I think few serious writers can earn this necessary time, legitimately, by the sort of writing they most wish to do. There are always the speed-kings, of course, but they pay heavily with blurred and half-seen images and phrases mutilated by the wind. A writer needs time to pause, to explore, to cultivate in detail the prospect before him. He needs to take time, and having taken it, to consume it in his own time.

But who among us is free to do this? Look at the panting cross-country novelists. Look at the six-day-bicycle-riding script writers, struggling at poems while changing tyres. Their doom is in the pace and the payout; they are paid off by the number of milestones they cover, and not by their discoveries of the country in between. These are the things which break their hearts and wind.

Old-day patronage was in many ways evil, but at least it gave the artist time without tears. Its modern counterpart—State or commercial sponsorship in their present forms—is a great deal worse, for this, geared to the speed-neurosis of industry, induces in the writer all the jumping-jack hysteria of the factory-worker faced with the dictatorship of the moving belt.

What are the present alternatives? A he-man's job as wood-cutter or crane-driver, with a couple of hours writing in the evenings? Romantic fallacy! The body's exhaustion is also the mind's. A State job, then—Ministry propagandist or B.B.C. hack? No; they fritter and stale like nobody's business.

What then? A State pension for all writers, with no questions asked? Not altogether; but that is more like it. Hardship and near-starvation are not bad for the young: they force the broader view, they stimulate, they atomize the coral-coasted island; they give birth to thoroughbreds of sublimation out of frustration. Let younger writers first serve this apprenticeship, and show something for it. Then, when they have passed the test, let the State provide them with sufficient pasture to live on, a free hand, and a bonus for special achievements. But do not let this be free altogether from the demands of commission. A fat pension, with no provisos, only encourages fatness; but extra sugar for spectacular leaps will keep the beasts in condition.

As to a present personal solution of the problem: my own serves me well enough, but I cannot say it would serve others. My rules are these: To avoid as far as possible the dissipation of regular work for others. Never to despise a commission unless I dislike it. Shelve any commission whenever the compulsion to do private work arises. But generally I welcome the rewards of scattered commissions; the discipline involved often provides channels for genuine personal expression. Anyway, I like writing for a waiting audience; and ever since my

schooldays I have enjoyed making poems to a set subject. I
only wish publishers and editors would issue that kind of
challenge more often. Records are never broken except on a
set course.

## Rose Macaulay

There can't be any general rule as to how much a writer
needs to live on. But whatever it is, it is very unlikely that he
will earn it at all early in his career, unless he happens to make
a lucky hit, get chosen by book societies in this and other
countries, perhaps even get filmed. The ordinary young writer,
whether serious or not, must depend on something else for
some years. If he (or she) has good-natured and moderately
well-off parents, they may consent to keep him (or, more
likely, her) till he finds his feet, or, alternatively, finds that he
had better adopt another career. If the parents refuse this
burden, as well they may, and if there are no other means of
support, the young writer should enter some profession, the
less exacting the better. If possible, he should choose a job that
does not run counter to and stultify his creative instincts;
either purely mechanical or physical work, whose hang-over
would not impinge on his leisure, but which he could forget
entirely when he laid down his tools each day and turned to
his writing; or work that ministered to his imagination. It
might be useful to get a job abroad for a time. Southey had a
notion that he would be happy and fruitful if only he could get
the consulship at Lisbon—' 'Tis a good thousand a year'—
though as a mater of fact the Lisbon consuls have always been
busier than he supposed, and have had little time for literary
pursuits. On the other hand, diplomats, whether ambassadors
or holding some lesser post in a legation, have often written a
great deal. Councillors and First Secretaries have been eloquent, and chancelleries have been nests of singing-birds or of
experimenters in prose. But diplomacy, of course, is out of the

reach of most young writers; it is a profession approached over stiff hurdles. Easier to be a tourist agent abroad (if you know any languages), or get a job in a café or a foreign bank or firm. That way, the writer will see life a little, which should be good for him. Much better not enter an intellectual profession, such as the law, medicine, or teaching, which will absorb his mind. In former times, the country parson's was often a life which gave scope for literature and scholarship; the fact that this is seldom now the case may indicate the decline of intellectual quality among clergymen. The number of our clerical authors in the past—and down almost to the present generation—is greater than in any other one profession; the quality of their work perhaps higher. However, if the writer succeeds in finding the job to suit him—preferably a series of jobs—his professional work should enrich his talent.

The State might well consider helping young writers with temporary maintenance. 'Let there be patrons,' as Herrick (himself patroned by Emmanuel Porter) urged in moving verse. Patrons have gone out; the State might do something to fill the gap. There might be a committee for the purpose of selecting worthy candidates. As no one can tell at first whether a serious writer is a bad serious writer or a good one, a few risks would have to be taken, and a few bad writers helped, as they were often helped by patrons of old. This does no great harm; better that than good young men and women should be forced to earn their daily bread by work that uses up all their energies and stultifies their talent. All the same, writers should be ready to live a little hard; to travel cheaply if at all, to eat and drink simply. They had better not be in a hurry to get married; this leads to expense, and, if they are young women, to devastating distraction of energy. (Unless, of course, they manage to marry money, which solves the problem at once.)

## J. Maclaren-Ross

Your questionnaire arrived at an opportune moment, when I was at my wits' end to know which way to turn for money. This situation is always arising with me. Hence, my answer to your first question is: A writer needs all he can lay his hands on in order to keep alive.

How much he actually should have depends on the writer himself: his tastes and habits. In other words, he should be able to live comfortably, in a style that suits his temperament. If he is a drinker he shouldn't have to worry whether he drinks beer or spirits or wine, though he shouldn't necessarily have enough to get sozzled every night. If he is a smoker he shouldn't have to buy Woodbines if he prefers Perfectos. If he wants to buy a book he should be able to buy it, not wait until it is sent to him for review or lent to him by a friend. If he doesn't drink, smoke, read books or go the cinema, then he almost certainly has other vices, or else a wife or mistress to spend money on; well, he should have enough to spend. A writer's standard of living should be at the least as high as that of a solicitor, or any other professional man.

I am a metropolitan man and I need a minimum of £20 a week to live on, given the present cost of living; and that's *not* including rent. Whether I get it or not is another matter.

Which brings me to your second question: How can a serious writer earn this sum by writing? It's very difficult. Suppose, like myself at the moment, you have written short stories but now want to write novels. How do you raise the sum of money needed to sit down and concentrate on writing a novel in moderate peace of mind? You can't do it except by more short stories, radio plays, or what have you, the writing of which takes up most of your time and vitiates your energy. So the novel doesn't get written, that's all.

Suppose, however, you are fortunate enough to obtain an advance of £300, you certainly spend more than that while writing the book, so you're no better off; in these days of small editions and reprints at long intervals, your advance almost covers the total royalties on your sales. Then there is the interval between delivery of MS. and the appearance of the book: nine months to a year if you are lucky, three years if you are not, as in one case I know. After that there is a further period until statements of sales go through and royalties are paid up; any attempt to obtain money in between is regarded by the publisher as an imposition, or, if he doles out some small sum, as an act of charity.

Besides, advances are rarely anything like £300. They are more likely to be, at the most, £75 or £100. The *Artists' and Writers' Year Book* is still talking about £25 as a suitable advance, 'but only in rare cases can publishers be made to see this'.

Therefore a novelist is supposed to spend six months writing his book and then live for a further eighteen months or so on his advance—about £100. Plainly impossible, with the present cost of living, even for a man of the most spartan tastes.

Publishers should be made to acknowledge the higher cost of living and to pay advances in proportion; a minimum of £300 should be forced upon them, and even that will not keep anyone for eighteen months. The rates paid by editors for poems, articles, stories, are far higher now than they were before the war. Why haven't publishers raised their rates accordingly?

Until they do, the writer is compelled to exist by means, in my opinion, detrimental to his serious work. In many occupations, like film-script writing, the B.B.C., etc., he has neither the leisure nor the energy, when the day's dull work is done, to settle to what he really wants to do. I don't think there can possibly be any occupations suitable to the writer other than that of writing what he wants when he wants and of being well paid for doing so.

I don't think, either, that the State or any other institution should support writers. Such a state of affairs would inevitably lead to limitation or control of subject-matter and theme. It is the publishers and editors, who make money and reputation out of printing writers, who should do more for the people on whose work they in turn depend for their living.

But this solution to the problem does not satisfy me, since I see no hope of the present vicious system being altered; and if I have advice to give to anyone who wants to write for a living, it is this:

(*a*) Don't attempt it.

(*b*) If you are crazy enough to try, be tough; get all you can. Price your work high and make them pay. Don't listen to your publisher's sob-stories about how little he can afford. He'll have a country-house and polo ponies when you are still borrowing the price of a drink in Fitzrovia. Remember, *he* makes the money; make him give you as much as you can extort, short of using a gun or pincers. Art for art's sake is all cock, anyway.

And by the same token, please pay promptly for this contribution, because I am broke.

## *George Orwell*

1. At the present purchasing value of money, I think £10 a week after payment of income tax is a minimum for a married man, and perhaps £6 a week for an unmarried man. The *best* income for a writer, I should say—again at the present value of money—is about £1,000 a year. With that he can live in reasonable comfort, free from duns and the necessity to do hack-work, without having the feeling that he has definitely moved into the privileged class. I do not think one can with justice expect a writer to do his best on a working-class

income. His first necessity, just as indispensable to him as are tools to a carpenter, is a comfortable, well-warmed room where he can be sure of not being interrupted; and, although this does not sound much, if one works out what it means in terms of domestic arrangements, it implies fairly large earnings. A writer's work is done at home, and if he lets it happen he will be subjected to almost constant interruption. To be protected against interruption always costs money, directly or indirectly. Then again, writers need books and periodicals in great numbers, they need space and furniture for filing papers, they spend a great deal on correspondence, they need at any rate part-time secretarial help, and most of them probably benefit by travelling, by living in what they consider sympathetic surroundings, and by eating and drinking the things they like best and by being able to take their friends out to meals or have them to stay. It all costs money. Ideally I would like to see every human being have the same income, provided that it were a fairly high income: but so long as there is to be differentiation, I think the writer's place is in the middle bracket, which means, at present standards, round about £1,000 a year.

2. No. I am told that at most a few hundred people in Great Britain earn their living solely by writing books, and most of those are probably writers of detective stories, etc. In a way it is easier for people like Ethel M. Dell to avoid prostitution than it is for a serious writer.

3. If it can be so arranged as not to take up the whole of his time, I think a writer's second occupation should be something non-literary. I suppose it would be better if it were also something congenial. But I can just imagine, for instance, a bank clerk or an insurance agent going home and doing serious work in his evenings; whereas the effort is too much to make if one has already squandered one's energies on semi-creative work such as teaching, broadcasting or composing propaganda for bodies such as the British Council.

4. Provided one's whole time and energies are not used up, I think it benefits. After all, one must make some sort of contact with the ordinary world. Otherwise, what is one to write about?

5. The only thing the State could usefully do is to divert more of the public money into buying books for the public libraries. If we are to have full Socialism, then clearly the writer must be State-supported, and ought to be placed among the better-paid groups. But so long as we have an economy like the present one, in which there is a great deal of State enterprise but also large areas of private capitalism, then the less truck a writer has with the State, or any other organized body, the better for him and his work. There are invariably strings tied to any kind of organized patronage. On the other hand, the old kind of private patronage, in which the writer is in effect the dependant of some individual rich man, is obviously undesirable. By far the best and least exacting patron is the big public. Unfortunately the British public won't at present spend money on books, although it reads more and more and its average of taste, I should say, has risen greatly in the last twenty years. At present, I believe, the average British citizen spends round about £1 a year on books, whereas he spends getting on for £25 on tobacco and alcohol combined. Via the rates and taxes he could easily be made to spend more without even knowing it—as, during the war years, he spent far more than usual on radio, owing to the subsidizing of the B.B.C. by the Treasury. If the Government could be induced simply to earmark larger sums for the purchase of books, without in the process taking over the whole book trade and turning it into a propaganda machine, I think the writer's position would be eased and literature might also benefit.

6. Personally I am satisfied, i.e. in a financial sense, because I have been lucky, at any rate during the last few years. I had to struggle desperately at the beginning, and if I had listened

to what people said to me I would never have been a writer. Even until quite recently, whenever I have written anything which I took seriously, there have been strenuous efforts, sometimes by quite influential people, to keep it out of print. To a young writer who is conscious of having something in him, the only advice I can give is not to take advice. Financially, of course, there are tips I could give, but even those are of no use unless one has some kind of talent. If one simply wants to make a living by putting words on paper, then the B.B.C., the film companies, and the like are reasonably helpful. But if one wants to be primarily a *writer*, then, in our society, one is an animal that is tolerated but not encouraged—something rather like a house sparrow—and one gets on better if one realizes one's position from the start.

## V. S. Pritchett

1. Before the war I remember J. Middleton Murry held that a writer could honestly earn about £400 a year. Aldous Huxley estimated the need at about £700. The post-war equivalent would be about £1,200 to £1,400 gross.

2. A vastly successful novelist, playwright, etc., can, of course, earn much more. But the promising, the rising, the merely successful, cannot earn anything like the above sums, by writing books or serious criticism or good short stories or poems, alone. The good creative writer will have to supplement his income from journalism, broadcasting, publishers' reading, editorial work, some other job—or a private income.

3. Any secondary work.

4. But it is essential that it should take up very little time and energy. This hardly ever happens, and the result is an evident decline in the quality of creative literature. The writers are worn out, overworked; they are not worn out by creation but by the various grindstones by which they earn the major part of their living. I would say that up to the age of thirty it

does not matter what a writer does with his time. An outside job may be valuable. After thirty, the outside job is inevitable in our high-costing, highly taxed society, where the private income is vanishing—inevitable, and in the long run fatal.

5. The question really amounts to this: should the State replace the support given by sinecures and the private income? No. State writers are bought and censored writers. I am against writers' co-operatives. I am in favour of the people who now have the large private fortunes being obliged, by the State, to support literature. These private fortunes are not in private hands. They are in the hands of the Boards, the shareholders of the great industrial firms. Shell-Mex, Unilever, London Transport, etc., should be obliged to give patronage—but not in return for publicity.

6. Advice to a young writer: discipline yourself to the *habit* of writing. Write every day. Keep office hours. Inspiration comes from the grindstone, not from heaven. Do not hope to move up from popular writing to more distinguished levels. Popular journalism corrupts very quickly. Write for yourself alone as long as you can; the conditions of the profession will gradually vitiate the highest standards. The failures of over-work are fewer than the failures of idleness. Move heaven and earth to get time, and put time before money whenever you can. Be born with a small private income; or get yourself supported by a husband or wife.

## Herbert Read

1. How much a writer needs to live on will depend on his personal appetites, but if he is married, has two or three children, likes decent food and a comfortable house, he will need with present costs at least £1,000 a year.

2. A serious writer cannot possibly earn this sum by writing. A serious book takes two or three years to write. To earn the necessary sum by book royalties, he would have to sell between

thirty and fifty thousand copies of each book: in all probability he will sell only three to five thousand copies.

3. The most suitable second occupation for him is one which is no drain on either his intellectual or physical energy. 'A nice job in a museum', jobs in publishers' offices and cultural organizations like the British Council and the B.B.C., are the worst possible kinds of occupation. They are too interesting: they overlap into his literary work. They create mental confusion and lead to all kinds of trivial activities which are intellectually exhausting and completely unremunerative.

Farming and small-holding, which have superficial attractions (especially for romantic writers) are physically far too exhausting. They drug the mental faculties with a poisonous fatigue.

The best kind of occupation is represented by Spinoza's lens-polishing. If I were beginning my life again, I should seek a job in the light engineering industry, especially one in which, by piece-work, the necessary amount of work could be varied according to the needs of the moment.

4. The more a writer has experience of the normal activities of human beings, the better it is for his writing. I can think of no great writer in the past who has not benefited from non-intellectual activities. I can think of many whose work has suffered from academic or hedonistic seclusion.

5. No. The State can only demoralize and debase literature.

6. I am far from satisfied with my own solution of the problem. I have tried several solutions—Civil Servant, museum assistant, university professor, editor of a magazine, and now a publisher. They have all been unsatisfactory, for the reasons given in my answer to Question 3 above. They bristle with the 'grappling-irons' which Cézanne so rightly feared, and although a strong-minded individual might be able to avoid the public responsibilities which will eventually attach to eminence in such a position, nevertheless all such jobs are

by their nature 'contact jobs', and whichever way one turns one meets the devouring pack—until in the end one is reduced to a condition of dazed indifference, the paralysis of the cornered animal.

My advice to young people who wish to earn their living by writing is at all costs to avoid following my example.

## *Henry Reed*

I find it easier not to answer Question 1 first. Question 2: I believe that after three or four years of practice a writer who is willing to do subsidiary literary work should be able to keep himself by writing. The position of the poet and the novelist is much the same: both have to earn their leisure to write; I think it is best, for most writers, to earn it by subsidiary writing of a civilized type; this is often extremely helpful in loosening a writer's tongue. The avenues open are obvious: free-lance journalism (especially for the 'good' provincial daily papers); commissioned reviewing (which should not be difficult to get, since reviewers are always drifting *out* of it); broadcasting, and writing for broadcasting. After a time it is wiser for a writer to confine this honourable hack-work to commissioned work. There is less risk and more money in it. I think it bad for any writer to write down; I deplore the writer who, *without enjoying it*, writes low fiction (e.g. detective stories) or dance-lyrics in order to earn money. To do so is to give play to a cheap part of the mind (present in all writers, I suspect— cf. some of James's plays) of which a writer must, in fact, strive to rid himself. There is a danger—though clearly a decreasing one—in writing for films.

3. The trouble with most secondary jobs available to writers is that you often have to write as well in order to bring your income within bearable limits. The best job is teaching, because of its incomparable holidays. It is, however, a job very exhausting to the brain, the emotions, the throat and the legs; I have

found that office-work is less tiring mentally and physically, but its hours often make work in the evening impossible. A university life is ostensibly ideal for writers; but here there is the grave disadvantage of your company; with angel-exceptions (some of whom I have met) the don is by nature prejudiced against the creative artist; in no profession is the belief more strongly held that all art *ceased* just before Mummy got married; there is a Freudian explanation of this, but it remains one of those obstinate psychological cloggings which get round the bend where the brush cannot reach. Its atmosphere savages the soul. A disadvantage of *all* secondary jobs is that they are apt to become primary. This induces in a writer self-pity and lethargy, both fatal.

4. You have but to look round to see how badly 'literature' suffers from the diversion of a writer's energy elsewhere. Very serious writers do not let their knowledge of outside *milieux* intrude unduly in their work; but minor writers are not very strong-minded about this. On the other hand, think what we should miss if Melville had never gone whaling, or Joyce Cary never been in the African Service; not, however, that they both digested these experiences before writing of them, and that they are great enough writers to order their recondite experiences into art.

5. I believe emphatically in the value of State help, and help from other institutions who will be willing to risk no returns. But the funds should *not* be administered by the donating institution, least of all by the State. Artists—cf. the Soviet novelists and our own official War Artists—are only too ready to play the whore and the toady to any institution which will pay them to do so. The universities, and particularly the provincial ones, should, I think, administer such funds; and as soon as practicable those who have benefited should help to choose future recipients. This brings me to Question 1. I think the three hundred pounds offered for one year by the Atlantic

Awards is an admirable basic sum (it is, I believe, free of income tax). It is enough for various forms of existence, including, I venture to think, married life and possibly a fairly small child. Three hundred pounds a year, however, still entails worry in the background; I think a youngish writer (i.e. younger than thirty-five) can live fairly happily on £800 to £1,000 a year.

6. I am quite content with my own 'solution'. I have a good deal of advice to offer. For writers without a private income, it is advisable to face the process of a possibly slow *conversion* to a position where they have to make fewer and fewer concessions for the sake of money: i.e. it is advisable for them to put up with the more reputable forms of hack-work till they need no longer do so. When they can, they should drop hack-work like hot bricks, however easy it has become. In any case, they should be very chary of the implications of each *kind* of hack-work: specifically, and without frivolity, I would advise all young writers not to take on regular novel-reviewing. It is one of the most exacting and lowering jobs in the world.

And poets: the poet must (but above all secretly) think of himself as a potential Shakespeare, *and not less than this*; he will rarely find difficulty in excusing to himself his occasional failures. He must manage his relations with his novelist-colleagues very carefully. The novelist is always kind to the poet, but the income-difference is always there. How true it is that every novelist would prefer to have been a poet I am not sure; I rather doubt it. At any rate the poet feels among novelists like a poor tolerated relative who has the good looks of the family but nothing else. Try to avoid a stab of anger and jealousy at the thought that even a good novelist earns about fifty times as much from his novels as you do from your poetry. Finally, no writer should live too far below his income; avoid cheap or irregular meals; and if he stays on after a party, he should try to insist on a proper bed, not the floor or the sofa.

## John Russell

All true writers exist in the hope of creating a masterpiece. This fact must be the central chimney and warming flue of their lives, and all other activites are, in the last resort, merely ways of buying the time which they need for their best work. All such writers write ultimately for themselves, and in obedience to inner canons of perfection; vanity, want and lust are potent local stimulants, but to the central impulse we must ascribe, if hesitantly, a certain absolute, moral grandeur. This quality is held by modern society in organized disrespect; and nobody needs telling that, although good work occasionally meets with a copious financial reward, it does so only by luck or accident. Writers need, therefore, some auxiliary limb or iron lung, if they are to make a living. This can be acquired within their own field; for although few people live by literature, a great many live off it; and a life, for instance, of desultory writing for periodicals must now exert a great charm. Most other employments for young men offer a crushing load of work and a nugatory initial reward. Herbert's rectory, Stendhal's consulate and Pater's fellowship at Brasenose seem gone for ever, and leisure, even purposeful leisure, is difficult to secure. As against this, good writing will always be rare, and will always be sought after; for the first five or ten years an aspirant with unusual or acceptable talent will earn, with relative ease, as much in this way as would be paid to him during his first years in diplomacy, at the bar, or in any learned profession. He will see himself at a bound among those whom he had hitherto regarded as Delphic arbiters of taste and judgement. His way of life is itself delightful; he can stroll up from the country on Tuesday afternoon; he need never be early for breakfast or late for the theatre; he can pass a normal life in society—or, if he wishes, a fruitfully abnormal one. Spring migrations are his for the asking; and on wet November mornings he can spare a glance, from his study window, for the dutiful bowlers of his friends as they splash along towards Whitehall.

In twenty years, however, his memory and ear will have been debauched by the habit of rapid composition to order; he will have lost the power of disinterested reading; his income will not have increased, though his commitments may well have trebled. He will never have dared to take a sabbatical year of travel and rearmament, for fear of that Tartar horde so vividly evoked by Sir Max Beerbohm—'younger men, with months of work before them'. His habits of mind will be known to the last twitch, and editors will dread his fixed grin or unvarying scowl. Most galling of all, he will see his beastly, dull contemporaries soar high above him; collocations of letters will hang to the tails of these comets; K.C.B., P.C., K.C.M.G., K.C., he will read. And as the junior Ministers move from N.W.3 to S.W.1, they will quietly drop him, and forbid their children to play with his. Illness will beggar him, and in perhaps another twenty years they will get him put on the Civil List, at forty pounds a year.

Writers are born, of course, with all their preservative instincts in a state of exceptional strength and tenacity. Most horny and tusky is this vital part of their being, and enclosed in a protective belt of Asian guile. Sublimest of spongers, the Duinese elegist has shown how the highest ambitions of the spirit need not exclude a deft and rapacious instinct for comfortable living; and I have heard it said, perhaps in envy or malice, that among our ranks long-sighted legacy-hunters and successful stalkers of rich wives occur in unusually high proportion. Be that as it may, I believe that the only serious enemies of a writer's best work are within himself; all outward obstacles can be overcome, and many may even do useful service as goads and challengers; and the advice or suggestions of others count ultimately for little. Most writers work, in Aubrey's phrase, 'as boars piss—scilicet, in jerks', and it is for the weeks and months of creative idleness that they and their patrons have to plan; but it would be difficult to convince any legislature of the realism of this view. Our task should rather be to improve the quality of the audience, and in this to begin with ourselves; it is arguable that, though the number of readers (or rather, of persons able to read) must be many times greater than at any other period in literary history, the informed audience has never, in proportion, been smaller. The State also has its duty here; for now that writers cannot hope to find the indulgent patrons or the commodious sinecures by which at one time they might have hoped to tide over their years of fasting and preparation, there is surely a case for the temporary endowment of at least a few young writers, and a stronger one for the protection of those who, in middle or later life, deserve better than indigence. If a small tax were levied upon all lending libraries, and the proceeds given to the Civil List, this might at last become a roll of honour, and its benefits be enlarged to the level of a decent subsistence.

## *Edward Sackville-West*

Another interrogatory! As if writers hadn't enough to do to keep their heads above water! But I see I have already begun to answer your questions, so I may as well go on.

The amount of income a writer needs to live on must, I should have thought, differ according to the kind of work he does. If he is a journalist with a family living in a town, he will need a lot more money than a novelist living alone in the country. But even then, what does 'need' mean? Some writers can be happy living very simply; others actually need what some would call superfluities—pictures, gramophone records, travel, lovers—to enable them to do their work properly. What appears to me certain is that a basic ration of *unearned* increment is essential to a 'serious' writer—so that he can afford to turn down hack-work that will fritter away his time, and not to be obliged to hurry his work, and even to lie fallow for a year or so if he feels the necessity of it. The only way a writer can earn a sufficient income today is by driving his quill as hard as it will go and harder, regardless of the results to his style, his taste and his sensibility.

There is no such thing as a 'suitable second occupation' for a writer—except in the sense that writing books on philosophy was a suitable second occupation for the late Lord Balfour. Serious writing is a whole-time job, and a very hard one, too. When a writer takes to regular pot-boiling, his work is bound to suffer sooner or later. (Those who think this doesn't matter are unfit to live in a civilized country.)

Your fourth question is less easy to answer. Of course nearly all writers must accumulate a certain capital of emotional and practical experience. In some cases this has to be replenished from time to time, in others not. But—at any rate when first youth is over—any employment that continues to absorb most of the would-be writer's energy can hardly fail to sap his creative vitality and will quite soon destroy it altogether. On the other hand there are, of course, all kinds of daily chores and interests which, far from diverting a writer's energy, nourish and promote it.

I certainly do not think the State a good substitute for the private patron of past times. In theory the State may have all the right intentions towards artists, but in practice its patronage is bound to be far too rigid, since the 'benevolence' is entrusted to little men in ivory offices, who either fear to carry out their instructions in a liberal and imaginative way, or else interpret them according to ignorant personal prejudice. Look at the way Shostakovitch has been ruined by the dogmatism of the Soviet regime. Subsidiary institutions (university colleges, publishing houses) are an improvement in this respect, but even they tend to upset the situation by insisting on too quick a return for their money. In this connection it is worth recalling the case of Robert Bridges who, during his tenure of the laureateship, wrote practically no occasional verse at all; devoting all his energies to the completion of *The Testament of Beauty*. Which, in the circumstances, was exactly as it should be.

Am I 'satisfied with my own solution of the problem'? Of course I am not! If I were, I shouldn't be wasting my time answering your questionnaire: I should have chucked it into the waste-paper basket and gone on working at the novel which I ought to have started long ago, had the demon of journalism not got me by the throat. Rightly or wrongly, I consider myself as first and last an imaginative writer who is forced, by the pressure of present-day English life, to fritter away the years in purely ephemeral activities.

My advice to the young writer? First: cajole, bully or blackmail your parents, guardians or whatever, into giving you an independent income just large enough to keep the wolf from the door. Time—quite a short time—will show whether or not you have the root of the matter in you. If it becomes clear to yourself, as well as to others, that you have not, then will be time enough to take to some sort of hack-work.

One final word: don't begin by reviewing other people's books. Many—even most—young writers think this the easiest way of starting on the career of letters. In fact, it is among the most difficult of all literary undertakings. While your lyrical faculty lasts (and it is unlikely to last as long as you imagine), write novels and poetry; there will always be time for criticism later on, when middle age has cooled your imagination, and deepened and sharpened your judgement. You can write several good novels, and even more good poetry, with next to no experience of life; but criticism is essentially the business of maturity.

## William Sansom

1. At the present cost of living, I should say a minimum of
£400 to £500 a year—this to obtain privacy and a certain
mobility, but not to support a family or remove pressure-
forming anxieties as to the future. But averages are difficult to
suppose: a writer, I expect, is usually in some way not normal
—and according to his character might prepare his best work
in restrictive or normally unsavoury conditions. Prisons,
gardens, slums, society, have all produced literature. Perhaps
the most reasonable average desideratum would be some comfortably private ivorite tower with the habit (and even the
necessity) of frequent sorties therefrom.

2. At the moment, with luck, yes. Provided his output is
regular, and he is to some extent established. But he must
necessarily risk the complete failure of experiments.

3. No commercial writing. However limited this sphere may
be, there is the temptation to excel within the rules of the game
and the creative cells are sapped. Manual work is probably
the best alternative, though this only rarely could bring in
sufficient extra income. Perhaps the usual—one of the quieter
Civil Services, if they exist any more? Teaching? Librarian?
Somewhere are to be found individually suitable libraries and
lighthouses. But again these are severely personal choices: it is
always possible, for instance, that a metropolitan mind isolated
with a gross of mixed stuffed stoats in a small museum, not a
hundred miles from Hadrian's Wall, might at some time begin
rather to pity itself.

4. Any fresh experience can provide its stimulation. But if
the writer feels imprisoned, he is likely to spend all his effort in
dreaming himself free. A state of free leisure is the really
important condition. In degree, the enrichment of experience
must be accompanied by enough privacy and leisure to absorb
and record it.

5. There is the chance always of a decline into directed State inspiration—but this should be risked. Patronage from any source is invaluable. It is wrong to assume that strings are attached to every generosity, right to marvel that fairly disinterested good does exist at all in the human arena.

6. Yes. Over a period of years I decided to save, and did. These savings gave me the chance to live and write freely for a couple of years. (Since, I have been so fortunate as to receive a bursary; this naturally has further eased matters, removed further the temptation of a salaried job.) So I suppose any advice I could give would be save, save, save. If you can. Modest living, if you can bear it, discovers a greater interest in simple things, and reduces the headache of desire. And any accumulating money develops a fair feeling of security, and thus a freer mind.

## D. S. Savage

So many social, cultural and religious issues are raised by the question of the writer's economic position that it is impossible to deal with them in a small compass. The position of the 'clerisy' is determined by the distribution of wealth/power/ privilege and by the cultural standards obtaining in society. Wealth in our racketeering society is distributed, to put it mildly, unjustly; and our cultural standards are debased. I am dead against the theory which, raising the banner of 'the artist', would make of writers a privileged *élite* existing in aesthetic detachment from, and yet actual dependence upon, an enslaved and militarized people.

How much does a writer need to live on? What sort of a writer; what are his responsibilities, liabilities? But it's quite useless to discuss this matter in general terms. For myself, I am not interested in earning a living by writing. I am interested in writing. Also, I have to earn a living for myself and my family—if only to be able to continue writing. In fact, I've never yet been able to earn the barest living for the five of us out of the rewards of authorship. I have been compelled to improvise, taking up one ill-paying job or occupation after another in the vain hope of eventually getting into a position in which I should have the more leisure and mental ease to read, think, write, in accordance with my irrepressible urge to those activities. My employments and my writing have each hindered success in the other.

There is no precise answer to Question 3. Question 4 raises the point of the relationship of writing to living. In the daily struggle which is my life I am brought up against the brute facts of human existence; through experience I get to know them, to comprehend something of the very structure of existence. This knowledge is inevitably reflected in my writing at the same time as the necessity for coming to terms with the material conditions of living puts a practical obstacle in my way as a writer. Naturally I'd like the obstacle removed—in which event the struggle would be transposed elsewhere.

I am cynical about State support for writers. I don't give a damn for the State either way. No, I'm not satisfied; in fact I haven't a solution. And I'm not a bit interested in the fate of people, young or old, who merely 'wish to earn their living by writing'. I am interested only in those who wish 'to write', and not even, very much, in all of those.

But I admit it's a problem, and the question still remains, what, under existing bad conditions, can be done to take some of the obstacles out of the way of serious writers (always remembering that there are degrees of 'seriousness') so that they can get on with the job? I have often wondered why, under the conditions of a capitalist society, no collective action has been taken to improve the writer's position—why it is that there is apparently no intermediate stage for the writer between that of outcast and celebrity, and how it is the celebrity shows so complete an unconcern with the tribulations of the outcast. If anything practical is to be done (and whatever is done is bound to be unsatisfactory), rather than State interference I should recommend the setting up of a commission by, say, the Society of Authors, to investigate the economic position of writers—particularly young writers—and to institute a fund for the purpose of making grants for needy writers to proceed with specific works of literary value. This fund, within the unwholesome conditions of a competitive economy, might well be swollen by some diversion of the proceeds from out-of-copyright works of dead authors, period of copyright being extended by law for this specific purpose, while celebrated writers, as well as publishers and other middlemen who profit from literature in one way and another, might be bullied and shamed into making substantial regular contributions to the fund. This would be used not merely for making direct cash grants but for financing one or more journals of a solid character which would provide a market for serious work, in much the same way as some American Universities support and finance independent quarterlies. An authors' publishing corporation, even, might be developed, co-operatively run and setting an example to the commercial publishing houses in its concern for the welfare of writers and for literary standards.

## Stephen Spender

1. Of course, what a writer needs depends on many things, such as his age, whether he is married, etc. The one impregnable position is readiness to make every economic sacrifice to his vocation and, if necessary, to involve everyone round him in such sacrifice. But very few writers can do this. Allowing for travel and occasional treats, I should say an unmarried writer needs £500 or £600 a year (free of tax) if he lives in London. A married writer, if he makes his wife his cook, needs £700. However, if he has children, if he does not wish his wife to be a

domestic slave and if he has any social life, he needs £1,000 a
year or more.

Directly he needs as much as this, difficulties of income tax
arise, for he needs actually to earn £1,500 a year. Writing is a
social occupation and in London he will find that entertaining
is one of his chief expenses. If he were a business man, the
government would pay for his lunches with his colleagues, but
as he is an artist, entertainment of other writers will not be
recognized as a legitimate expense of his profession.

2. Try to earn £1,000 a year or more from writing today and
see what happens. If you write books your publisher will not
have paper to print more than 5,000 copies, which will bring
you in £250 to £350. This means you must either write four to
six books a year, or you must turn to journalism. Assuming you
are paid, on the average, £3 3s. for 1,000 words, you will have
to write 333,000 words a year to gain £1,000. Myself, I find that
if I write three or four articles a week (*a*) I become irritable,
(*b*) I get into a condition in which I find it very difficult to read
seriously, (*c*) least of all can I read what I write myself. I can
write an article far more easily than I can bear to read it, for
the purpose of proof-correcting, (*d*) there follows a general
disgust with my own ideas, my way of thinking and talking,
and (*e*) a tendency to write more and more journalism and less
poetry, because I feel unworthy to write serious work.

3. I can only state the problems in general terms. These are
(*a*) to avoid expressing merely in words on a level which lowers
one's standards, (*b*) to avoid exhausting oneself physically
and/or mentally, (*c*) to avoid becoming absorbed in some task
which eventually becomes more important to one than one's
writing, (*d*) to avoid being forced to play some role in life—
such as an official or a pedagogue or an important person
—which usurps one's creative personality.

The safest part for a writer to play in a job is a return to
childhood. Do some job which enables one to learn something

which will be useful in writing. Accept the fact that one is once again the stupidest boy in the class, the backward son in the family. One's best relationship with one's colleagues is for them to think of one as slightly mad but full of good will. Be a cog and allow oneself to be gently ground between the heads of departments. Reassure people by allowing them to think that one is distinguished without one's ever menacing their own position. For God's sake never be in a position of responsibility and have no ambitions. Do not seek honours and do not refuse them. One should aim at being a rather superior and privileged office clown who excites no one's envy, and on whom one's colleagues project a few fantasies. One encourages all this by arriving always a little late (but not too late). Prepare for the worst, when the boss shows you his (or his wife's or his son's) poems. Pretend to like them, ask for a testimonial and resign immediately when this happens.

4. This depends entirely on the quantity of the writer's energy. If he has the energy to do another job and to write, I cannot help thinking that his writing gains by a contact with the machinery of ordinary life. A scientist, a managerial leader or a statesman who realizes an idea which has to pass through the whole machinery of a modern organization, is creative in a way parallel to an artist who overcomes technical problems in order to state an idea in his particular medium. If one can retain the sense of a creative attitude in one's environment and not be crushed by a routine, one will learn much from ordinary work. Myself, I think that the best and most serious modern literature suffers from unworldliness. Literature should be made of the same worldly muck as are the historic plays of Shakespeare, the courtly drama of Racine and of Lopé de Vega, the materialistic novels of Balzac and the Duchy of Parma in *La Chartreuse de Parme*. Byron was the last worldly poet. What we want is a fusion of Byron and Blake.

5. Only in the way of recognizing and protecting the writer's professional position, by providing paper for modern books, giving creative writers the travel facilities of journalists, allowing the social contacts of writers with their colleagues to count as tax-free business expenses, etc.

6. At the moment I am happy because I work with an intelligent and sympathetic international group of people who, not being English, expect of me what I can give, do not make me feel guilty and have an unobtrusive recognition of my value in their work and also in my own which has a certain value for them. I am not unpatriotic, but I fear that the mainspring of English industriousness is a sense of guilt and for this reason the position of writers who have to work for their living in this country is particularly difficult. They are forced into the dilemma of feeling they have to choose between two kinds of work. In France, this is not so, with the result that many French writers combine official positions with writing.

I advise the young writer to be perfectly honest with himself about the all-important problem of how he is expending his energy. The only rule in this work is to know what you want to do and do it, at all costs. If you can do other things as well, you will probably gain by it. But if you can't, you're *foûtu*.

## *Dylan Thomas*

1. He needs as much money as he wants to spend. It is after his housing, his feeding, his warming, his clothing, the nursing of and looking after his children, etc., have been seen to—and these should be seen to by the State—that he really needs money to spend on all the luxurious necessities. Or, it is then that he doesn't need money because he can do without those necessary luxuries. How much money depends, quite obviously, on how much he wants to buy. I *want* a lot, but whether I *need* what I want is another question.

2. A serious writer (I suppose by this you mean a good writer, who might be comic) can earn enough money by writing seriously, or comically, if his appetites, social and sensual, are very small. If those appetites are big or biggish, he cannot earn, by writing what he wishes to write, enough to satisfy them. So he has to earn money in another way: by writing what he doesn't want to write, or by having quite another job.

3. It's no good I suppose, saying that I know a couple of good writers who are happy writing, for a living, what they don't particularly want to write, and also a few good writers who are happy (always qualified by words I'm not going to use now) being bank clerks, Civil Servants, etc. I can't say how a writer can make money most suitably. It depends on how much money he wants and on how much he wants it and on what he is willing to do to get it. I myself get about a quarter of the money I want by writing what I don't want to write and at the same time trying to, and often succeeding in, enjoying it. Shadily living by one's literary wits is as good a way of making too little money as any other, so long as, all the time you are writing B.B.C. and film-scripts, reviews, etc., you aren't thinking, sincerely, that this work is depriving the world of a great poem or a great story. Great, or at any rate very good, poems and stories do get written in spite of the fact that the writers of them spend much of their waking time doing entirely different things. And even a poet like Yeats, who was made by patronage financially safe so that he need write and think nothing but poetry, *had*, voluntarily, to give himself a secondary job: that of philosopher, mystic, crank, quack.

4. No, to both questions. It neither suffers nor is it enriched. Poems, for instance, are pieces of hard craftsmanship made interesting to craftsmen in the same job, by the work put into them, and made interesting to everybody, which includes those craftsmen, by divine accidents: however taut, inevitably in order, a good poem may appear, it must be so constructed that

it is wide open, at any second, to receive the accidental miracle which makes a work of craftsmanship a work of art.

5. The State should do no more for writers than it should do for any other person who lives in it. The State should give shelter, food, warmth, etc., whether the person works for the State or not. Choice of work, and the money that comes from it, should then be free for that man; what work, what money, is his own bother.

6. Yes and No, or *vice versa*. My advice to young people who wish to earn their living by writing is: DO.

\*　　\*　　\*

STILL slowly digesting the answers to our questionnaire on the 'cost of letters', I feel that it has somehow revealed only one or two external symptoms of the complicated illness of our culture and our times. Thus, when I write 'complicated illness' I already betray a certain pleasure in being ill. It is more interesting. We live in an age in which normality (health, peace, happiness) seems dull. Are these things dull? No one with toothache thinks the absence of toothache dull, yet health, peace, happiness, convey to us who are mentally sick and yet don't want to be cured an impression of stagnancy. But we know that these qualities are not really stagnant; health as skiers, for example, experience it, is a kind of intoxication. They seem stagnant because we are feverish. Our illness, then, is a fever, a rise in temperature which makes us impatient of the tempo of normal living. It expresses itself in our talk of another war, wherein we forget death and the black-out, but re-member the heightened historical consciousness which flushed our cheek and brightened our eye, and the importance which we derived from expressing our opinion on each new crisis. It also expresses itself in our inability to settle down, to use our money to buy leisure: in fact the claim of so many writers in the questionnaire that they need a thousand pounds a year to

live on could be translated to mean 'it is not until fully occupied on the thousand-a-year level that one entirely ceases to be
bothered by the books one hoped to write'. The courage required to surrender a good job in some area of culture-diffusion
in order to create that culture can be gained only through a
sense of vocation. But how can an unknown or under-paid
writer make that choice? The times are against it. Where is
the writer who stays home in the afternoon and has crumpets
for tea? Where is the disdainful unworldly group, the new
Pre-Raphaelite brotherhood? It is here that the State (in the
opinion of nine out of twenty-one writers) must step in. It
must give young writers scholarships and older writers Sabbatical years; it must, with its official blessing, thrust leisure
as well as money on them and punish those who sneak back to
London, to reviewing or the B.B.C. It was an older writer,
Robert Graves, who remarked that, where the State and the
artist are concerned, 'he who pays the piper, calls the tune'.

What is that tune? Here is the crux. We are now at the
beginning of a socialist regime. 'The State' to most artists
(ninety per cent of whom are by origin bourgeois indivi-
dualists) is a large, sprawling, well-meaning young giant,
dangerous as 'Rex' to criminals, but tolerant to artists and
anxious to avail itself of them. Writers who have been pacifists
or revolutionaries see the dangerous 'Rex' aspect, others who
have done well as Civil Servants envisage it as wise and adult,
but I am convinced that, to the average writer, the State is a
clumsy new master, amiable and ready to be teased or bullied
in a way which the private patron, with his human vanity,
would have resented. So far, in fact, the infant Hercules, while
far from paying out to every piper, has warbled only approval
of the tune. 'Graham Sutherland, Benjamin Britten, Henry
Moore, very nice I'm sure, very pretty—how much?' The
attitude of the artist to the State is still that of the middle-class
child to the working-class window cleaner who is graciously

asked in to admire his toys. But supposing the window cleaner says 'I've no time for such rubbish now—you help clean my windows'. Immediately the other facet of the relationship appears—the bourgeois terror of the working class: 'you nasty, big, horrid man, go away. I'll tell my Daddy, he'll never let you clean these windows again.' But Daddy is outside, clearing the drains.

Thus one might say that, under a Conservative government the artist is either the 'good son' (Kipling) or the problem child, the mischievous adolescent Prince Hal (Byron, Wilde, Shaw). He invents Colonel Blimp. Under a Socialist government (unless he is a Socialist), his top layer of gentlemanly condescension peels away to reveal an obscure guilt at not doing manual labour, beneath which is a sense of helplessness which will drive these artists who can't hit it off with the new Father figure into exile or the despised arms of the Conservative opposition. But supposing there is no opposition? Supposing party government (which really implies four possible attitudes of the artist to the State) comes to an end through a series of Socialist victories and the State, now all-powerful, since the vague cultural opposition of an educated leisured class will have lost all political reality, begins to ask for the art it likes, then the answer will be social realism. Be a social realist or starve—(social realism and, for Conservatives, the pretty-pretty, are the only two kinds of art for which a politician can spare the time). If in addition to liking social realism there are to be found patriotic reasons for encouraging it (i.e., increase of coal production, dismay of capitalist rivals, etc.), then the State will begin to feel positive anger against those artists who are not social realists. They must be brought into line. This is happening today in Russia, in an atmosphere which recalls an immorality scare in a bad public school, and what is happening is so important that *Horizon* feels it necessary, at the risk of saturating our readers, to give a much fuller report of the case

than has so far appeared, so let us pretend that we have heard
nothing about it, that the writers mentioned, Zoshchenko and
Mme Akhmatova are their English equivalents, Zoshchenko
something of Evelyn Waugh, of Nat Gubbins, of G. W.
Stonier, Mme Akhmatova something of a Virginia Woolf or
Edith Sitwell, but in their seventies; and that the terrible new
headmaster, Zhdanov, is Bevan or Strachey. And now we take
you over to


# THE FIFTH FORM AT ST. JOE'S

### I. TROUBLE BREWING

From the editorial, first number of new Propaganda Department magazine *Culture and Life*, 28 June 1946:

A new historical period has begun in the life of our country . . .
Life demands of us a development of ideological and cultural work
in accordance with the historic tasks confronting the Soviet State . . .
In forming the awareness of Soviet people, literature and art have
enormous importance. Our people have a high opinion of the Soviet
literary productions which appeared during the war years, but our
writers, dramatists, directors and artists are lagigng behind the
demands currently being placed on Soviet literature and art. Publishing houses and literary journals frequently print mediocre works
of little artistic value. There are still people among our *littérateurs*
who stubbornly avoid contemporary themes and prefer to depict
only the very distant past. A hopeless error is being made by the
directors and writers who are assuming that the Soviet people after
the war want only relaxation and diversions. Soviet literature and
art must produce works full of passion and profound thoughts,
penetrated with ideas of life-giving Soviet patriotism.

Literature must, by means of artistic words, reveal the world
historical significance of the victories of the Soviet people, must
show the vitality and invincibility of the Soviet democracy. Literature is called upon to show the spiritual wealth, the moral firmness,
the moral cleanliness and loftiness of spirit of the Soviet man. Only
an idealistically advanced, really just literature, based on the living

experience of our peoples' struggle for Communism, can be a force raising Soviet people to the resolutions of the historic problems confronting them.

In order that literature may be able to fulfil its duty to the people, analyse the complex problems of modern life, explain the nature of the social processes in our country, an authoritative literary criticism based on principle must come to the aid of literature.

But we do not have such criticism yet. The state of our criticism is unsatisfactory and its public authority is low. Criticism is not having the necessary effect on the forming of Soviet literature. Criticism is anything but exacting as to artistic form, is poor in thoughts and generalization.

Worthless and fruitless is the criticism which neglects the principle of the party-nature of literature and places the interests of the shop or department above general State interests. It loses its significance as the champion of advanced ideas of our time and becomes petty, servile, or fretfully impatient.

The chief sin of contemporary criticism lies in its having placed itself in the service of particular agencies and writers, lauding mediocre productions of these writers and frequently lamenting the valuable productions of other writers.

Modern criticism is detached from life which means that the literary critics are not in a position properly to evaluate and analyse the great productions of Soviet literature, to define the tendencies of its development.

Our critics do not know how to combine an analysis of the idea content of literary works with an analysis of artistic form.

## II. BEFORE THE WHOLE SCHOOL!

The magazines *Zvezda* and *Leningrad*. Decree of the Central Committee of the Communist Party of the Soviet Union, of 14 August 1946. From *Pravda*, 21 August.

The Central Committee of the Communist Party of the Soviet Union notes that the literary-feature magazines *Zvezda* and *Leningrad* which are published in Leningrad are operating in a very unsatisfactory manner.

In the magazine *Zvezda*, alongside significant and successful works by Soviet writers, there have recently appeared many works which are devoid of ideas and ideologically pernicious. The grave error of *Zvezda* lies in offering a literary rostrum to the writer Zoshchenko, whose works are alien to Soviet literature. The editors of *Zvezda* were aware that Zoshchenko has long specialized in writing empty, inane and trivial things, propounding rotten works without ideology, which are trivial and indifferent to politics and calculated to disorientate our youth and poison its consciousness. The most recent of the published stories of Zoshchenko 'The Adventures of an Ape' (*Zvezda* Nos. 5–6, 1946) is a vulgar lampoon on Soviet life and Soviet people. Zoshchenko portrays Soviet customs and people in ugly caricature form, slanderously depicting the people as primitive, uncultured, stupid with Philistine tastes and customs. The maliciously hooligan description by Zoshchenko of our life is accompanied by anti-Soviet attacks.

To offer the pages of *Zvezda* to such vulgar dregs of literature as Zoshchenko is the more inadmissible since the editors of *Zvezda* were thoroughly familiar with the character of Zoshchenko, and with his unworthy behaviour during the war when Zoshchenko, not at all helping the Soviet people in their fight against the Germans, wrote such an abominable thing as *Before Sunrise*, an evaluation of which, along with an evaluation of all the literary 'creations' of Zoshchenko, was given on the pages of the magazine *Bolshevik*.

The magazine *Zvezda* also broadly popularizes the works of the writer, Akhmatova, whose literary and social and political personality has long been familiar to Soviet society. Akhmatova is a typical representative of the empty poetry without ideas which is alien to our people. Her poems, which are imbued with a spirit of pessimism and decadence, expressing the tastes of old drawing-room poetry which have never progressed beyond the attitudes of bourgeois aristocratic aesthetics and decadence—'art for art's sake' —and which did not wish to keep in step with its people, damage the task of bringing up our youth and cannot be tolerated in Soviet literature.

The effect of granting Zoshchenko and Akhmatova an active role on the magazine was doubtless to introduce elements of ideological disjunction and disorganization among Leningrad writers. Works began to appear in the magazine which cultivated a spirit of obsequiousness to modern bourgeois culture of the West, a spirit which is not characteristic of Soviet people. The magazine began to publish works saturated with nostalgia, pessimism and disillusionment in life (the poems of Sadofev and Komissarova in No. 1 of 1946, etc.). In publishing these works the editors aggravated their errors and still further lowered the intellectual level of the magazine . . .

The Central Committee notes that the magazine *Leningrad* is operating particularly badly. It has constantly opened its pages to the vulgar and slanderous writings of Zoshchenko, and to the inane and apolitical poems of Akhmatova. Just as the editors of *Zvezda*, the editors of the magazine *Leningrad* have permitted grave errors in publishing a number of works saturated with a spirit of obsequiousness to everything foreign . . .

How could it happen that *Zvezda* and *Leningrad*, published in the hero-city, known for its advanced revolutionary traditions, a city which was always a nursery of advanced ideas and advanced culture, permitted apolitical works without idea content, and alien to Soviet literature, to creep into its magazines. What is the significance of the errors made by the editors of *Zvezda* and *Leningrad*?

The leading employees of the magazines, in the first place their editors, Comrades Sayanov and Likharev, forgot the thesis of Leninism that our magazines, be they scientific or artistic, cannot be politically indifferent. They forgot that our magazines are a powerful means whereby the Soviet State brings up the Soviet people and, in particular, the youth, and for this reason must be guided by the phenomenon which comprises the vital foundation of the Soviet structure—its politics. The Soviet system cannot suffer its youth to be educated in a spirit of apathy towards Soviet politics, in a spirit of disrespect and lack of ideas.

The strength of Soviet literature, the most advanced literature in the world, is that it is a literature in which there are not and cannot be any interests other than those of the people and the State. The task of Soviet literature is to help the State properly to bring up the youth, answer its needs, educate the new generation to be brave, to believe in its cause, to be fearless before obstacles and ready to overcome all barriers.

For this reason any preaching of lack of ideas, indifference to politics, 'art for art's sake' is alien to Soviet literature, pernicious to the interests of the Soviet people and the State and can have no place in our magazines.

The lack of ideals on the part of the leading employees of *Zvezda* and *Leningrad* also had the effect of their setting, as a cardinal point in their relations with such literary figures, not the interests of the proper education of the Soviet people and of the political direction of the activity of the *littérateurs*, but personal interests of friendship. Criticism was dulled in order to avoid spoiling relations with friends. Clearly worthless works were permitted in the Press out of fear of offending friends. This sort of liberalism in which the interests of the people and the State, the interests of the proper education of our youth, are sacrificed to friendly relations and in which criticism is stifled, results in writers ceasing to perfect themselves and in losing awareness of their responsibility to the people, the State and the Party, and of ceasing to go forward.

All the above proves that the editors of *Zvezda* and *Leningrad* have not measured up to the duty with which they were charged, and have permitted serious political errors in directing their magazines.

The Central Committee decrees that the leadership of the Union of Soviet Writers and, in particular, its Chairman Comrade Tikhonov, have taken no steps to improve *Zvezda* and *Leningrad* and have not only not fought against the pernicious influences of Zoshchenko, Akhmatova and other non-Soviet writers like them on Soviet literature, but have even tolerated the penetration of tendencies and habits alien to Soviet literature into the magazines . . .

The propaganda administration of the Central Committee of the Communist Party of the Soviet Union did not assure the necessary control over the work of Leningrad magazines.

### III. EXPELLED!

The Central Committee of the Communist Party of the Soviet Union decrees:

1. The editors of *Zvezda*, the board of directors of the Union of Soviet Writers, and the propaganda administration of the Central Committee of the Communist Party of the Soviet Union are to take steps for the unconditional elimination of the errors and weaknesses of the magazine indicated in our decree, are to correct the line of the magazine and guarantee a high idealistic and artistic level while forbidding access to the magazine for the works of Zoshchenko, Akhmatova and others like them.

2. In view of the fact that at the present moment there are no suitable conditions for publishing two literary artistic magazines in Leningrad, the magazine *Leningrad* is to cease publication and all literary forces in Leningrad are to be concentrated around *Zvezda*.

3. In an effort to introduce the necessary system in the work of the editors of *Zvezda* and a serious improvement in the magazine's

content, the magazine is to have an Editor-in-Chief and an editorial board under him. It is decreed that the Editor-in-Chief bears full responsibility for the ideological and political direction of the magazine and the quality of the works published in it.

4. Comrade A. M. Egolin is appointed Editor-in-Chief of *Zvezda* while retaining his functions as Acting Chief of the Propaganda Administration of the Central Committee of the Communist Party of the Soviet Union.

### IV. ALL WE LIKE SHEEP . . .

[SEVERAL PAPERS]

A few days ago in Leningrad there was a meeting of the 'Aktiv' of Leningrad Party Organization at which the Secretary of the Central Committee of the Communist Party, Zhdanov, made a statement with regard to the decree of the Central Committee of the All-Union Communist Party of 14 August of this year 'with regard to the journals *Zvezda* and *Leningrad*'. The meeting discussed the statement made by Zhdanov, and in accordance with it passed the following resolution:

> *Resolution passed at the meeting of the 'Aktiv' of Leningrad Party Organization on the statement of Zhdanov on the Decree of the Central Committee of the Communist Party 'On the journals* Zvezda *and* Leningrad'.

Having heard and discussed the statement of the Secretary of the Central Committee of the All-Union Communist Party, Zhdanov, on the decree of the Central Committee of the Communist Party with regard to the journals *Zvezda* and *Leningrad* which are published in Leningrad, the meeting of the Aktiv of the Leningrad Party organization unanimously acknowledges this decree to be just, entirely approves it, and undertakes to be guided by it and to carry it out precisely.

The meeting of the Party Aktiv considers that the City Committee of the Communist Party, being occupied with the decision of practical economic questions, has neglected questions of ideological work, has not concerned itself with the direction of the journals, has overlooked very big mistakes in the work of the editorial staffs, thus giving an opportunity to people who are alien to Soviet literature, such as Zoshchenko and Akhmatova, to take a leading position in the journals. Having forgotten that the journal of the Central Committee of the Communist Party *Bolshevik* strongly condemned the non-ideological, worthless writings of Zoshchenko, the Bureau of the City Committee of the Communist Party and its Secretaries, Kapustin and Shirokov, made a gross political mistake in admitting Zoshchenko as a member of the editorial staff of the journal *Zvezda*.

The City Committee of the Party, and first and foremost its Propaganda and Agitation Section, have forgotten the instructions of Lenin and Stalin to the effect that literature is a most important Party and State matter, that its task is to strengthen the Soviet system, to assist the Party and the State in the Communist education of the workers, to inculcate in the young generation the best qualities of Soviet peoples—courage, faith in their cause, love and devotion to the Socialist Motherland, the capacity and knowledge for overcoming any difficulties. The absence of daily guidance on the part of the City Committee of the Communist Party led to the result that the Leningrad journals instead of being a powerful weapon in the education of Soviet peoples and especially of youth, by profoundly ideological, contemporary productions, correctly reflecting Soviet life, opened their pages wide to such trivial and worthless writers as Zoshchenko, whose writings are full of a rotten lack of ideology, triviality and ignorance of politics, which libellously portray Soviet people and mock their Soviet readers. The journals widely popularized the production of a typical representative of empty poetry which is alien to our people, Akhmatova. The journals also printed the formally pretentious and false productions of Yagdfeld, the verses of Sadofev, which are decadent and permeated with melancholy, the similar verses of Komissarova, and other productions which are weak from an ideological and artistic standpoint.

The meeting of the Party Aktiv notes that although Leningrad writers have composed a number of good, ideologically valuable productions, the general level of their work lags behind the growing tasks of Soviet literature. Many Communist writers have lost the feeling of responsibility and of Bolshevik regard for the high calling of Soviet literature. More than this, some of them have joined the tag-end of writers—the vulgarians and merchants of literature. In the Leningrad section of the Union of Soviet Writers a situation was created in which the interests of the State and the Party were subordinated to private interests, and to personal friendships, a situation of clannishness and mutual admiration.

All this led to the result that in the productions of Leningrad writers there was no portrayal of the heroic deeds of Soviet people, of its inspired creative work in the post-war restoration of works and factories, collective farms, cities and scientific and cultural institutions. Artistic productions did not portray the laborious exploits and life of the workers of Leningrad who had been strengthened in the flame of the Great Patriotic War, and who are now working to restore their city, a hero city, to consolidate further the strength and might of their country . . .

Noting that the governing body of the Union of Soviet Writers and in particular its President, Tikhonov, did not effectively direct the work of the Leningrad section of the Union, did not engage in struggle with the harmful influences of non-Soviet writers, did not take any measures to improve the journals *Zvezda* and *Leningrad* and permitted the infiltration into these journals of tendencies and habits foreign to Soviet literature, the Party Aktiv considers it necessary to ask the Central Committee of the Communist Party to strengthen the governing body of the Union of Soviet Writers, and to put at its head a stronger leader, capable of directing the work of the Union.

The meeting of the Party Aktiv calls upon all writers of the city of Leningrad to resolute improvement of their work as is demanded by the decree of the Central Committee of the Communist Party, to deep study of Marxism-Leninism, and heightening of their ideological understanding, to intensive creative labour aiming at a new development and flowering of Soviet literature, which is called upon to reflect the interests of the people and the State, and to inculcate the noble qualities of Soviet patriotism amongst the workers and amongst youth.

### VI. ALL'S WELL THAT ENDS WELL MAYBE

The meeting of Writers regards the decree of the Central Committee of the Communist Party with regard to the journals *Zvezda* and *Leningrad* as a document of immense significance both as regards principle and programme, determining the direction and the path of development of Soviet literature.

By its decree the Central Committee of the Communist Party points out to us that the strength of Soviet literature, the most progressive literature in the world, lies in the fact that it is a literature which has not and cannot have any other interests except the interests of the people, the interests of the State. The function of Soviet literature is to help the State in the correct education of youth, to answer its demands, to educate a young generation to be bold, confident in its cause, without fear of obstacles, ready to surmount all difficulties.

The meeting demands of every Leningrad writer that he should devote all his creative powers to the matter of producing ideologically valuable productions of high artistic merit, portraying the greatness of our victory, the fervour for re-establishment and socialist reconstruction, the heroic deeds of Soviet people for the fulfilling and over-fulfilling of the new Stalin Five-Year Plan. In our productions there must be found a worthy and clear portrayal of the Soviet citizen, educated by the Communist Party, steeled in the fire of the Great Patriotic War, devoting all his powers and talents to the great cause of Socialist construction, capable of surmounting any obstacles.

The governing body of the Union must take all steps for strengthening the contacts between writers and the broad masses of the workers, whose demands and just criticism must guide every writer in his work.

It is a matter of honour for Leningrad writers to carry out the decree of the Central Committee of the Communist Party and to rally the best forces of Soviet writers around the journal, to make the journal *Zvezda* the foremost literary journal in the country . . .

The meeting unanimously assures the Central Committee of the Communist Party and Comrade Stalin that the writers of Leningrad will within a short space of time overcome the grievous defects in their work, and under the leadership of the Leningrad Party organization will find within themselves the powers and the possibilities for the creation of works worthy of the great Stalin era.

What is this verdict in Western terms? It is as if the magazines *Horizon* and *New Writing* (whose present editorial deals with another aspect of the same problem: Soviet attacks, encouraged by *The Times* correspondent, Mr. Parker, on 'escapist' English literature and periodicals) were suspended; one suppressed, the other given a new editor and our composite writers, Waugh-Gubbins, and Woolf-Sitwell publicly censured, with all those who have written favourably of them, and forbidden to publish another line (i.e., condemned to starve). Pasternak-Eliot is also involved and elsewhere reprimanded and Spender-Tikhonov retired from his high function.

It is not to be expected that *Horizon*, which exports about twenty copies to Russia, can be of the slightest help to Messrs. Zoshchenko and Akhmatova whose books at this moment are probably being withdrawn from all circulation, as if they were Celine's or Giono's, and for us even to hint that Western culture approves of them is the worst thing we can do. But we can deduce one or two conclusions for our Western readers.

(1) Better a 'State' which can't read or write than one which begins to take a positive interest in literature.

(2) There is only one judge of books whom we *dare* trust—with all its faults—the Reading Public. A Buy-more-books Campaign with writers and publishers touring the country in a ballyhoo travelling circus is safer than the best-intentioned crumb of State patronage.

(3) Yet the State is ourselves, *l'état c'est toi*, and after enjoying the beginnings of the Third Programme (so admirably free from such doctrinaire rantings) we can envisage a State which does not necessarily adopt social realism but encourages art for its own sake. The Russian attitude betrays a complete ignorance of what art is about and why people like it, and we must be constantly on the look-out against its implications.

(4) The artist who cares truly for individual freedom, aesthetic merit or intellectual truth must be prepared to go once more into the breach against the Soviet view with all the patience, fervour and lucidity with which, ten years ago, he went into action against the nascent totalitarianism of the Nazis. This is a terrible and tragic conclusion, but the situation is no less tragic. The Soviet conception of art, with the intolerable bullying of artists to which it leads, is a challenge to every writer with liberal opinions—it is the extreme of illiberality.

(5) We must accept the probability that literature will die out in Russia, because the State is trying to force it artificially. All we can do is to see that does not happen here, and proclaim at once to our well-meaning and as yet inoffensive little Hercules the truth that Art is not a product of patriotism or policy or mass-demand, or the yells of a political commissar with a youth movement, but of internal conflict in the sub-conscious. The artist is a self-cured neurotic—the origins of Art are not in the State but in the family, and the one golden recipe for Art is the ferment of an unhappy childhood working through a noble imagination.

### SAYING OF THE MONTH

*La justice humaine est d'ailleurs pour moi ce qu'il y a de plus bouffon au monde; un homme en jugeant un autre est un spectacle qui me ferait crever de rire s'il ne me faisait pitié, et si je n'étais forcé d'étudier maintenant la serie d'absurdités en vertu de quoi il juge.*     FLAUBERT, *Letters.*

*September–October* 1946


# THE ENVY BELT

WE have now considered two main factors in the condition which we call 'Inflationary Decadence': the economic in-security of the artist and the ambiguous role of the State. There remains a third: the collapse of criticism. This, of course, is interlocked with the other two, for since his books take a long time to write and seldom command a large sale, a critic will fall back on reviewing. The salient observation which a visitor from Mars would make, if asked to admire our foremost critics, is the extreme brevity which they have adopted. Mr. Desmond MacCarthy is generally considered our best but it must be a long time since he has written (except occasionally on the theatre) an article of more than eight hundred words—the length required by the opulent Sunday newspapers. Critics, in fact, may be divided into the eight-hundred-word Sunday and the sixteen-hundred-word weekly classes. The book-reviewers for daily papers, since they have to review several books at once in their eight hundred words, rarely find space for more than a few general indications.

Now the sixteen-hundred-word critic (V. S. Pritchett and Raymond Mortimer are examples) can give a very good picture of one item. On the weekly level an author is likely to get justice done to him on his last book, however skimped it will be elsewhere, but he can never obtain it for the bulk of his work. No author is now allowed the space of one of Macaulay's essays for the criticism which unravels the skein in the carpet, making clearer the stages in an author's development, helping him to see his way ahead. Here two factors enter in. It is not only difficult to place articles of considerable length on living writers and be paid for them, it is an arduous task to get them written. For, apart from the best critics, often too over-trained as sprinters to enter for these marathons, one encounters a stubborn field of resistance. This is the Envy Belt. The Envy Belt encircles every writer of talent at about the middle distance. Immediately round him are his friends and fellow craftsmen who either like him personally or are sufficiently obsessed with their own task not to experience the green-eyed monster. Below them stretches the Envy Belt, beyond it again a vague Fan Belt that fades out into the wastes of ignorance. It is the aim of the Envy Belt to increase its power by constantly detaching groups from the zones above and below. When these have been destroyed and there are no more friends, and no more fans either, it sets about devouring someone else. Yet were twenty of our outstanding authors to name the writers and editors from whom they invariably got bad reviews the lists would be surprisingly homogeneous, and these reviewers would also be found not to differ very much from their predecessors, who used to maul the youthful Tennyson or Keats. 'Righteousness is the hall-mark of unconscious guilt,' profoundly remarks Dr. Glover in this issue, and the characteristics of the Envy Belt are usually intense moral indignation (often concentrated on occasional errors in grammar or spelling), a vanity in proportion to their envy (for envy is the price we pay ourselves—and exact from others—for being vain), and a bitter sense of their own frustration. If, in particular, some writer has in youth shown considerable promise, especially promise of a quite outstanding sterility, he will never be forgiven by his ex-colleagues. Flap-eared, sphincter-mouthed pin-heads, donnish journalists or journalist dons, old soaks who have written nothing for twenty years, join the chorus of detraction.

> Out of England have we come
> Great hatred, little room.

Almost as bad is the tendency among other reviewers to indiscriminate praise which is a kind of guilt-offering made to the writer by those who know they lack both the time and the space to evaluate him properly, and who say a few nice things because such things are generally said and because in our close and convivial society mercy makes for so much less trouble than justice.

*November* 1946

# INTERPLANETARY

ONE doubt is ruining Christmas for intending visitors to the moon. *Will their papers be in order?* Compared with this problem the few remaining technical difficulties pale into insignificance. I recently put the question to a High Official. He replied, 'The moon is somewhat younger than the earth and

consequently may not have attained to so complex a civilization. However, we may expect that they would wish the first
visitors from our planet to give a good account of themselves,
and I would suggest something in the nature of a tryptichal or
rather heptatichal passport, with visa, priority indication, identity card, vaccination, legitimacy, and currency certificates,
and ration book rolled into one. But a visa for the moon should
clearly specify which part of it is intended as well as the
duration of the visit; it should give the name of the proposed
port of entry and here, incidentally, it's no good putting down
"Tyco Brahé" if this region is not provided with proper
clearance facilities or is known to our lunar colleagues by some
outlandish name. But it's not your visa to the moon I'm worry-
ing about,' he said heartily, 'for, as I say, they may be as
backward up there about these matters as we all were before
1914—it's your re-entry permit to the British Isles. Why
should we let you in? Technically we can give you a visa to the
moon and of course you may take your seventy-five pounds
there, if it's in the Sterling Area, and apply for a further
expenses allowance if you can convince me of the value of your
trip for the export drive, giving references of the firms with
whom you propose to do business. But what guarantees can you
offer us in support of your return? Who will endorse your re-
entry visa for us at the other end? Under what statute are we
impelled to accept their authority? In whose name will permission be granted? A visa from one country to another is
evidence of a reciprocal arrangement; what documentation is
there to indicate that such an arrangement exists? Frankly,
I see none. If they possessed a competent bureaucracy, I think
by now we should have heard from them. At least at my level.
Perhaps you can get a letter sent down by hand from my
opposite number. And besides, another point, the faintest
deviation of the compass in your return rocket may land you,

most inconveniently, in a part of this earth for which you have no transit visa or, worse still, where the general regulations governing the issue of passports do not apply.'

'One more thing,' I ventured shyly, 'as you know, you can't get a temporary visa to visit the United States now without very properly being asked what aliases you have lived under, whether you have been to prison or taken part in political agitation and, in addition, without having your finger-prints taken. Twenty-one of them, with all the combinations—the old ladies love it. Well, supposing they have only these flippers in the moon, will they accept this form of identification?'

'It's very ticklish—I think I shouldn't risk it, in your place I would offer the selenic authorities a dozen photographs: two full, two of each profile, two quarter, two three-quarters, two back, taken, as a delicate compliment, by moonlight. And finger-prints, by the way, are never really satisfactory— nothing's easier, with all this modern machinery, than to take your fingers off, and then nobody knows *who* you are.'

He looked tense and grim. I drew the conversation towards his favourite hobby. 'Tell me, is it because you felt misgivings about finger-prints that you turned your attention to the feet— your Big Scheme, you remember?'

His face softened. 'No, no, nothing so prosaic. I was put on the track, no, on their tracks'—his glance was almost shy—'by my particular weakness, a fondness for poetry. You remember the verse Gray suppressed from the Elegy which ends:

The redbreast loves to build and warble there
and little footsteps lightly print the ground.

It must have been that, coming on top of innumerable odes to the nightingale that gave me, one sleepless night, my brain-wave, my revelation! Exit permits for swallows—identity cards for birds. Think of it, man, think first of all of the general

untidiness, the aimless lackadaisical squalor under the present
dispensation. The human population reasonably docketed, an
adequate watch kept on their goings-out and their comings-in,
while the feathered world wanders all over the place, treating
our island as if it were habitable only six months of the year:
swallows, nightingales, geese, duck, snipe, quail, starlings—
who include, I'm certain, some very undesirable elements, all
the cosmopolitan rag, tag and bobtail, the feathered gangsters,
the international play-birds living on the fat of the land,
gorging themselves on what it has taken us months of toil to
produce, billing and cooing and necking and petting, playing
their dirty little games in the hedges, making shameless noises
all night, ruining the farmer, loosening morals. Look what the
cuckoo stands for in our language—both fool and knave.
Little footprints indeed! Well, I shall put an end to it. I'm not
going to rest till I've got every one of these little footprints into
the filing machine—identity card first, a neat little ring round
the leg, and then we'll see who's to be allowed to go where they
like, when they like, mollycoddling themselves, exporting
capital in their fat, pampered little crops, treating the world
as if the whole system of controls and ramifications which go
to make up that triumph of the human will and intelligence—
a valid passport for a viable frontier—were a thing of naught.
'You remember the lines of Victor Hugo,' he concluded:

Vite! A tire d'ailes!—
Oh! c'est triste de voir s'enfuir les hirondelles
Elles s'en vont là-bas, vers le midi doré.

Well, I don't find it *triste*. I find such behaviour incompetent
and impertinent, a reflection on my terms of reference and,
incidentally, not very British, and somehow I don't think,
when I've framed my little wing-clipping regulation with the
Minister, that Sister Swallow will recur.'

*December* 1946

# THE COMING OF THE CRISES—I

IT was said two years ago in this column that 'every European war means a war lost by Europe' and recent events have brought home to us that in the last conflict we were defeated from an economic though not from a moral or military standpoint. 'We shall treat England like a beautiful flower,' Goering is supposed to have jested, 'but we shan't water the pot'—and something very like that is now happening. The advantages which position, coal, skill and enterprise won for us in the nineteenth century have been liquidated and we go back to scratch as a barren, humid, raw, but densely over-populated group of islands with an obsolete industrial plant, hideous but inadequate housing, a variety of unhealthy jungle possessions, vast international commitments, a falling birth-rate and a large class of infertile rentiers or over-specialized middlemen and brokers as our main capital. Surrounded on all frontiers by a loosened belt of good eating, we yet suffer from undernourishment, dearth of vitamins and sunshine, lack of hope, energy, leisure and spirit. Thus the outstanding difference at this moment between English and Americans is that in America one is conscious that everyone is tuned up to a positive individual quality; a man is completely a man, or a woman a woman—vain, confident, affable and aggressive. Here, the ego is at half-pressure; most of us are not men or women but members of a vast seedy, over-worked, over-legislated, neuter class, with our drab clothes, our ration books and murder stories, our envious, stricken, old-world apathies and resentments—a careworn people. And the symbol of this mood is London, now the largest, saddest and dirtiest of great cities with its miles of unpainted half-inhabited houses, its chopless chop-houses, its beerless pubs, its once vivid quarters losing all personality, its squares bereft of elegance, its dandies in exile, its antiques in America, its shops full of junk, bunk, and tomorrow, its crowds mooning round the stained green wicker of the cafeterias in their shabby raincoats, under a sky permanently dull and lowering like a metal dish-cover.

But soft! What forms are these? Why, the first quarter of a million tourists climbing on our trains, with their torn seats, pilfered bulbs and stinking lavatories, rushing through empty churches and derelict country-houses, grappling with our moribund telephone system, languishing through our Sunday afternoons by the porridge-grey ocean, freezing in our provincial hotels with their vest-pocket electric fires and shilling meters, where an immutable phalanx of cross-word puzzle widows are clamped to the arm-chairs, waiting for death on a thousand a year.

'So young and so untender?

So young, my lord, and ****!'

'Oh dear, I can't think what that word can be; four letters.'

'Sounds like a quotation to me.'

'Sh—it's time for the News!'

In the general speculation about the British crisis there has been constant reference to decadence, but decadence in its exact sense—a decay of the vital principle—is not very evident; the symptoms are rather of breakdown and stoppage, of sudden illness rather than senility, and the improved prospects of the working class and petty bourgeoisie must be set against the impoverishment and restriction of enterprise among the upper and middle classes. The falling birth-rate, also, is an almost universal phenomenon. What we are really witnessing is the collapse of the Industrial Revolution, of that British Empire which was founded on geographical position, business daring, foreign investments, cheap labour, food and goods, wise administration, coal, iron and sea-power. We are decadent only if we fail to replace it by another, and we can replace it only by thinking clearly and directing the inventive genius of our country to that end.

The first question we must ask ourselves is whether, if we had the choice, we still want to remain a great power. It is customary to admire Sweden, Holland, Switzerland, but do we really wish to become like them; should we reduce our population by two-thirds? I think the answer must be NO—that we cannot retreat into an enlightened provincialism as a small, smug community of industrialized sheep-breeders; that it is part, as it were, of our biological role as a nation to take on responsibilities, to expand our trade, to police and to administer, to take a leading part in an eventual world government, even if our country thereby becomes but a nursery and an almshouse. Therefore, having decided against becoming a minor power we must see how we can plan to avoid it. We must consider our actual resources, assuming India and the Dominions to be practically lost to us, but that we retain for a while the tin and rubber of Malaya, Ceylon and various scattered possessions in the South Seas and West Indies. There remains a very large proportion of the continent of Africa. With an intelligent arrangement with France and Belgium the development of all pastoral Africa from Rhodesia to the Mediterranean could be planned in relation to the industrial output of Western Europe. Having assured our markets and raw materials, the scientists could then be called in to solve the home crisis, which is largely due to the obsolescence of our industrial methods and machinery. London, for example, is an obsolete city. If we give complete wartime priorities to scientists most of our technical disabilities can be overcome and the mistakes of Victorian industrialization avoided. After the turn of the scientist would come that of the artist. Thus if we could only produce a great architect, a man or a group who could create a new three-dimensional poetry in a material suitable to our climate and our time, then the whole nightmare of war-destruction, housing schemes, ruin and dilapidation would vanish. There may have been people who bewailed the disappearance of Tudor timber, bear gardens and back alleys to make room for Wren's churches, Lincoln's Inn or Queen Anne's Gate, but they do not win our sympathy. On the other hand the proposals for rebuilding Regent's Park revealed the bankruptcy of contemporary architecture, for since we have no proper understanding of the values of our present civilization, we cannot design an architecture which embodies them.

After the search for an architecture the next priority will be a College of Taste, for it is clear that we cannot for long maintain our export trade without a rebirth of that quite vanished quality. The *Queen Elizabeth*, for instance, though a magnificent ship which will always be admired for its vast and silent engines, is at the decorator's level exactly on a par with the Cumberland Hotel. We are still lamentably slow to ask our best artists to advise and help with our minor arts such as furniture, glass, china. The Americans snap up the modern Portuguese ware with its pineapple coffee pots and banana leaf dishes. When will Graham Sutherland design our breakfast sets? Or Henry Moore our garden sofas? 'Let us make all the good, fine and new things we can and so far from being afraid of other people getting our patterns, we should glory in it and throw out all the hints we can, and, if possible, have all the artists in Europe working after our models.' This is not, alas, the voice of twentieth-century England, but the bold mid-eighteenth-century accents of Josiah Wedgwood.

Over the last few months *Horizon* has been quite rightly pre-occupied with the decline in literary values, for it is a decline which must end by affecting our own standard. Thus for the first time there will be no article on last year's poetry as we do not consider the volumes produced in 1946 to justify one. It is disheartening to think that twenty years ago saw the first novels of Hemingway, Faulkner, Elizabeth Bowen, Rosamond Lehmann, Evelyn Waugh, Henry Green, Graham Greene, to name but a few, for no new crop of novelists has arisen commensurate with them. Viewing the scene of 1947, moreover, one is conscious of the predominance of a certain set of names, the literary 'Best People', who somewhat resemble a galaxy of impotent prima donnas, while round them rotate tired business men, publishers, broadcasters and Civil Servants who once were poets, novelists, and revolutionary thinkers. The State and International Charity are now beginning to bestow patronage on the young and promising; I know of a young writer who has received three separate financial awards on the strength of one unpublished book—but when will the middle-aged author of proved merit receive his due? I could name half a dozen excellent writers in their early forties, who might one day make a valuable contribution to literature in return for a couple of years of complete idleness at a patron's expense and who are now wearily grinding themselves into hacks. Literature is becoming a spare time hobby (except for the novelist who sells his work to Hollywood) and is consequently losing its authority. As fewer people think clearly and feel strongly, so the power of the written word declines along with the ability to write, for though people may turn to great art in moments of national disaster, there is no deterrent to aesthetic adventure like a prolonged struggle with domestic difficulties, food shortages, cold, ill-health and money worries. Art is not a necessity but an indispensable luxury; those who produce it must be cosseted. It would be a nice concession if all who could prove that they contributed to the culture of this country were allowed additional allowances for foreign travel—but when poets are excused Austerity and painters winter abroad we will be decadent with a vengeance, what?

*W. H. AUDEN*

# THE FALL OF ROME

### TO C. C.

THE piers are pummelled by the waves;
In a lonely field the rain
Lashes an abandoned train;
Outlaws fill the mountain caves.

Fantastic grow the evening gowns;
Agents of the Fisc pursue
Absconding tax-defaulters through
The sewers of provincial towns.

Private rites of magic send
The temple prostitutes to sleep;
All the literati keep
An imaginary friend.

Cerebrotonic Cato may
Extol the Ancient Disciplines,
But the muscle-bound Marines
Mutiny for food and pay.

Caesar's double-bed is warm
As an unimportant clerk
Writes I DO NOT LIKE MY WORK
On a pink official form.

Unendowed with wealth or pity,
Little birds with scarlet legs,
Sitting on their speckled eggs,
Eye each flu-infected city.

Altogether elsewhere, vast
Herds of reindeer move across
Miles and miles of golden moss,
Silently and very fast.          *April* 1947

# THE COMING OF THE CRISES—II

EVERY year around Budget-time appear the inevitable statistics dealing with our expenditure on betting, films, tobacco, alcohol and, occasionally, books. As far as Anglo-Saxons are concerned, it is clear that books, though free of purchase tax, play hardly any part in the Great Escape. Even with their increased cost they register but a paltry gain, and reading—'that unpunished vice'—remains also one of the least attractive. Yet for an outlay of five shillings a week (less than half the sum expended by the addict of barley or tobacco) many a lily-livered refugee from the Pink Bliss, the Red Devil, or the Blue Boredom, gluing his eye to the print, can footle through life in a benevolent daze.

This neglect of letters is a result of bad advertising. If we compare the inducements to buy beer or cigarettes with the advertisements for books, we find that, while the first two are based on the pleasure principle, the last concentrates on uplift. Publishers insist on elevating when they should be parading the essential agreeable uselessness of the written word. Listening to the Portuguese *fados* Beckford wrote, 'You think you are drinking milk but all the time the poison of voluptuousness is stealing through your veins'. That is how we would have you look at *Horizon*, and to the occasional reader who still complains that it is 'above his head' we would add that to bumble around half understanding and half not, in a maze of useless information, is in itself a bewildering and quite fatuous pleasure.

Yet if I were Chancellor of this—or indeed any other country—with what horror and despair would I view the human situation! Forty-six million people every year more unhappy, more discontented with their lot—spendthrift flies crawling towards the sun, ready to pay any sum for the weed that calms anxiety, the liquid that generates illusion and

oblivion, paying out fortunes in betting (which means buying
the right to daydreams of yet more alcohol and nicotine or still
untaxed sensual pleasures), flocking to the cinema to see what
Hollywood considers best for them; a people (like most others)
whose pleasures are both vicarious and sterile; not constructive play-therapy but a monotonous alleviation of pain and
boredom. When one considers as well the emigration and
would-be emigration figures the picture of desolation seems
complete. While we smugly christen the present 'The Atomic
Age', the statisticians (if any) of the future may rather describe
ours as the age of alcohol or trace our changeover from the
ancient standard of gold to the new currency of the cigarette,
while noting playfully how the modern State, which is responsible for the happiness of those who compose it, draws an
increasing revenue from their misery. A more profound
moralist would add that smoking increases in proportion to the
strain of modern life, drinking in proportion to its monotony;
in both we take a vegetable revenge on the machine which
robs the worker of the pleasure of craftsmanship and sets a
standard of efficiency (the telephone, or traffic lights) with
which ordinary humans cannot compete. Descending deeper
still he would find that the advance of the opiates is characteristic of the terrible transitional epoch in which we live, a
generation which has destroyed God without knowing how to
create Man.

Man without God is immensely lonely: we should treat
everyone alive today as a friend on his deathbed or the inmate
of a condemned cell. The Americans have a society called
'Alcoholics Anonymous' (great revenue producers, I imagine)
who rally to each other's side when a bout is due: were
'Human Beings Anonymous' with its motto 'we must love one
another and die' ever to get on its feet, we might experience
a new world in which budgets were unbalanceable, where

people enjoyed their work, where men were not sick under lamp-posts, and women didn't cough, and where a magazine like *Horizon* was as desirable as a packet of Churchman's or a stick of gum.                                          *May* 1947

## LONDON AND PARIS

THE predicament of the modern writer which was first discussed at length in *Horizon's* inquiry on the Cost of Letters and the series dealing with 'Inflationary Decadence' has now been most forcibly taken up by the *New Statesman*, Mr. J. B. Priestley and others. Nothing will be done, because the roots of the evil go down too far into our society for any financial top-dressing which the State might tardily administer to be of any use. There are already signs of a return to that inertia, which is the natural mental climate of these islands. The sales of serious literature are diminishing, the golden moment of periodicals is past, the flirtation between art and politics forgotten, while the affair of the Bankside Power Station proves that though experts may produce an admirable plan for making London once more an agreeable place to live in, it cannot stand up to a strictly material short-term priority. And if South London cannot be saved, what chance is there that the proposed linking of Hampstead Heath, Regent's Park and Hyde Park, with the necessary demolitions, will ever be tolerated? Or that artists will ever receive as a favour (since they cannot strike) the concessions which miners can demand as a right? Yet in the long run our export trade depends (through industrial design) nearly as much on art as on coal.

It is interesting to compare the situation here with that in France. In France, if anything, the plight of the artist is worse. The sales of a serious writer are generally on a smaller scale than here, the royalties are less, seldom exceeding ten per cent.

The price of a book is lower and the formidable hurdle of translation has to be taken before the vast Anglo-Saxon public can be reached. A writer is not likely to make more than two hundred pounds from a book (which undergoes the same endless delays in appearing as here), nor do any magazines exist which pay large sums for articles or extracts. There is in addition an acute crisis in the production of both magazines and newspapers. There are too many newspapers, and those without large funds or subsidies are being forced to the wall. There are also too many luxury magazines, too many specialized literary ones; the rates of pay are generally low because, owing to competition, the circulations are limited and the same kind of article by the same author has a way of appearing over and over again. Inflation and the high cost of living also reduce the value of a writer's earnings and there is nothing to set against this black picture except the fact that poverty is less humiliating in literary Paris, where nearly all are poor, than perhaps anywhere else, and that the exciting liberty and anonymous independence of the free-lance writer have not yet acquired that taint of irresponsibility with which they are associated in our civic-minded termitaries. There are said to be forty thousand *artistes-peintres* by profession in France today and how most of them live is a mystery, for they are not employed on newspapers, magazines, or by the giant publishing house in whose offices many of the most brilliant intellectuals are to be found. It is an ironical reflection that the contents of an ordinary still-life—a loaf of white bread, a cheese, part of a ham, some butter and a bottle of wine—can now be obtained only at a fabulous price on the black market, and a studio not at all. It is the prohibitive price of these necessities which remove painter and writer from the natural tranquil domestic environment enjoyed by their great predecessors and forces them to teach, copy, or betray.

Externally Paris has never looked lovelier. Except for the prices it is astoundingly as it was before the war. The black-market *bistro* is vanishing, the normal pre-war restaurants of each quarter coming into their own, there is no longer the feeling that outside the luxury district and the artists' quarter all is want and decay. The small parallelogram between the Palais Royal and the Luxembourg, the Île St. Louis and the Rue de Bourgogne, still contains what is most alive in the arts of Europe. It is the final stronghold of free spirits against the Anglo-Saxon worship of money and respectability, the bogy of nationalism, or the Slav idols of social realism and the party line. It is the last place were races mingle as easily as the Present and the Past. There is a crop of new and inexpensive 'existentialist' bars and night-clubs which recall the first be-ginnings of Montparnasse. The new permanent Impressionist museum in the *Jeu de Paume* contains all that was most sensuous and most scattered in the Museums before the war. All cafés, not just one or two, within that lovely lozenge are now delight-ful, and the small hotels of the left bank are all habitable again. Yet, as an American observer pointed out, 'This is the summer —and terribly like Vienna between the wars, when what was once a great capital came to life only between May and September, with the dollars and the tourists and the fine weather, to sink back for six months into poverty, hunger, cold and darkness when the last of those who thought "Vienna hadn't changed at all" had returned home'. But this verges on the political problems of France, on the endless discussions about Communism and de Gaulle. Rather than make pronouncements on that, we give our readers the trans-lation of a short controversy which has appeared recently in *Combat* (Editor, Albert Camus) and other papers and which reflects the political tension in left-wing circles and the eternal problem of the relations between the democratic belief in the rights of the individual and the Marxist conception of tactics.

## THE NIZAN CASE

PAUL NIZAN may be known to some of our readers through his visit to England during the Spanish War. He was at that time one of the Editors of *Ce Soir* and was also known here as the author of two novels *La Conspiration* and *Le Cheval de Troie*, part of which appeared in *New Writing*. When war broke out he resigned from the Communist Party. As a soldier he was not allowed to publish articles, but he sent a letter announcing his resignation, which was published in the Socialist newspaper *L'Œuvre*. He was in liaison with the British 14th Army Field Workshop when he was killed in action at St. Omer on 23 May 1940. From that moment rumours began to circulate to the effect that he had been employed by the French police as a spy on Communist activities during his membership of the Party. His widow has for long tried to obtain a denial of these rumours, and it was finally to establish their falsity that Sartre and others addressed the original statement to the newspaper *Combat* after an attack on the critical honesty of Nizan had been made by M. Lefebvre in his book *On Existentialism*. Below we give the text of the statement.

'From time to time we are reminded that Jacques Decour, Jean Prevost and Vernet died for us, and it is well that it should be so. But a silence has fallen on the name of Nizan, one of the most gifted writers of his generation, who was killed by the Germans in 1940; no one dares speak his name and it seems as though he was being buried for a second time. Nevertheless, in certain political circles the whisper goes round that he was a traitor. Aragon told one of us that Nizan had informed the Vichy Minister of the Interior of certain military secrets of the Communist Party. If you ask for proof of this, you won't get any. You will be told that it is common knowledge that shortly before he died, Politzer affirmed this to be so, and that, anyhow, you need only read Nizan's books to see that he was a traitor. In his latest book, *On Existentialism*, M. Lefebvre writes: "Paul Nizan had few friends, and we wondered what was the reason for this. Today we know. All his books have treason as a central theme;" and "He came from reactionary, and even Fascist, surroundings. Perhaps he was one of them, since he pretended to be spying on them."

'Now, to the best of our knowledge, the Communists can only reproach Paul Nizan with the fact that he left the Party in 1939 at the time of the Russo-German pact. Each individual can think what he likes of this: it is a strictly political matter, and it is not our intention to discuss it. But when, without adducing any proof, people accuse Nizan of being a police spy we cannot forget that he was a writer, that he died fighting, and that it is our duty as writers to defend his memory. Thus, we address ourselves to M. Lefebvre (and to all those who, like him, spread these infamous accusations), and we ask them the following question: "When you say that Nizan is a traitor, do you simply mean that he left the Communist Party in 1939? If this is the case, say it quite openly, and everyone will agree with you or not according to his ideas. Or do you mean that, long before the war, Nizan undertook in return for money to inform an anti-Communist government of the activities of your Party? If this is the case, prove it. If we remain without an answer, or if we are not given the proofs for which we ask, we will act on your silence, and will publish a second manifesto affirming Nizan's innocence."

'The undersigned:

'R. Aron, G. Adam, A. Breton, S. de Beauvoir, P. Bost, A. Billy, P. Brisson, J-L. Bost, J. Benda, Roger Caillois, A. Camus, M. Fombeure, J. Guehenno, Henri Jeanson, J. Lescure, M. Leiris, J. Lemarchand, R. Maher, M. Merleau-Ponty, F. Mauriac, Brice-Parain, J. Paulhan, J-P. Sartre, J. Schlumberger, Ph. Soupault.

'M. Louis Martin-Chauffier, in an attached letter, "associates himself fully with the intention of our request, but not with its expression".

'He adds: "Paul Nizan was one of my friends . . . I think I knew him fairly well, and I would say entirely if it were a question of clearing his good faith or his honour. Thus, I associate myself fully with the intention of your manifesto. But I can only do it on the margin of the document which you sent me. My relations with my

Communist friends, whom it involves, are such that I cannot address them in this tone." ' From *Combat* and *Le Littéraire*.

'A manifesto has appeared in the Press which pretends to have the object of defending the memory of Paul Nizan against the accusation "spread by rumour" of having sold information to the Minister of the Interior.

'This protest would have seemed fairly natural if the fact that a member of the National Committee of Writers had not been cited by name as an originator of this "rumour" which makes the manifesto appear far more as a manœuvre to discredit one of us, and, through him, our whole committee, than as a defence of the memory of Paul Nizan.

'This kind of personal backbiting obliges us to remind the signatories of the text in question (moreover, themselves, not all equally well equipped to rise up in the name of morality) that by writing as they have, they have made themselves guilty of or accessories to a dishonest accusation against an unnamed person.

'Acting as they do, these signatories are expressly committing the very crime against which their indignation has been aroused.

'Take note.

(sgd.) The Managing Committee of the
National Committee of Writers.'
From *Les Lettres Françaises*

## LARGE SCALE SPRING MANŒUVRES

'A headline in a paper started a train of thought: "The anti-Communist offensive is in full swing in the United States". But it seems to me that it is also at its height in France. I am not only referring to the unequivocal campaigns of a well-known section of the Press, but also to the manœuvres in which a certain number of intellectuals are engaging.

'Is it pure chance that at this very moment *Paris Presse* is serializing Hemingway's *For Whom the Bell Tolls* which, under the guise of a novel, is no more than an anti-Communist pamphlet?

'Is it pure chance that, under the excuse of defending Paul Nizan's memory, the militant anti-Communist writers, joined by a few trusting spirits, have united to append their signatures to a revealing elbowing match? Contemplating this eloquent piece, where, beside more literary names, that of the former editor of the

German-controlled paper *Aujourd'hui* shines with a rare brilliance, everyone will understand the meaning of such a document.

'I knew Nizan personally—I did not like him because he was a cold character, jealous, above all, of his own reputation. His public repudiation of his Party and his comrades, at the moment when they were persecuted and in danger, filled me with disgust. He reserved his announcement of this event for *Temps*, the organ of the Comité des Forges and for *L'Œuvre*, run by Marcel Déat. A man of good faith would have remained silent. I am not afraid to write this because I know it to be true.

'I concede that his friends should now be anxious to rehabilitate his memory because he died for France. But is this a good enough reason for disseminating these accusations which are injurious to those whom Nizan betrayed?'

C. M.

*Les Lettres Françaises*

### THE WATCH-DOGS OF ANTI-COMMUNISM

'A few days ago we received a document entitled THE NIZAN CASE and signed by a certain number of writers.

'These gentlemen complain that a great deal is said about Jacques DECOUR, Jean PREVOST and other writers who died in the cause of freedom, and that no one DARES speak of NIZAN and that there are WHISPERS that he was a traitor. They lament, they sigh, and, without a shade of doubt, they attack the Communists, particularly Aragon.

'Because it goes without saying that the aim behind their present manœuvre is not to RESTORE THE MEMORY of NIZAN, for which these Gentlemen don't give a hoot, but to attack the French Communist Party. Thus, it is only necessary to read the names of these protestors to understand the deep meaning behind their move:

'Brice PARAIN, dismissed from *L'Humanité* because he was Editor of a police newspaper, *Detective*; André BRETON, a former guest of Trotsky, the most important servant of the international Political Police against the workers' movement, André BRETON who, in his magazine, denounced his co-signatory of today as a police spy; Jean PAULHAN, the man for whom Roman Rolland was a traitor by the same title as Alphonse de CHATEAUBRIANT; Henri JEANSON, founder and editor of the Nazi newspaper *Aujourd'hui*. And a host of others who do not seem uncomfortable in the company of these "specialists".

'Naturally enough, certain newspapers have already espoused the cause of these gentlemen: *Littérature*, *Carrefour*, *Gavroche*. At the moment when, after the scandalous incidents provoked at the Assembly by Pierre ANDRÉ and others tarred with the same brush over the debates on Indo-China, all the anti-Communists fling themselves into the attack, those who have just taken up the defence of the "patriot" HARDY, can only be rejoicing at the diversion created in the name of another "patriot", whose claim to this title is immediately considered as incontestable since he is an enemy of our Party.

'NIZAN left the Communist Party in 1939. He left it with a great deal of noise, surrounding his gesture with ostentation, immediately participating in the abominable campaign of calumny which was let loose against the most far-seeing and courageous citizens of France. He left it in the same manner as did GITTON and CAPRON, men of the Political Police ... Traitor to his Party, he became by the same action a traitor to France because his public pronouncements helped such men as Daladier and Bonnet—against whom he had been writing on the eve of his decision—and the whole fifth column in their criminal political activities. Can we believe that this attitude was anything but the development of previous activity?

'But his present defenders pay no attention to all that. Their preoccupation is fighting the Communists; anything is grist to their mill and their best weapon still remains provocation, cold and deliberate provocation which clothes itself in literary prestige and dissimulates itself behind a hypocritical appeal to morality.

'These gentlemen don't even recoil before the fact of combining with a person like JEANSON, for instance, against the men of the Resistance.

'Enough!

'Five years of suffering have in themselves been a sufficient revelation of what is disguised as anti-Communism, for this manœuvre to be in itself the judge of those who instigate it, and those who defend it.'

GUY LECLERC<br>L'Humanité

'Monsieur Lefebvre, who has been explicitly implicated, has not replied.

'M. Sartre, on the other hand, has written to us as follows: "Since the National Committee of Writers has shown itself to be so solicitous of the honour of its members, I wish, *in the first instance*, to state that I am still a member of the Committee and I am not aware of any defence that it has put up on *my* behalf against the attacks of which *I* have been the object. Secondly, it was to me that M. Aragon made the statements which have been quoted. Does he think, then, that they are of such a nature as to discredit their originator by the simple publication of them? Or did he in fact make them to me? In which case it is a question of his word against mine. He should state the facts from his point of view and everyone can then judge as they think fit."'                                   J-P. SARTRE

'The writers who signed the protest take note of the declarations made by *L'Humanité* and the National Committee of Writers; they also take note of Monsieur Lefebvre's silence. We know that Nizan left the Communist Party in 1939: everyone must judge this according to his views. As for the insinuations about his conduct before that date, no proof of their veracity has been forthcoming.'

*Combat*

*June* 1947

# THE LITERATURE OF DISENGAGEMENT

IN order to prepare an edition of essays from *Horizon* for translation into German it was necessary to run through all ninety-odd numbers. Surprisingly enough the later essays turned out to be the best, that is to say the most solid; and these long articles sometimes possess (as in Tangye Lean's 'Study of Toynbee' or Gerald Brenan's 'St. John of the Cross') a depth and grasp which is quite out of the run of current literary journalism, while many of the fireworks which achieved immediate popularity in earlier numbers are now inclined to appear superficial and shoddy. One is also conscious of a change of policy which would appear to be justified. This change is expressed in our belief that the honeymoon between literature and action, once so promising, is over. We can see, looking through these old *Horizons*, a left-wing and sometimes revolutionary political attitude among writers, heritage of Guernica and Munich, boiling up to a certain aggressive optimism in the war years, gradually declining after D-Day and soon after the victorious general election despondently fizzling out. It would be too easy to attribute this to the policy of the editors, their advancing years, and war-weariness. The fact remains that a Socialist Government, besides doing practically nothing to help artists and writers (unless the closing down of magazines during the fuel crisis can be interpreted as an aid to incubation), has also quite failed to stir up either intellect or imagination; the English renaissance, whose false dawn we have so enthusiastically greeted, is further away than ever. Even Socialist magazines like *Tribune* and *The New Statesman* seem desperately short of new talent and the sole outstanding Socialist writer remains J. B. Priestley. Somehow, during the last two years, the left-wing literary movement has petered out, with Europe's new golden age, or the dream of a merry and aesthetically minded Socialist State. The atomic bomb renders most individual action futile; our fate is in the hands of four men, Truman, Stalin, Marshall, Molotov, and there is but little we can do about it; the one answer to the atomic bomb is an international world state based on a religion of absolute pacifism founded on the sacredness of human life. If we can be exploded by the hundred thousand into brown dust, like a rotten puff-ball, then we must at all costs believe, as the truly great have believed, that the hairs of our heads are numbered and that every thing which lives is holy.

In the light of the comparative failure of the 'progressive' movement of the last few years to rise above intelligent political journalism into the realms of literature, we must look else-where, either to the mad and lonely, or to those who have with a certain angry obstinacy meticulously cultivated their garden. Among these the Sitwells shine out, for during the darkest years of the war they contrived not only to produce their best work, to grow enormously in stature, but to find time to be of immense help to others. Many poets and writers were consoled by their encouragement as well as by their intransigent example, and so this number, at the risk of the inevitable accusation that we support a literary clique, is wholeheartedly dedicated to them. In order to dominate the present one must withdraw from it, such would seem the lesson of these sages, and let us hope that they can overcome even the gathering acedia of the reading public, corrupted by summer heat and murder trials, gnawed by anxiety and post-war disillusion, stricken by shortages, hourly more unable to concentrate, always ready for a lark until the skies darken with a new black-out, and the winter of cold, poverty and famine induced by their own folly compels them again to try a bit of reading. *July* 1947

# STENDHAL

## THE PRIVILEGES OF 10 APRIL 1840[1]

MAY God grant me the following diploma:

### ARTICLE I

Never any serious pain right up to advanced old-age; then, no pain but sudden death in bed from apoplexy, during sleep, without any moral or physical distress.

Every year, not more than three days of ill-health. The body and all its by-products to be quite odourless.

---

[1] These daydreams represent a very little-known text of STENDHAL, composed towards the end of his life (when a man of fifty-nine). They were first printed in *Les Quatre Vents*, No. 6 (Paris 1946) from which they are now translated. *Horizon* considers that Stendhal's wishes, besides making pleasant summer reading, are of permanent interest, and show that a great genius, even when death approaches, can sometimes prefer the air of humanism—however adolescent—to the odour of sanctity.

### ARTICLE 2

The following miracles will neither be observed nor suspected by anyone.

### ARTICLE 3

Whenever desired, the member to be as the index finger in regard to firmness and agility. Its shape two inches more than the big toe and of the same thickness, but pleasure by means of the said member to take place only twice a week. Twenty times a year the privileged one to be able to change himself into the being that he wishes, provided that that being exists. A hundred times a year he will speak for twenty-four hours any language he wishes.

### ARTICLE 4

The privileged one having a ring on his finger and pinching this ring while looking at a woman, she will fall passionately in love with him as we know Eloise did with Abelard. If the ring is slightly moistened with saliva, the woman becomes only a tender and devoted friend. By looking at a woman and taking the ring from the finger, all sentiments inspired by virtue of the foregoing privileges shall cease. By looking at a hostile being and stroking the ring on the finger hate changes into good-will.

These miracles can only take place four times a year for *l'amour passion*; eight times for friendship; twenty times for the disappearance of hate, and fifty times to inspire simple good-will.

### ARTICLE 5

Fine hair, a good skin, excellent fingers which never peel, a delicate and gentle body odour. The 1st of February and the 1st of June every year the clothes of the privileged one revert to the condition they were at the third time he wore them.

### ARTICLE 6

Miracles in the eyes of all who don't know him: the privileged one shall have the face of General Debelle, who died in St.

Domingo, but without any imperfection. He shall play fault-lessly whisk [*sic*], écarté, billiards, chess, but never make more than 100 francs at them. As a pistol shot, a horseman and a fencer he shall be perfect.

### ARTICLE 7

Four times a year he can change himself into any animal he wishes, and afterwards change back into a man. Four times a year he can change himself into any man he wishes and further-more concentrate that man's life into that of an animal. In case of death or impediment to the being into which he has changed, he shall revert immediately to the shape of the privileged one. Thus the privileged one can, four times a year, and for an unlimited time, in each case, occupy two bodies at the same time.

### ARTICLE 8

When the privileged one is wearing on his person or his finger for two minutes a ring which he has kept for a moment in his mouth, he shall become invulnerable for the time he has decided upon. Ten times a year he shall possess the sight of an eagle and be able in running to make five leagues in an hour.

### ARTICLE 9

Every day at two o'clock in the morning the privileged one shall find in his pocket a gold napoleon plus the value of forty francs in ready money in the currency of the country in which he finds himself. Any money of which he has been robbed will be found the following night at two o'clock in the morning on a table in front of him. Murderers at the moment of striking or giving him poison will have a violent access of cholera for eight days. The privileged one can shorten these pains by saying, 'I entreat that so-and-so's sufferings stop altogether or are diminished in severity'.

Thieves will be seized with an access of extreme cholera for two days at the moment when they shall be ready to perform the theft.

### ARTICLE 10

Eight times a year while out hunting a little flag shall reveal to the privileged one an hour in advance what game there is and its exact location. One second before the game takes to flight the little flag will be luminous. It is understood that the flag shall be invisible to anyone except the privileged one.

### ARTICLE 11

A small flag shall point out to the privileged one statues hidden underground, under water or by walls. Also what these statues are, when and by whom made and the price one could receive for them after discovery. The privileged one can change these statues into a ball of lead of the weight of a quarter of an ounce. The miracle of the flag and the successive changing of the statue into a small ball and back again into a statue to take place not more than eight times a year.

### ARTICLE 12

The beast which the privileged one mounts or which draws the carriage in which he travels will never fall ill or fall down. The privileged one can unite himself with this animal in such a way as to inspire him with his wishes while participating in his sensations. Thus the privileged one when riding a horse will make but one animal with him and dictate his own will. The animal thus united with the privileged one will have three times the strength and courage which it possesses in its normal state.

The privileged one transformed into a fly, for example, and united with an eagle will form one being with that eagle.

### ARTICLE 13

The privileged one is unable to pilfer; if he tries to do so, his organs would not permit the action. He can kill ten human beings a year, but no one to whom he shall have spoken. For the first year he can kill a human being provided he has not spoken to him more than twice.

### ARTICLE 14
Should the privileged one wish to relate or reveal one of the articles of this diploma, his mouth would be unable to form any sound and he will have tooth-ache for twenty-four hours.

### ARTICLE 15
The privileged one taking a ring in his finger and saying, 'I entreat that noxious insects be annihilated', all insects within six metres of the ring in every direction to be smitten with death. These insects are fleas, bed-bugs, lice of every description, crabs, gnats, flys, rats, etc.

Snakes, vipers, lions, tigers, wolves and all poisonous animals, seized with fear, will take flight and shall withdraw to a league's distance.

### ARTICLE 16
Wherever he is, the privileged one, after having said, 'I pray for my food', shall find: two pounds of bread, a steak done to a turn, a leg of mutton *idem*, a dish of spinach *idem*, a bottle of St. Julien, a carafe of water, dessert and ice-cream and a *demi-tasse* of coffee. This prayer to be granted twice every twenty-four hours.

### ARTICLE 17
Ten times a year by request the privileged one will never miss either with rifle or pistol or with a blow from any kind of weapon. Ten times a year he can perform feats of arms with twice the strength of his opponent, but he shall be incapable of administering any deadly wound or one which causes pain or disablement for more than 100 hours.

### ARTICLE 18
Ten times a year the privileged one by request, will be able to diminish by three-quarters the suffering of anyone he sees; or

this person being at the point of death, he can prolong his life by ten days while diminishing his actual suffering by three quarters. He can also by request obtain for the person in pain a sudden and painless death.

### ARTICLE 19

The privileged one can change a dog into a beautiful or an ugly woman: this woman will offer him her arm and will have the intelligence of Madame Ancilla[1] and the heart of Melanie.[2] This miracle can renew itself twenty times a year.

The privileged one can change a dog into a man who will have the figure of Pepin de Bellisle and the intelligence of Monsieur Koreff, the Jewish doctor.

### ARTICLE 20

The privileged one will never be more unhappy than he has been from 1 August 1839 to 1 April 1840. Two hundred times a year the privileged one can reduce his sleep to two hours which will produce the physical effects of eight hours. He will have the eyes of a lynx and the agility of Debureau.

### ARTICLE 21

Twenty times a year the privileged one can read the thoughts of everyone who is around him up to twenty metres distance. A hundred times a year he can see exactly what the person he wishes is doing, with the complete exception of the woman whom he loves the most.

There is also an exception for dirty or disgusting actions.

### ARTICLE 22

The privileged one can earn no more money than his sixty francs a day by means of the privileges here announced. One

[1] Madame Ancellot.

[2] Melanie Louason with whom he was in love in 1808. At fifty-nine years of age after thirty-two years of separation it is worth noting this reference in his wishful thinking.

hundred and fifty times a year he can obtain by request that such and such a person entirely forgets his existence.

### ARTICLE 23

Ten times a year the privileged one can be transported to any place he wishes at the rate of one hundred leagues an hour. During the journey he will sleep.     *Translated by C.C.*

*August* 1947

## AMERICAN INJECTION

'I HOLD, as some have done before me, that the human mind degenerates in America, and that the superiority of the white race, such as it is, is only kept up by intercourse with Europe.' PEACOCK (*Gryll Grange*), 1860.

\*     \*     \*

'If material life could be made perfect, as (in a very small way) it was perhaps for a moment among the Greeks, would not that of itself be a most admirable achievement? . . . And possibly on that basis of perfected material life, a new art and philosophy would grow unawares, not similar to what we call by those names, but having the same relation to the life beneath which art and philosophy amongst us ought to have had, but never have had. You see, I am content to let the past bury its dead. It does not seem to me that we can impose on America the task of imitating Europe.' SANTAYANA, letter to Pearsall Smith, 1921.

\*     \*     \*

'America is no place for an artist. A corn-fed hog enjoys a better life than a creative writer.' HENRY MILLER, 1945.

\*     \*     \*

### FIRST IMPRESSIONS

*Thursday, 28 November.* Nantucket light. In cold, sunny afternoon the bright red lightship bobbing to starboard is the first sign that our ten-day prep-school voyage is coming to an end, we are as happy as the discoverers of Virginia in 1584. 'We found shoal water, where we smelt so sweet and so strong a smell, as if we had been in the midst of some delicate garden abounding with all kind of odoriferous flowers, by which we were assured that the land could not be far distant.' No more dull dormitory life, eight to a cabin, no hurried monotonous meals (without drink, for our ship, the *Highland Governess*, is dry), no more scrambling for chairs, or searching for conversation, no more the pitching and tossing of the battered old bureaucrappy troopship over the endless empty heaving dishwater of the autumn Atlantic. Tomorrow our personalities will be handed back to us. Agitation amongst the young Canadian engineers in my cabin. 'Gee, I can't wait to be sweating over a corpse.'

To bed excited, with lights and lighthouses visible, and in the distance the Long Island beaches. All the voyage an immense euphoria about U.S.A., Baedeker alternating with Baudelaire: prospect of seeing California and far south-west! Europe seems infinitely remote; England like a week-end cottage which one has abandoned with all the washing-up undone. I understand the New World *motif*. Actuality, the ideal of inhabiting a continuous present . . .

*Friday*. Up at six to see New York in the darkness—sunrise, the Narrows, the first houses, the ferries, *l'aurore rose et verte*, the Statue of Liberty, skyscrapers in fog, general impression much more European than I had expected. Interminable wait before going ashore during which the passengers all look exactly as they did on the first day—'their sweating selves, but worse'. Off about 12.30, then through customs and in taxi to hotel; my driver asks—and gets—six dollars. Tony and Wystan are there and we go off to lunch at my choice, the *King of the Sea*, exotic and rather bad, but Third Avenue, red and raffish, has a fascinating Continental charm. Auden warns us of the perils of the big city, he seems obsessed with hold-ups, the proper use of the subway system, and with jumping to it at the traffic lights; his welcome is like that of the town mouse to the country mouse in the Disney film. I discover only later that his battle with the traffic lights is a kind of personal obsession with the machine age, a challenge to his desire to pass efficiently in the crowd. Hugging our wallets tightly and plunging over the crossings we proceed in short rushes to the Holliday book-shop, an oasis where carefully chosen books are sold like hand-made cushions; here Wystan introduces the two new mice and leaves us, with instructions on how to take the subway back. That evening an elaborate dinner with Peter at Voisin's, much anticipated on the *Highland Governess* (disappointing except for avocado pears). The new mice compare notes. Peter says the U.S.A. is a place where only the very rich can be the least different from anyone else, but where the poor are not crushed and stunted (as in England, where the upper class is twice as tall as the lower). Here, he said, the poor are picturesque and often beautiful—the true creators of the American dream—and that there was also a great poetry about the country when one travelled over it. On the other hand it was awful seeing nothing but copies—of buildings, houses, furniture, pictures, and where the originals were in private hands they gave no intimacy. I found the skyscrapers depressing, a huge black ferro-concrete architecture of necessity shutting out the light from the treeless streets

> Whose constant care is not to please
> But to remind of our, and Adam's curse
> And that, to be restored, our sickness must
>    grow worse.

*Saturday.* To the Lafayette after strolling round delicious Washington Square which in the morning sun considerably revives me from the gloomy thoughts of the night before, sleepless beside the sizzling radiator. Greenwich Village, which reminds me more and more of Soho, is still cheap, and apparently not quite spoilt, 'the one place in New York where different income groups are still mixed up, and where the queers and misfits from the Middle West can all find sanctuary'. 'There is an immense cleavage here', says Tony at lunch, 'between the intellectuals and everyone else, who are really quite uninterested in books, though they like to keep up with the best-sellers. Intellectuals thus have to join political movements or attach themselves to causes or become dons for they cannot otherwise survive. They become over-serious, "culture" requires one hundred per cent efficiency and is a whole-time business, everyone becomes extremely bellicose and erudite; publishers work so hard that even they have no time for pleasure, and without pleasures the intellectual becomes uncivilized, a pedantic variation of the business man.'

After lunch to the top of Rockefeller Center. Asked the bald elevator boy on the last lap why we were told to face outwards. He made no reply at first, then broke down into helpless laughter; the only words to come from him were, 'It's all so silly'—mountain sickness, perhaps. The view was the first beautiful thing I had seen in New York, where one can go for weeks without the knowledge of being surrounded by water. If one need never descend below the fortieth floor New York would seem the most beautiful city in the world, its skies and cloudscapes are tremendous, its southern latitude is revealed only in its light (for vegetation and architecture are strictly northern); here one can take in the Hudson, the East river, the mid-town and down-town colonies of skyscrapers, Central Park and the magnificent new bridges and curving arterial highways and here watch the evening miracle, the lights going on over all these frowning termitaries against a sky of royal-blue velvet only to be paralleled in Lisbon or Palermo. A southern city, with a southern pullulation of life, yet with a northern winter imposing a control; the whole nordic energy and sanity of living crisply enforcing its authority for three of the four seasons on the violet-airy babel of tongues and races; this tension gives New York its unique concentration and makes it the supreme metropolis of the present. Dinner with Auden's friend Chester. At last the luxury of poverty; stairs, no lift, leaking arm-chairs, a bed-sitting-room with bath-kitchenette curtained off, guests with European teeth (who was it said that Americans have no faces?), a gramophone library, untidy books not preserved in cardboard coffins, an incompetent gas stove—and an exquisite dinner cooked and served by C. Clam-juice mixed with chicken broth, chops with a sauce and lima beans, lederkranz cheese and pumpernickel, dry Californian wine. Argument afterwards about poetry interspersed with selections from Wystan's favourite operas. They are many. Much conversation about the U.S. and W. continues to propound his point of view (see his introduction to James's *The American Scene*). Though very pro-British (his bedside bible remains a work on the mineralogy of the Lake District compiled by a friend of his father's), he reverts always to the same argument, that a writer needs complete anonymity, he must break away from the European literary 'happy family' with its family love and jokes and jealousies and he must reconsider all the family values. Possibly he could do this in any large impersonal society, but only in America is it so easy for the anonymous immigrant to make money. He is, of course, extremely lonely, but then so is every American; 'you have no idea', he says, 'how lonely even the married are'. I make the inevitable point that surely it is important to live in attractive surroundings, and in New York (where all want to live) only the rich can afford them. Why live an exile in a black slum, looking out on a fire-escape, in a city which is intolerable in winter and summer, when for the same money one might flourish in Regent's Park or on the Île Saint Louis? But then,

I imagine Auden replying, you would at once have the family all about you, and he concentrates on planning my return journey to Washington Square. Walking back from the subway station at two in the morning I find a second-hand bookstore open all night in West Eighth Street, I go in and buy more Cummings. To purchase early works of Cummings in the small hours, in the heart of

> the little barbarous Greenwich perfumed fake

and march home with them in the frosty night, while the tugs hoot and central heating plants under the long black street puff away through its many manholes like geysers on the moon, that is to enjoy that anonymous urban civilization that Auden has chosen, and of which Baudelaire dreamed and despaired!

★    ★    ★

Long now past diary-keeping, I am a slave of my telephone and engagement book. Europe is a dream, and Auden's anonymity equally remote. We are plunged in New York literary life and try to analyse the swirl and eddy of that vigorous, intricate, cordial group of groupings. America is not Europe, in neither its places nor its people nor its values, and it is only by making the most desperate adjustment that a true European writer can remain himself here. Thus in the United States literature is fighting a losing battle against the Book Business which we can hardly comprehend. The crucial factor is the high cost of book-production which renders the printing of small editions (under 10,000) uneconomic; the tendency is therefore to go all out for the best seller and, with a constant eye on Hollywood, to spend immense sums on publicity so as to bring about one of these jack-pots. But even without Hollywood there are large sums to be made from book-of-the-month clubs, cheap pulp editions, serial rights, and so the result of this pressure is a transformation of the literary scene into mass-production. The American public are cajoled into reading the book of the month, and only the book of the month, and for that month only. Last year's book is as unfashionable as last year's car. The standard of living among publishers is also ridiculously high; huge offices among skyscrapers employ armies of bright and competitive young men. I know of one whose lawyers forbade him to start a business of his own as his capital was but a hundred thousand dollars. The hunt for young authors who, while maintaining a prestige value (with a role for Ingrid Bergman), may yet somehow win the coveted jack-pot, is feverish and incessant. Last year's authors (most of the names that have just reached England) are pushed aside and this year's—the novelist Jean Stafford, her poet husband Robert Lowell or the dark horse, Truman Capote—are invariably mentioned. They may be quite unread, but their names, like a new issue on the market, are constantly on the lips of those in the know.[1] 'Get Capote'—at this minute the words are resounding on many a sixtieth floor, and 'get him' of course means make him and break him, smother him with laurels and then vent upon him the obscure hatred which is inherent in the notion of another's superiority. 'In Ngoio, a province of the ancient kingdom of the Congo,' Frazer relates, 'the rule obtains that the chief who assumes the cap of sovereignty is always killed on the night after his coronation.' But in civilized Ngoio the throne is generally vacant. America is the one country (greatly to its credit) where an author can still make a fortune for life from one book, it is also the country where everyone is obsessed with that idea, where publishers live like stockbrokers, and where authors, like film-stars, are condemned to meditate from minute to minute last year's income tax, next week's publicity. It is all part of the American tragedy —that, in the one remaining country where necessities are

---

[1] For this reason we have tried to avoid literary prize-givings in this number and to present a cross-section of a living ant-heap, not a case of mounted butterflies fast-fading and wrongly named.

cheap, where a room and food and wine and clothes and cigarettes and travel are within everyone's reach, to be poor is still disgraceful. The American way of life is one of the most effective the world has known, but about the end of life Americans are more in the dark than any people since the Gauls of Tacitus. What *is* the American way? It may be summed up as a creed which is partly the effect of climate, partly of vitamins and calories, partly of pioneer experiences, partly of the inherited memory of what was bad in Europe. The American way assumes a world without God, yet a world in which happiness is obtainable, but obtainable only through a constant exertion of the will towards a practical goal and of the mind towards solution of present problems. Riches and success are the outward signs that this goal is being attained, that the human organism is making full use of its energy and faculties; a whispering of wives, expert at farewell (three is the lucky number), indicates that the proper stages on the journey are being reached, and handsome, healthy, indifferent children are present to carry on when the wage-earner passes over; any moments of disquieting leisure are rendered innocuous by extraverted social activities with colleagues of similar status and their families, or sent flying by alcohol. The esteem of society is enormously important and can only be held by a decent, kindly and acquisitive way of living. Courage, humour, hard work and the affectionate co-operation of uncles and cousins make endurable the darker side: sickness, insolvency, hangovers, death and Mother. Seldom has a more harmless or profitable philosophy of life been evolved, a more resolute opponent of art, remorse and introspection, or one further removed from the futile European speculation about the Soul or the Past, the moping about sin and death, the clinging to moribund methods, ideals, the pangs of ennui. If one were but permitted to take human beings at their own valuation, the American way would seem the most desirable solution to our predicament, offering us a full life built round the notions of freedom, independence, hard work and the family; the personality without a thought stoically working itself out through action. But the end? What is old age in America? After sixty, where do old people vanish? Why are the bustling battalions of unwanted Moms so elegantly pathetic? And the rich who have pocketed their winnings, why are they so glum? And what is this 'way,' in reality, but forty years' drudgery in an office while the divorced wives play bridge together and the children drift apart? What is the getting of money but a constant source of ulcers and anxiety, till apoplexy or heart-failure clamp down? And why does alcohol, which should oil the wheels of intercourse, so flood and clog them that there is a Drunk in each so respectable family? And why the immense rush to psychiatry, the high rate of madness and suicide? Why, after midnight, do so many Americans fight or weep? Grown-up while still a child, middle-aged at thirty, a boy only among his cronies of the golf course or the lunch club, coffined or cremated at about sixty-three, the American business male with his forceful, friendly, unlined face carries within him a dust-bowl of despair which renders him far more endearing and closer to Europe than his dutiful efforts to conceal it. Action, often violent and destructive, not contemplation, is his remedy, but his awareness of the tragic human predicament goes very deep.

This leads us on to one of the finest traits in American character. At a time when the American way, backed by American resources, has made the country into the greatest power the world has known, there has never been more doubting and questioning of the purpose of the American process; the higher up one goes the more searching becomes this self-criticism, the deeper the thirst for a valid mystique of humanity. Those who rule America, who formulate its foreign policy and form its opinion, are enormously conscious of their responsibility and of the total inadequacy of the crude material philosophy of life in which they grew up. The bloody-minded, the smug, the imperialist, the fascist, are in a minority. Seldom, in fact, has an unwilling world been forced to tolerate, through its own folly, a more unwilling master.

The New York scene reveals many traces of this unrest. Insecurity reigns. Almost everyone hates his job. Psychiatrists of all schools are as common as monks in the Thebaid. 'Who is your analyst?' will disarm any interviewer; books on how to be happy, how to attain peace of mind, how to win friends and influence people, how to breathe, how to achieve a cheap sentimental humanism at other people's expense, how to become a Chinaman like Lin Yutang and make a lot of money, how to be a Bahá'i or breed chickens (*The Ego and I*) all sell in millions. Religious houses of retreat merge imperceptibly into disintoxication clinics and private mental homes for the victims of traffic lights and nervous breakdowns. 'Alcoholics Anonymous' slink like house detectives around the literary cocktail parties. A most interesting phenomenon is the state of mind apparent in *Time*, *Life*, *The New Yorker*, and similar magazines. Thus *Life*, with its enormous circulation, comes out with excellently written leading articles on the dearth of tragedy in American literature or the meaning of suffering, and a closer acquaintance reveals them to be staffed by some of the most interesting and sensitive minds in that insensitive city.

It is easy to make fun of these three papers, but in fact they are not funny. Although they have very large circulations indeed, they only just miss being completely honourable and serious journals, in fact 'highbrow'. Hence the particular nemesis, ordeal by shiny paper, of those who manage them; they work very hard, and deliver *almost* the best work of which they are capable. But the gap is never quite closed between the public and the highbrow writer, because the American organism is not quite healthy. I mention this at some length because it indicates how very nearly New York has achieved the ideal of a humanist society, where the best of which an artist is capable is desired by the greatest number. Thurber's drawings, Hersey's *Hiroshima*, the essays of Edmund Wilson or Mary MacCarthy, *Time*'s anonymous reviews, show that occasionally the gap *is* closed; when it is closed permanently the dream of Santayana will be near fulfilment.

But these anxiety-forming predicaments (*Time*-stomach is a common trouble) are for those who live in New York and have to earn their living. To the visiting non-competitive European all is unending delight. The shops, the bars, the women, the faces in the street, the excellent and innumerable restaurants, the glitter of Twenty-one, the old-world lethargy of the Lafayette, the hazy view of the East River or Central Park over tea in some apartment at the magic hour when the concrete icebergs suddenly flare up; the impressionist pictures in one house, the exotic trees or bamboo furniture in another, the chink of 'old-fashioneds' with their little glass pestles, the divine glories—Egyptian, Etruscan, French—of the Metropolitan Museum, the felicitous contemporary assertion of the Museum of Modern Art, the snow, the sea-breezes, the late suppers with the Partisans, the reelings-home down the black steam-spitting canyons, the Christmas trees lit up beside the liquorice ribbon of cars on Park Avenue, the Gotham Book Mart, the shabby cosiness of the Village, all go to form an unforgettable picture of what a city ought to be: that is, continuously insolent and alive, a place where one can buy a book or meet a friend at any hour of the day or night, where every language is spoken and xenophobia almost unknown, where every purse and appetite is catered for, where every street with every quarter and the people who inhabit them are fulfilling their function, not slipping back into apathy, indifference, decay. If Paris is the setting for a romance, New York is the perfect city in which to get over one, to get over anything. Here the lost *douceur de vivre* is forgotten and the intoxication of living takes its place.

What is this intoxication? Firstly, health. The American diet is energy-producing. Health is not just the absence of disease but a positive physical sensation. The European, his voice dropping a tone every day, finds himself growing stouter, balder, more extroverted and aggressive, conscious of a place in what is still, despite lip-service, a noisily masculine society. Then there is the sensation of belonging to a great nation in its present prosperous period of triumph. But, in addition to 'feeling good', the Americans are actively generous and kind and it is this profusion of civilities which ravishes the visitor. American hosts are not only thoughtful; it is almost dangerous to express a wish before them—to such unobtrusive lengths will they go to fulfil it. American hostesses bring their ingrained perfectionism into daily living. It is a society more formal, more painstaking, more glamorous and more charitable than our poor old bitter, battered, pennywise European equivalent —we may pine inevitably for a whiff of honest English malice, outspokenness and bad manners but we should not be proud of such nostalgias for we have largely forgotten the degree to which leisure, money, goodwill and taste can still make life agreeable. One thing only seems to me impossible in New York—to write well. Not because the whirl and pleasurable bustle of the gregarious life built around writing is so irresistible, not because it is almost impossible to find a quiet room near a tree, or to stay in of an evening, not because intelligent conversation with a kindred spirit is hard to come by (it is not), but because this glowing, blooming and stimulating material perfection over-excites the mind, causing it to precipitate into wit and conversation those ideas which might have set into literature. Wit and wisecrack, not art, are the thorny flowers on this rocky island, this concrete Capri; they call the tune for which our proud new bass is lent us. 'Yah', one may say instead of 'yes', but when 'fabulous', 'for Chris' sakes', 'it stinks', 'way off the beam' and 'Bourbon over ice' roar off our lips, and when we begin to notice with distaste the Europeanism of others—it's time for flight, for dripping plane-trees, misty mornings, the grizzling circle of hypercritical friends, the fecund London inertia where nothing stirs but the soul.

What are the alternatives? We may stay on and coarsen— many English writers do—into shapely executives or Park Avenue brandy philosophers; we can fight like Auden for privacy and isolation, or grow bitter and fitzrovian in the 'Village atmosphere'—or we can try elsewhere. Cape Cod or Connecticut have their devotees, but these havens are the rewards of success, not its incubators. Boston, last stronghold of a leisured class, offers a select enlightenment of which a contemporary Englishman is just downright unworthy. Washington has immense charm, the streets of Georgetown with their ilexes and magnolias and little white box-houses are like corners of Chelsea or Exeter, but a political nexus offers few resources to the artist who is outside the administration, and the lovely surroundings (the shores of the Chesapeake Bay and its tributaries form the most insidiously appealing of all American landscapes to the home-sick European), are not places in which he can hope to earn a living.

Let us try California. The night plane circles round La Guardia, leaves behind the icy water of the Sound and that sinister Stonehenge of economic man, the Rockefeller Center, to disappear over the Middle West. Vast rectangles of light occasionally indicate Chicago or some other well-planned city, till at six in the morning we ground in the snow of Omaha. As it grows light the snow-fields over the whole agricultural region of the Middle West grow more intricate, the Great Plains give way to the Bad Lands, poison ivy to poison oak, the sinuosities of the Platte rivers to the High Plains, the mountains of Wyoming, the Continental Divide. All semblance of European structure vanishes; Salt Lake appears as a radiant lunar landscape in the wan sunshine, with the Great Salt Lake desert glistening beyond it, fading into other deserts, and, at last, into the formidable Carson Sink. It is hard to picture the immense desolation of the West in winter, the wilderness of snow lying over fifteen hundred miles of plateau and mountain, till suddenly, unfrozen, among the pine woods of the Rockies a blue alpine lake appears, Lake Tahoe, and beyond a great glowing explosion of orange sky, woods without snow, green hills with no trace of winter, the darker patches of citrus orchard, the line of irrigation canals, the Sacramento Valley— California and the enormous pale Pacific.

San Francisco is a city of charming people and hideous buildings, mostly erected after the earthquake in the style of 1910, with a large Chinatown in which everything is fake—except the Chinese—with a tricky humid climate (though sunny in winter), and a maddening indecision in the vegetation—which can never decide if it belongs to the North or the South and achieves a Bournemouth compromise. The site is fantastically beautiful, the orange bridge, the seven hills, the white houses, the waterside suburbs across the Golden Gate give it a lovely strangeness, the sunset view from the 'Top of the Mark' is unique—but the buildings lack all dignity and flavour. Yet San Francisco and its surroundings, Marin County, Berkeley, Sauselito with its three climates, San Mateo where lemon and birch tree grow together, probably represent the most attractive all-the-year-round alternative to Europe which the world can provide. If I were an escapist, that is, rather more determined to escape, I would fly from the delirium or coma of the countries I love and settle in Central California. There Europe is twice as far as from New York which itself is so remote that it becomes a kind of Europe, a delicious object of the annual holiday, yet the temperate European climate and way of life still prevail. A hundred miles to the south is some of the

loveliest country I have ever seen, the Monterey peninsula and
the evergreen hills of Big Sur. At Monterey the Pacific for once
imitates the Mediterranean, the vast cold treacherous sail-less
ocean flows in sunny, sandy coves round the pine and cypress
woods of the peninsula, the enormous sea-lions bark all night
off the shore. South of Carmel the wild Santa Lucia mountains
with their forests of holm-oak and holly roll southwards
for two hundred miles of green Dorset downs, five thousand
feet high. Here the Pacific roars at the foot of inky cliffs,
pouring in immense black strands of weed, whose roots bob
like human heads, while out to sea the whales, drifting south in
pairs, spout lazily by. On one of these cliffs surrounded by
editions of Rimbaud lives Henry Miller with his wife and
child. His house is a romantic shack, built by the convicts while
making the road, for which he pays six dollars rent a month.
A mile or so farther is a hot open-air sulphur bath. Once a
week the groceries come out from Carmel. There is some fog
in winter, but generally it is sunny. The sea is there, the mountains and a bathing pool in the redwood forest. Here is one
writer who has solved the problem of how to live happily in
America without hacking, by writing unstintingly of himself and
the Cosmos, decently impervious to this remote grandiose
wilderness of mountain and sea.

   Hollywood and Los Angeles are well described by Isherwood.
On the whole those who have loved the Mediterranean will not
be reconciled here and those who care deeply for books can
never settle down to the impermanent world of the cinema.
Those who do not love the cinema have no business to come.
There are exceptional cases of intellectual adaptation of which
Aldous Huxley's is the most remarkable. The Californian
climate and food creates giants but not genius, but Huxley
has filled out into a kind of Apollonian majesty; he radiates
both intelligence and serene goodness, and is the best possible
testimony to the simple life he leads and the faith he believes

in, the sole English writer entirely to have benefited by transplantation and whom one felt exquisitely refreshed by meeting. Huxley and Isherwood incidentally join hands with Auden in that all three believe (somewhat masochistically) that the peculiar horrors of America—its brashness, music at meals, and racial hysteria—by being emphasized there to a degree not found in other countries, force the onlooker into a rejection of the world which might otherwise come too late. As Auden puts it, 'the anonymous countryside littered with heterogeneous *dreck* and the synonymous cities besotted with electric signs . . . without which, perhaps, the analyst and the immigrant alike would never understand by contrast the nature of the Good Place nor desire it with sufficient desperation to stand a chance of arriving'.

Miller, in his *Air-Conditioned Nightmare*, writes with more desperation: 'In the ten thousand miles I have travelled I have come across two cities which have each of them a little section worth a second look—I mean Charleston and New Orleans. As for the other cities, towns and villages through which I passed I hope never to see them again. Everything that was of beauty, significance or promise has been destroyed or buried in the avalanche of false progress. We have degenerated; we have degraded the life which we sought to establish on this continent . . . Nowhere have I encountered such a dull, monotonous fabric of life as here in America. Here boredom reaches its peak.'

Well, maybe it does, perhaps Americans have destroyed their romantic wilderness on a grander scale than our own rodent attrition at the beauties of our countryside—but I feel a change is coming. As Europe grows more helpless the Americans are compelled to become far-seeing and responsible, even as Rome was induced by the long decline of Greece to produce an Augustus and a Vergil. *Our impotence liberates their potentialities*. Something important is about to happen, as if the wonderful *jeunesse* of America were suddenly to retain their idealism and vitality and courage and imagination into adult life, and become the wise and good who make use of them; the old dollar values are silently crumbling, and the self-criticism, experimental curiosity, sensibility and warmth which are so well represented, I feel, in this number, are on their way in. For Americans change very fast. 'Do they?' 'Very fast and all at once,' he said, 'and nothing ever changes them back.'

*October* 1947

# IN JUGULAR VEIN

GENTLEMEN,

The offensive against Art is developing according to plan. It is too early yet to prophesy total victory, too early even to talk of a break-through or to indulge in wishful thinking about a complete mopping-up of art and artists. We must not underestimate the foe. But it is worth while recapitulating what has been done. A year ago this magazine, under the title of 'The Cost of Letters', published a bundle of documents which revealed that the morale of our enemy was sinking fast. Economic warfare was making itself felt all along the line. Last winter a brilliant exploit deprived the enemy of all paper supplies for more than a month, and another daring fuel raid put their dangerous radio station, Third Programme, out of action for a considerable period. What was particularly encouraging about this brief campaign was the feebleness of the enemy's response. Meanwhile our blockade was not ineffective. We may now proudly claim that, while the steady shipment to America of the entire antique collections of Britain proceeds unhindered, it is almost impossible for a contemporary work of art to pass from one country to another. If it is extremely difficult for a painter to move around the world or export his wares, it is quite impossible for anyone else to go abroad to look at painting. There is only one cause for alarm. We have effectively sealed off the whole civilian population from access to the Continent and its dangers; we have even reimposed a rudimentary censorship. But have we been sufficiently thorough in preventing foreigners from coming here? The autumn has seen the blockade of pictures, tourists, etc., one hunded per cent successful—with films and sheet music added to the list. But the most daring coup was the banning of the import of foreign books; a feat which held that quality of surprise, rapidity and ruthlessness which indicates the born commander. Though the contents can never rival our own, foreign books are—were, I should say—sometimes speciously well printed; the margins immorally wide and the paper indecently thick; the sentiments expressed often well informed and subversive. I don't think we will any of us regret them.

And now I have to pass on to a very unpleasant subject. There exists, as you know, a fifth column in this country. There are artists, writers, poets, crypto-artists and crypto-writers, survivors from the bad old days, over whom the authorities have insufficient powers. There are even one or two publishers or reviewers who compose in their spare time. I blame no one for this; I blame the system. But something must be done. The paper control has just cut the ration of periodicals by ten per cent. That is a step in the right direction, a most salutary step. It will be followed, I hope, by further cuts and by the rationing of fuel to printers and binders in such a way that these very inessential industries are compelled to liberate their manpower for the national effort. It will become increasingly difficult, I am afraid, for gentlemen of the literary and artistic persuasion, when forced out of their Bloomsbury bed-sitting-rooms by cold and hunger, to avoid taking a few tottering steps in the direction of the welcoming sign 'Labour Exchange' where 'guidance' will be freely given to them—

with perhaps a shave and a haircut thrown in. But these are slippery creatures—and this is where the public can help. You all hate a spiv (Yes, SIR!)—You all hate an Eel (I'll say we do!) —You know what to do with a Drone, a second-helping wallah, a lipstick lovely, an aesthete (Leave 'em to us); You know the right noise to make when you see a Butterfly (Brrrrerp!) You've been put on your guard against the Gander in his club window—you've been warned against the Royal Turbot, with her French perfume and gigantic hat. I want to warn you against the Artist: I want you to learn to hate him like a whale. We've made short work of the whales lately (cheers); it's no secret that there soon won't be a whale left. (Loud cheers.) Radar, depth charges, blubber bombs—their number's up. Why is it that we all love a journalist, a civil servant, a Public Relations Officer, or a Member of Parliament when we see one? Yet we all hate instinctively an artist! I'm going to call them 'bats' to you, because they squeak, because they have no morals and hang upside down and stink and spend the day in a terrible fug and look revoltingly like human beings. (Laughter.) I'm going to appeal to you to rid our island workshop of our flitter-mice friends—every one of them from the greedy Flying Fox to the dirty little Pipistrelle. *You* don't have to interfere with them. Leave that to *us*. (Laughter.) The public has a perfect weapon ready. Apathy. (A voice—Spell it!) Just don't think about them. That's all. You've got plenty to think about. Rations, the new cuts, the potato shortage, bigamy, the last six murders, the latest currency fine, the long-skirt controversy, the Royal Wedding, the airplane disasters, the Marshall Plan (all aid short of peace), the new combined electric cheater and staggered geyser, holidays with P.A.Y.E. And I'm glad to see that you're reading less. I'm told that books are getting nearly as hard to sell now as before the war. I hope we shall soon live to see the book and periodical entirely superseded by the bulletin and communiqué. (Cheers. For He's a Jolly Good Fellow!)

A word about morale. Morale is good. There is nothing wrong with the people. Their fettle is fine. We are all too busy to read or think; our minds are entirely occupied with material problems; there's nothing so healthy as having to devote all one's energies to the next meal. But sometimes we get a bit blue and then we like to wrap ourselves in the Union Jack and pass moral judgements. Here are a few slogans which I find of great comfort, and which I hope some of you will.

'Thou shalt hate thy neighbour as thyself!' This, I think, is all we really need to know about the bogus modern science of psychology. 'Hatred begins in the home.' Fair enough! That is why we invented the State. 'He preyeth best who hatest best all things both great and small.' 'Hate and it shall be given unto you.' This I take to mean that if we can hate a class and then all other classes, a nation and then all other nationalities, the old and the young, the rich and the poor, the male and the female, then we can end by hating not only the living but life itself. And not until we hate life are we ready to take a creative part in shaping the twentieth century. And remember, Art is the flower of life; it is what is most living. We must cut down the blossom till we have learnt how to uproot the plant.

At present we are passing through a phase of voluntary compulsion. That will fail and be succeeded by a phase of 'guidance' which will restore the controls and penalties of our 'finest hour'. I see one ray of hope: remember, whatever miseries we endure, they are endured to the full by other nations, and among those nations there are rulers so forward-looking as to regret the good old days of war (sound, if not safe) as much as we do. I don't think we shall have to wait long, gentlemen, before I return to my old and treasured post as *Horizon*'s military spokesman.

> Decay along with me
> The worst is yet to be.   (Ovation.)

*November* 1947

## EYES RIGHT

THE award of the Nobel prize to André Gide just after his seventy-eight birthday is one of the few strokes of felicity in this miserable year. Gide represents that spirit of creative doubt which, with its antithesis, the spirit of reflective action is a twin hall-mark of Western civilization. On the whole the creative doubters (Gide, Valéry, Joyce, Proust) represent an older generation than the reflective doers (Malraux, Montherlant, Camus, T. E. Lawrence) and certainly a wiser one. It is pleasant that a knowledge of Gide (still referred to by the *Daily Mail* as 'the esoteric writer') should at last be spreading in England, which he visited this summer.

Otherwise it has been a year of disappointment. One long poem by Dr. Sitwell, one original experiment in the form of the novel by Philip Toynbee and the catalogue of that branch of our literature which can be described as 'experimental' is complete. In France Surrealism and even Dada continue to exert an influence, the poems of the 'Lettristes' are similar to those of Jolas and Rutra in early numbers of *transition*; Jabberwocky is in fashion. Here one can say that such a thing as *avant-garde* in literature has ceased to exist. And a literature without an *avant-garde* soon becomes a literature without a main body. It is but one more sign of what a distinguished critic has called 'The Twilight of the Arts'.

There is an intimate connection between the Twilight of the Arts and the twilight of a civilization. There was a certain twilight of the arts at the end of the eighteenth century, but it was to be dispelled by the marvellous moonshine of romanticism; it remains to be seen whether we are on the verge of a new Dark Age, lasting for several hundred years or if our greatest writers are just around the corner. If the break-up of Europe corresponds to the break-up of the Roman Empire, with Communism replacing primitive Christianity, then the arts are in peril, for Communism exploits art but cannot produce it and scientific optimism excludes the sense of tragedy and mystery which forms an ingredient. The prerequisites of an artistic revival are freedom to travel and enough to eat; it is just possible the Marshall Plan may secure these for Western Europe. There remains an even more essential condition—that Western Europe believes in itself. At present Russia and the United States are the only two countries with such a faith, which are convinced that they are about to fulfil an historical mission, even though it be only to destroy each other. Western Europe has lost that belief until the moment arrives when it can be reintegrated with Eastern Europe and federated into the most civilized of the four or five units which comprise a world state.

Meanwhile, the effect of increasing the barriers between European countries is to bring the arts to a state of national and provincial bankruptcy. The spiritual problem of the artist in a world without hope is deeper than the economic, for most artists are secretly aware that if they could believe passionately in their mission their economic difficulties would either be solved or would cease to matter. At present most of us labour under a double disappointment, a disappointment with the state of the world which, two years after the last war, seems fast sinking into the apprehension which immediately preceded it, and a disappointment with our experience of Socialism, which some of us associated with the idea of joy. But a Government which conscripts labour, cuts paper, prohibits book imports, and does not even dare to propose the abolition of the death penalty (though the proposal was first incorporated in a Conservative Home Secretary's Bill) bears no relation to the kind of Socialism which many of us envisaged. Except in matters of colonial and foreign policy, and in certain elementary measures of social justice, the world situation (often another name for the intransigence of the Kremlin) has not permitted Socialism in this country to express its ideals, and the public may soon be taking the wretched material of its austerity suit to a tailor who promises a more dashing line.

# 'Horizon's' Christmas Message

**Rev. Dr. Opimian:** Science is one thing and wisdom is another. Science is an edged tool with which men play like children and cut their own fingers. If you look at the results which science has brought in its train, you will find them to consist almost wholly in elements of mischief. See how much belongs to the word Explosion alone, of which the ancients knew nothing. Explosions of powder-mills and powder-magazines; of coal-gas in mines and in houses; of high-pressure engines in ships and boats and factories. See the complications and refinements of modes of destruction in revolvers and rifles and shells and rockets and cannon. See collisions and wrecks and every mode of disaster by land and by sea, resulting chiefly from the insanity for speed, in those who for the most part have nothing to do at the end of the race, which they run as if they were so many Mercuries speeding with messages from Jupiter. Look at our scientific drainage, which turns refuse into poison. Look at the subsoil of London, whenever it is turned up to the air, converted by gas leakage into one mass of pestilent blackness, in which no vegetation can flourish, and above which, with the rapid growth of the ever-growing nuisance, no living thing will breathe with impunity. Look at our scientific machinery, which has destroyed domestic manufacture, which has substituted rottenness for strength in the thing made, and physical degradation in crowded towns for healthy and comfortable country life in the makers. The day would fail if I should attempt to enumerate the evils which science has inflicted on mankind. *I almost think it is the ultimate destiny of science to exterminate the human race.*

𝕷𝖔𝖗𝖉 𝕮𝖚𝖗𝖗𝖕𝖋𝖎𝖓: You have gone over a wide field, which we might exhaust a good bin of claret in fully discussing.

T. L. Peacock, *Gryll Grange*, 1866

*December* 1947

# THE CRUTCH FOUNDATION

FIGMENT of a powerful daydream, the name of Filmore Van Rensselaer Crutch is but little known in this country. Mr. Crutch is a very rich man, else he had but a small chance of being catapulted into existence. Public Utilities, one might say, were his middle name, in the distant days in which he was raking in the fortune which he has now chosen so worthily and brilliantly to disperse. Like many American millionaires who feel a certain guilty curiosity about the arts, Filmore looked around for a field where the weight of his patronage could still be put to advantage. 'Atlantic Awards'; 'Occident Prizes'; 'Thousand Pound First Novels'; 'Rockefeller Grants;' 'Publishers' Travelling Scholarships'—it would seem that never has the young author been better provided for; the mere intimation of a desire to write causes the cornucopia to pour into his lap. Filmore read through the terms of reference and studied the capital allotted to the various benevolent pressure groups with a sinking feeling. Too late, too late! Suddenly an idea gripped him. 'What about the guys who judge all this muck! Who pays *them*?' It was in this way that the foundation was laid for the now famous Society for the Redemption of Middle-aged Hacks. 'The proposition is this,' explains Filmore. 'A guy gives his dough to a promising young writer. What guarantee has he got that the writer will ever turn out anything or use the money except to spend it on drink and women? But with a middle-aged hack the probability is that he wrote at least one good book in the past, is used to working, and could do another. I'd rather pick an old car of a good make off the dump than buy a new Cheapie. Let's see what happens. I hear of a new hack. My boys look him over. We aim to give him back his self-respect. As a rule, he's got three or four jobs, all badly paid; he dabbles with the cinema, drones on the B.B.C., has a leathery face, wandering alcoholic eye, dirty suit, bald patch, scurfy collar, worries all night, anxious to please but forgotten how, once was thought a bit of a genius, now he's right out on a limb, a middle-aged hack if ever there was one. This is how we recondition—er—"redeem" him. First we study his type—find out what his four jobs were, analyse the books he hasn't written. Then we give him a psychological treatment. Explain to him that literature is an impossible career, that he must be damn good to have written anything. The treatment now starts. We reckon it costs twenty thousand dollars. The hack is taken off all his jobs. This is often very painful. "But who'll review the gardening books for the *Financial Times*," he screams. "Not you—you won't even have to read the damn thing," the Institute replies. Next we close up the hack's home. The kids go to school: the wife to her relations. The first year we spend in getting him back into the physical, mental and moral shape he was in when he did his best work. He goes on a cruise to the Bahamas, or we lend him a villa in Sicily; he visits tailors and hosiers again, we repay the publisher's advances. Hacks hate this. Mostly he just sleeps. "Where's my wife," they sometimes say. "Stuck in the fish-queue somewhere. Don't you worry about her." "Sometimes I wake up in the night and fancy I hear her cough." "Don't think about it. Here's a receipt for your income tax for the last three years. Here's your ticket to Paris. Here's your wallet. Here's your travellers'-checks for the next six months; visas, hotel reservations." "Oh, Mr. Crutch—" "That's all right, nothing's too good for the author of *Flittershins* or *Ramshackle Roger*."

'After a year of untroubled sleep and care-free leisure the hack is unrecognizable. But he's not middle-aged for nothing. That's the beauty of it. He *wants* to work: he thinks of nothing now but the book he might have written. Doesn't just chain-smoke in night-clubs like a "Promising". He settles down into the lucid glow of second adolescence in his suite at the *France et Choiseul*. The next year he usually writes it. All the healthy self-indulgence of the first year is canalized into hard routine and creative energy. All the drudgery of the past spurs him on. The third year he revises. Breakfast, work, a swim before lunch, a siesta, tea, a drive. Then another hour of revision before dinner and dancing, conversation or bridge. The Sicilian spring, the Alpine summer, the Venetian autumn pass in a flash! The book is finished, the publisher's crazy about it. He's famous again!' 'And, pardon me, Mr. Crutch, what do you get out of it?' 'Just the satisfaction of a job well done—of seeing these poor human wrecks saved from their platitudes; the feeling that I have helped an artist to realize all his potentialities, set a poor warped plant that once bore fruit in the soil where it can straighten up, expand and once more give a bumper harvest.' 'Don't make me cry *too*, Mr. Crutch. Haven't you any other reason?' Filmore put one hand over his mouth and sucked a tooth. 'Three of my hacks won literary prizes this year,' he said. '"The Lemuria Award", "The Forgotten Man Prize", "The Troubleday Trophy". Each time they beat the "Promising" candidate, and one of them was fifty-four. "Troubledays" and "Lemuria" are both financed by old acquaintances of mine who stem, like me, from Public Utilities.' He panted—then bellowed—'I'll break them now as I crushed them then'.

'Just one more question. What happens afterwards to these reconditioned hacks? Do you get any relapses?' I didn't like the look on his face, which was one of unimaginable disgust, as if he too smelled the mingled odour of wet pram and boiled cabbage and overheard the dear voice, from the back kitchen, reminding me of fingers worn to the bone, of the best years of her life freely given to one ungrateful, though waited on hand and foot—and so with a quiet oath, I redirected Filmore Van Rensselaer Crutch to the desolate corner of the mind from whence he sprang.

*January* 1948

# CENTENARY

THE appearance—amid the fears of war and the falling almond blossom—of the hundredth number of *Horizon* requires brief notice. The correct procedure is to offer a costly banquet at which a Minister of State with cultural leanings (if one can be found) delivers his congratulations; mentioning the great part which *Horizon* has played in improving international relations by making known the splendid achievements of British art and literature to a troubled world and earning dollars. High officials of the British Council, the Central Office of Information, the Arts Council, the Third Programme and such arbiters as Messrs. Joad, Wilson Harris, Walter Elliot, Douglas Woodruff, Ivor Brown, D. N. Pritt and Gracie Fields explain why they have not always seen eye to eye with us. Telegrams regretting their unavoidable absence are read from Bernard Shaw, E. M. Forster, Marshal Smuts, Gide, Jung and Zhdanov. The Editor, replying, makes a feeble joke about the recent paper cut, recalls the magazine's modest beginnings, hints at future expansion, delivers thanks to all present: the gorged columnists then retire to decide whether the event is worth a paragraph.

It would be more economical and more rewarding to tell the truth, to say that *Horizon* has reached or rather tottered to its centenary on two legs, the generosity of its proprietor and the obstinacy of its editor. Many another owner would have long ago abandoned the thankless task of financing a serious magazine, many another editor would have preferred resignation to the prolonged and widespread unpopularity which accompanies his position. But there is *certain plaisir aristocratique à déplaire* and in addition there are a few loyal friends of the magazine on whose support we have always been able to count.

Among our enemies I would list those hidden bureaucrats whose frustrating activities give us persecution mania, then a few malignant rivals and rejectees and, more serious, the devoted illwishers who spend their time announcing that we have ceased or are just about to cease publication.

During the eight years I have edited *Horizon* we have witnessed a continuous decline in all the arts. Literature has been robbed of Joyce, Yeats, Virginia Woolf, Wells, Valéry, Freud, Frazer, to name but a few, and their places are not being filled. This is not because there is a decline in talent, but on account of the gradual dissolution of the environment in which it ripens. There is a decay in communication owing to the collapse of that highly cultivated well-to-do world bourgeoisie who provided the *avant-garde* artists—writer, painter, musician, architect—with the perfect audience (compare the paintings bequeathed by Frank Stoop to the Tate Gallery with those within its present purchasing power). Yeats, Joyce, Rilke were largely supported by a few devoted ladies of this milieu. There is also disintegration in the material to communicate; the 'truth—beauty—goodness' soap-bubble which we could all blow and admire and waft to each other has vanished leaving no comparable illusion to replace it. All this, however, might well prove an inspiration to an artist and not a handicap were not the political uncertainties of the world so disquieting. Birds are silent in an eclipse and now that Hitler ruins us from his Bunker while Molotov, with every speech, makes Fascists of us all, there is no urge to make music. There is one solution to which artists may not have given enough consideration. Mr. Somerset Maugham says that a chief pleasure of money is the being able to tell any man to go to hell. But a little thought reveals that it is possible to do this without a penny. Every writer I know under sixty (except one or two prosperous novelists) is ruining his talent through hackwork and part-time jobs: there is always a fistula through which the juices of genius are leaking away into some disgusting receptacle. Perhaps—since the State won't help us and the patron can't—we should all learn to be much poorer, and should recognize poverty as the one decoration which the lover of art and liberty is awarded.

*Horizon* has become aware of the decline of literature through the increasing difficulty of obtaining contributions. If the reader will glance at the present issue he will see that there is a poem by Miss Sitwell. In point of fact, six eminent poets were asked for a contribution for our hundredth number; the other five had nothing ready. Sorry, no eggs. Of the six, Miss Sitwell, alas! is alone able to devote her time to poetry: all the others are hard-working officials, publishers, teachers, etc., in fact culture diffusionists, selling culture for a living like the Aga Khan his bath-water. We are sometimes attacked by professional Cornishmen or Fleet Street Welsh for not being adequately regional. Had we considered the whole British Isles as our region we would long ago have become extinct: that we have been able to fill so many numbers is due to the wealth which our international humanist bias has allowed us to glean from America, France and Italy. It is no accident, in fact, as Marxists say, that *Horizon* stands repeatedly exposed as a decadent organ of bourgeois formalist liberal humanism. Bourgeois, because we believe that the perfect medium for art and artists is an enlightened bourgeoisie with its guarantees of peace, privacy and a regular income and because an intense hatred of the bourgeoisie is one of its most rewarding features. Formalists, because we believe that the cup generally outlives the wine which it was made to hold. Humanists, because our mortality is the one fact of which we can be certain—'our only portion is the estate of man'—and that estate, as we are continually finding out, is much richer than earlier humanists guessed, containing as it does such unexplored tracts of beast and angel, ape and automat. Every human being enjoys an exquisite privilege, that of being alive, and suffers, in the knowledge that he must die, an unbearable torture. To all those so privileged we owe respect and honour, to all those under that common death sentence pity and love. Only the ineradicable human vices—cruelty, stupidity, vanity, thoughtlessness—can make nonsense of this theorem and prevent us from understanding that human life is sacred and that consciousness is one—for the sum of human consciousness is what is loaned to the living for the appreciation of the world and should be handed on in better shape to those who follow.

But we live in a world which has forfeited both the hope which was the promise of Christianity and the happiness which the philosophers offered. Our vices at last have found weapons which permit us to do evil on the scale which hitherto we had only imagined, and so while there are Russian militarists and American strategists and English physicists and Jewish terrorists and Arab Nationalists and Balkan Separatists and Social Realists and Marxist Theorists, and while the fate of the world rests between Congress and the Politburo, we would be rash to prophesy for *Horizon* a further existence of more than two years. This will enable us to have covered the whole of the forties and to have enslumbered the arts, like a skilled anaesthetist, into final oblivion.

*April* 1948

## HUMANISTS AT BAY

HORIZON was recently the subject of a full-dress attack in a multilingual Moscow magazine called *Soviet Literature*. An unfortunate critic, A. Elistratova, had to read through a lot of back numbers (mostly 1944–5) and tack them on to *The Loved One* for a general blast against our decadent English culture. The Editor, Mr. Evelyn Waugh and Mr. Herbert Read ('the reactionary decadent clique of *Horizon*') come in for most of the abuse; the Editor is accused of going so far as to simulate anti-Fascism in order to entrap unwary young writers in his reactionary policies. One of the most endearing features of Communism is the charming belief that editors are important: they scheme, they struggle for power, they instigate sweeping reforms and diabolical intrigues. Remove such strong and wicked juggernauts as edit *Horizon*, the *Cornhill*, *New Writing*, *Time and Tide* or the *Times Literary Supplement* and the misguided masses can breathe again. It's all so simple. Evelyn Waugh's sympathies were with the Italians in the war in Abyssinia. Ten years later *Horizon* publishes *The Loved One*. Therefore *Horizon* is Fascist. 'The British citadel of militant decadence in the arts.' One of the objects of the Soviet attack is a list we gave of signs that should mark a civilized community (abolition of death penalty, laws against homosexuality, etc.). This list was also the subject of a violent onslaught from Mr. Evelyn Waugh in *The Tablet*. Moscow here joins hands with Rome and causes us once more to reiterate that unless a writer be attacked by both Catholics *and* Communists he is not of his time.

Let us try to put our own position more clearly. *Horizon* describes itself as a review of literature and art. That is to say we believe in the aesthetic approach; that art and literature exist in their own right—not as symptoms of political attitudes nor *ad majorem Dei gloriam*. We have no proof that this is so;

we have no proof that any absolute values—Truth, Justice,
Virtue, Liberty—really do exist, and are not simply arrangements for our own convenience, yet we happen to belong to
that section of Western civilization who have been conditioned
to behave as if they existed. We acquired our values from
Greece, Rome and the Bible, from the Renaissance; we are in
fact humanists. The dilemma of the humanist is precisely that
his Reason—by which he lives—disqualifies him from believing
in these abstract values which paradoxically he is often prepared to die for:

> Our sphere of action is life's happiness
> and he who thinks beyond, thinks like an ass.

Humanistically speaking, Rochester's sentiment is impeccable
yet most humanists would find it impossible to live by: it is
'thinking beyond', however uncertainly or inaccurately, that
distinguishes us from the beasts. The scepticism inherent in
the humanistic attitude implies one virtue—tolerance, which
becomes to the agnostic what faith is to the believer. Intolerance
is the one underlying bond between the Church and Communism since both these bodies presume to know for certain
what is best for their adherents, and for neither of them does
Death exist. To the Church this life is the preparation for
another, to the Communist it is part of the undying life of the
State: it is only the agnostic humanist who can consider his
death as being as much his own property as his life and who
can regard the two major religions of today as perversions of
the magnificent original humanity of the Sermon on the Mount.
Anyone who is interested in the case that can be made for
humanism caught between these two authoritarian systems
should read Lionel Trilling's fascinating novel, *The Middle of
the Journey* (Secker & Warburg). Humanism is a discredited
word because it is associated with superficial academic gentlemen in easy circumstances: it is in fact as useful a name as

any for that intense preoccupation with the estate of man, with the human predicament, which leads to a refusal to accept any solution by which evil is done that good may follow. In the eyes of a humanist all living beings are wonderful and privileged creatures under sentence of death: however much he may suffer from the intolerance of those who claim to know better he must not allow himself to forget that the differences which separate him from a Catholic or a Communist are in fact exceedingly small and unimportant when seen against the things which unite him to them. This was constantly proved in the Resistance movements and what is human life but a resistance movement on too large a scale? One advantage of being a humanist editor is that one can print articles by both Catholics and Communists without necessarily agreeing with a word they say, but out of a general reverence for the human intelligence (a courtesy they can seldom return). The other great advantage is that humanism, whether right or wrong, is distinctly favourable to the arts whether we believe them to be mere social diversions or profound intuitive glimpses into The Unknowable or Unknown. In the last analysis one can only say of a work of art 'I happen to think it good'. Well, from now on several million Communists are going always to think *Horizon* bad, because they've been told to by *Soviet Literature*. That's all there is to say. And yet not quite— for one might add that the division of the world into two spheres both living under the fear of war, is doing incomparable harm to art, that the humanist editor never knows whether to be more appalled by the miserable persecution of esoteric writers which proceed behind the Iron Curtain or the incredible vulgarity which the success cult in the U.S.A. thrusts upon them. And peevish, overcrowded, bureaucratic England, land of cut films, banned books and little class-conscious moustaches, are we not also to blame? Always when I return I am overwhelmed by the ugliness of the architecture, the

gloom of the people, the drabness of the sky, the obedience to
authority—and yet I know there is more honesty, affection,
good sense, justice and tolerance to be found here than in most
countries of the world. But art? Fossilizing talent confronting
spiteful mediocrity, provincial stylists back on the farm, rustic
philosophers leaving the farm for the B.B.C. . . . A progressive
Socialist movement without a single first-rate writer or painter
who supports it (correct me please) or for whom (correct me
again) it has ever done anything. The artist here is like the
wolf in La Fontaine's Fable *dont la condition est de mourir
de faim*, who admires the culture-diffusing dog's sleek coat
but doesn't like his collar.

> 'Qu'est cela?' lui dit-il. 'Rien.' 'Quoi. Rien?' 'Peu de
> chose.'
> 'Mais encor?' 'Le collier dont je suis attaché
> De ce que vous voyez est peut-être la cause.'
> 'Attaché,' dit le Loup; 'vous ne courez donc pas
> Où vous voulez?' 'Pas toujours, mais qu'importe?'
> 'Il importe si bien, que de tous vos repas
>     Je ne veux en aucune sorte;
> Et ne voudrais pas même à ce prix un trésor.'
> Celà dit, maître Loup s'enfuit et court encor.

*November* 1948


# ON, STANLEY, ON!

THE Lynskey Tribunal is not a subject which bears any direct
relation to a review of literature and art, but there are one or
two things which should be said about it which only we militant reactionary aesthetes are capable of saying. The Tribunal
is a record of a love affair, and, like most love affairs, it is based

on illusion. It records the love which rakish Big Business bears for homely respectable Miss Bureaucracy and the delicate feminine backslidings of that lady (such a nice girl) when wooed by wicked rich financiers with their expense accounts and private dining-rooms. Nobody quite lost their virtue, but the findings will probably disclose that it was a very near thing. To a detached observer what stands out most is the complete and utter dullness of the two conflicting ways of life, both so highly honoured in our society. Which would you rather be? A business man bowling to and fro between London and Manchester, always looking for a fourth at cards, eating, for the sake of trade, innumerable bad luncheons with people you've never met, dining at dog-racing tracks with minor politicians, taking them to English seaside hotels for windy negotiations, waiting in ministries for permits to make profits which are at once removed by taxation, swapping Christmas presents, jollying up the wives of public figures—or a servant of the State, poor but enormously respectable, buoyed up by that sense of collective self-righteousness which obliterates every defect, inflated by touched caps and dispatch-cases, and so smothered by the ennui of routine, the gnawings of fear and envy that any old Park Lane jackdaw appearing on the window-sill bedazzles like a peacock?

For two months now the public have absorbed every detail of this confused attempt at seduction—in itself an unsavoury sign, for it shows the growing-up, in our happy little Socialist brotherhood, of exactly the same spirit which informed the Russian purges. Sir Hartley Shawcross in no way resembles Vyshinsky, but his role of public prosecutor carries with it the prestige of a prima donna and one can see arising through the increasing public interest in this affair a relationship between the people and their prosecutor which does not preclude an eventual complicity, as between mob and matador, were these tribunals to replace watching test matches, darts and football as the national sport. For the spectator, even the newspaper-reader, derives from their consideration a sense of virtue. He feels that he is all out to end corruption in public life: he does not perceive that the sentiment he experiences is in reality a form of resentment, a hatred of anybody enjoying advantages or privileges and so ultimately the pleasures which he does not enjoy himself, and that this resentment is a particular ailment of democracies and one which can just as easily be let loose against foreign travel, art exhibitions, long-hair, honeymoon couples, Oscar Wilde, actresses or bottle parties, as against the protagonists at Westminster Hall. There is probably not one of us who could stand up to the searching methods of such an inquiry without revealing much that was ridiculous, a little that was pathetic, and certainly a grain that was criminal in the conduct of our own lives over a long period of time. Let us hope we may never become so important in the public eye as to deserve one.

*January* 1949

## PEACOCKS AND PARROTS

IN this issue Stephen Spender, who has just spent fifteen months in America, gives his impression of the literary scene and the situation of American writers. It is a gloomy picture, though an even gloomier one could be painted here: indeed I wish I could paint, for it resembles the moment when the Sleeping Beauty pricked herself with a pin. There they all stand, our distinguished authors, exquisite puzzled petrified figures, professors of this, doctors of that, companions of honour; their glasses raised to their lips, 'gentlemen, Miss Austen', 'gentlemen, Mrs. Woolf', 'ladies, I give you Mr. E. M. Forster', great publishers, fine broadcasters, polished lecturers, keen editors as ever kept pen from paper, fierce in hall and kind in fray:

> The varying year with blade and sheaf
> Clothes and reclothes the happy plains.
> Here rests the sap within the leaf
> Here stays the blood along the veins . . .
> Here droops the banner on the tower
> On the hall-hearths the festal fires,
> The peacock in his laurel bower
> The parrot in his gilded wires.
>
> Roof-haunting martins warm their eggs:
> In these, in those the life is stayed.
> The mantles from the golden pegs
> Droop silently: no sound is made.

When, lured by dull daydreams of bread and butter, we tear ourselves away from the fine fastidious frozen spectacle it is to rejoice in the talent of young American writers, inhabitants of that 'other America' which Spender describes as in opposition to the America which we all dislike and its chief glory—as, in the days when there was an 'other' England we turned to Lawrence, Huxley, Auden, Isherwood. For many of the unknown and original contributors to this magazine are now American. In the last year we have published nineteen American authors in fourteen numbers, and they would seem especially to excel in poetry and the short story. And in much that we do not print, the American talent seems superior; the stories which are not quite good enough will be more original, fresh and vigorous, the poems will be modern—interesting failures—never that stream of Victorian cliché which continues to pour from so many aspiring hearts nearer home. Even American readers praise, attack, criticize—but at least write.

*March* 1949

# LONDON LETTER

THE first warm Sunday at the end of March is the unofficial beginning of Spring. The Park smells of new grass, the noise of the mower is heard, the crocus carpets are on display, the boats are set free on the lake, huge crowds saunter up and down in the sunshine, while as night falls other cries mingle with those of the waterfowl, contraceptives reappear in the gutters, a body (making the third unsolved murder of Regent's Park) is found in the thirteen-acre garden of Barbara Hutton's featureless house where once the dresses of the ballerinas invited by Lord Hertford, the 'Pasha' of the region, moving all night among the trees, would be glimpsed by the respectable guests arriving for breakfast. Soon the leaves will be out and the first American writers, on their way to Paris and a summer in Italy, will settle here for a day or two. These early migrants play an important role, for they reawaken the comatose winterbound group of hibernators who have not been able to get away to the sunshine by reminding them that they still have a reputation, that although their corporeal selves are bound to their native soil by drudgery and currency-restrictions, their books are free to wander where they will. Let us suppose that a young novelist, (we will call him Harold Bisbee), whose first novel so perfectly shaded off the social boundary between the Far and the Middle West, has collected enough prize-money to visit his London and Paris publishers on his way to the island of Procida, goal of so many Near-Far Western friends. What is he going to find here? His first disappointment will be his hotel, for there no longer exists in London a single hotel in which it is a pleasure for an artist to stay. That particular vision of the literary life which was conjured up (till a bomb removed it) by Garland's Hotel in Suffolk Place, by the old Royal York at Brighton, or by the Royal Bath at Bournemouth with its memories of Henry James and Gosse, the hotel with its aroma of the nineties, its gilt and plush, its red or green flock walls and mahoganied private sitting rooms where discreet and elderly waiters served pints of claret to literary gentlemen, the hotel we have imagined from so many memoirs, where Thackeray called on Turgenev or Conrad on Hardy or Maugham on Max, whose letter-heading plucks our heart in James's letters: Hotel de Russie, Rome; Grand Hotel, Pau; Hotel de l'Europe, Avignon; Hotel de l'Ecu, Genève; when we come to London—ah, Bisbee—it doesn't exist. The best hotels of London are large and anonymous, the smaller ones have all been renovated. The Russell in Russell Square is central for visits to publishers and the place has some Pompeian Art Nouveau and a period flavour, but it is essentially the hotel for Midland business men. The other hotels round the British Museum have had to be completely done over since the Gibraltar refugees or Ministry of Information were there. Of the fashionable hotels, the Connaught has the most atmosphere, but it is rather too chic for a serious young writer. If Bisbee stays at too expensive an hotel he will frighten off the elusive men of letters whom he is here to study, and only his publishers will call. The southern rooms of the Savoy and northern apartments of the Hyde Park give the nicest views of London in summer, or else high up in the Dorchester, but all these are expensive and somehow unsuitable. I think that the only place where Bisbee could stay without being disillusioned on his first day would be in one of those bachelor chambers, kept by retired butlers, round Clarges or Half Moon Street or Curzon Street. James, I see, lived at 3 Bolton Street when he first came to London in the Eighties. I expect Bisbee could live there too. Having arrived and unpacked, laid out the cartons of 'Luckies' which are to cut his swathe through European society and, alas, taken a pull at the bottle of Bourbon he is bringing over to his publisher, London loneliness will descend on poor Harold. He looks out at the waving maples, the long sad spring sunset; he rings up one or two people who are out and then sallies forth to dine alone and collect his first impressions. Critical moment. Where will he eat? I can't say I envy him. He should, of course, for that first evening, go to an oyster bar: Wilton's in King Street, St. James's, Driver's or Bentley's or Wheelers or Scotts and then look in at some 'pub'—such as the Red Lion in Duke of York Street—whose interior is a delight. Then it is time to wander sadly home through the asphalt evening, looking at St. James's, the Park, the buses, the prostitutes with their fur scarves and little dogs and back to the inevitable Henry James companion-volume ('When the warm weather comes I find London evenings very detestable') and so to bed. In the morning the telephone at 3 Bolton Street gets busy, his publisher takes him out to luncheon at the Etoile, literary London is at his feet.

What will be his sensations? As he looks round the crowded cocktail party, hugging a thimble of something warm and sweet with a recoil like nail-polish remover, he will certainly observe four facts about English writers. They are not young, they are not rich, they are even positively shabby; on the other hand they seem kind and they look distinguished and their publishers look hardly more prosperous and hardly less distinguished than they do. No one, certainly, can be in this for the money. Of the people he most wants to meet there will be a fair sprinkling, for private individuals can no longer afford to give cocktail parties and most writers will not miss this chance of a pleasurable spring reunion. The Sitwells are generally in the country but Mr. Eliot will probably be there accompanied by Mr. John Hayward (Dr. Johnson disguised as Boswell) and they already convey an atmosphere particularly English to the gathering (not angels but Anglicans, as Gregory said). Towering over the rest are Mr. Stephen Spender and Mr. John Lehmann, two eagle heads in whose expressions amiability struggles with discrimination (Bisbee's European visit will largely depend on their summing up). About nine inches below them come the rank and file, Mr. Roger Senhouse, Mr. Raymond Mortimer, Mr. V. S. Pritchett, Miss Rose Macaulay, Miss Elizabeth Bowen, Quennell, Pryce-Jones, Connolly, we all are there. But where is Bisbee's opposite number? Why is Mr. Dylan Thomas still the youngest person present? Where are the under thirties? If Bisbee is observant he will have remarked on the two outstanding peculiarities of English literary life. The absence of young writers at the bottom, the fusion of author with publisher at the top. In such a gathering nearly everyone will have two or three jobs. Authors are either publishers or editors; if they do not edit or publish they will be on the British Council or the B.B.C. Culture is made and diffused by the same people. The cow serves in the milk bar. This explains the amazing coherence of English literary life, which often surprises visitors. It is easy to get ninety per cent of English writers happily into the same room because nearly all work in the same business. Editor-author, publisher-author, B.B.C.-author, in turn the hunters and the hunted, they are in constant communication. Then again, they are nearly all of an age, which is now from about forty-five to sixty. But the remunerative pressure of culture-diffusion tends gradually to extinguish the creative spark and Bisbee would do well to make a point of never asking these charming, friendly and distinguished people what they are writing now, or what they plan to write in the future. Make clear that you have read our books, at least one of them, that you regard us as authors first and as publishers, editors, broadcasters, or village explainers afterwards, and then try to understand the endless struggle which goes on with unfeeling demands for income-tax, with rising costs and standards of living, or the impossibility, for an English writer, of living cheaply in a sun-warmed cottage by the Pacific, and condone the fatal mixture of intelligence, administrative ability, humour and good sense with imagination that makes it so hard for us to exist only as artists, to suffer only as artists, to be deprived as artists of the human right to bring up and educate a family. We live in a time when none but successful novelists can make a living by their pens. Poets are doomed; essayists, critics fare little better; biographers may just survive. These mellow, sensitive, elderly and so individual faces who surround young Bisbee are perhaps the last known herd in existence of that mysterious animal, 'the English man of letters'—if there are no young people in the group, is it entirely due to the retardation of war, or is it not, perhaps, that they find so little to tempt them?

One might continue the day dream further. Let us picture Harold Bisbee, with his clear eye, charming mouth, slow western accent, his anecdotes of Cody, Neb., his passion for the 1920's, his success-story ties, his Bebop records, his wonderful *trouvaille*, James's butler's granddaughter his cook in Bolton Street! Let us picture him truly endearing himself to all our tired literary business men and women, who fling open their doors with a welcome they have long ceased to keep for each other, as he in turn slowly falls under the spell of their charm and taste and conversation—that wonderful conversation which uncovers as it proceeds the skeleton of the book they have not written. Might he not find in us the ideal subject—always such a problem—for a second novel? What could be a better field for his energy and powers of analysis than to disentangle this trusting group of middle-aged friends and lay bare, quite ruthlessly, what has gone wrong? Lies the fault with our schools? With our families? With the war? Is it taxation? Is it the Socialist Government? Is the Government not Socialist enough? Or is it with the next war? The uncertainty of living *entre trois guerres*? I see summer coming; Bisbee's ticket to Paris expires; now he's lost his booking at the Pont Royal, now the season at Procida's over; and, lo, the squares and parks of London are thick with golden maple leaves; autumn mists curl through Bolton Street; in leafy Kensington or river-scented Chelsea all doors open to Bisbee. 'Yes, I knew Lytton well.' ' I once met David Garnett.' One night an English girl, struck by something poetical in his fading youth, his flinty drawl, takes him to her bed *sauter pour mieux reculer*, as is the English way, and, after talking about frigidity there for an hour and a half, she tells him about her former lover, and bursts into tears. November is here, and all the other prize-winning novelists have long returned home. Haggard, unshaven, a fugitive now from his account at Bolton Street, Bisbee walks the streets. He has discovered George Moore. It is by a busman's café in Ebury Street that a tall grey head, a hawk-like glance bends over him one night. 'You're Harold Bisbee, aren't you? I used to know your stuff. You may remember mine. Been with us a long time now, son, haven't you? Almost one of us. How would you like a job? Publishing—but there's a bit of editing to do as well. Good. My office, tomorrow, at nine!'

*April* 1949


# VIVA LA MUERTE!

Dwight Macdonald, editor of *Politics*, is a representative of the non-Communist extreme left. Christopher Hollis is the Roman Catholic Tory M.P. for Devizes. A certain similarity in their point of view reveals the extent to which Communist policy is uniting Western thought by causing all those who make a study of the Ends *v.* Means fallacies of Marxism to contribute an alternative doctrine which invariably is based on a positive restatement of spiritual values and of the rights of man. To take our own example. The attacks on *Horizon* from Communist sources always picture us as reactionary, decadent, lost elements who have no contact with the working class and whose extinction is a matter of minutes. These attacks are usually launched in a breezy, hearty manner, whether they proceed from *Pravda* or the English fellow-stragglers. There is a special voice for talking to decadents whether you address them as a Communist or as a Fascist, as a key-jingling Conservative business man or a pipe-smoking Socialist planner, and it always makes the decadent feel thoroughly guilty. Suppose these people are right and that the only salvation for the artist lies in his representation of the problem of the working class? 'All we, like sheep, have gone astray.' Then where are the productions of those who have not gone astray and which we should take as a model? So far as we know they don't exist, or, if they do, our deviation has so intoxicated us that we don't even like them. We are driven on to the ultimate conclusion that 'decadence' is the only living force in the arts today, and that if the whole world were to go Communist tomorrow, despite all the commissars in the universe, it would cry out for 'decadent' modern art. The workers are just as tired and bored with themselves as anybody else, and, wherever they have a chance to exhibit their art and not what they are told ought to be their art, it appears more 'decadent' than bourgeois art because its neurotic quality is not enriched by competent technique. How many times have we 'decadents' not quailed before the roar of our political sergeant-majors only to find they have a rejected poem in their pocket? So when we are attacked as 'decadent' we should go forward, confident that we are on the right track. 'Decadent', 'Reactionary', 'Morbid', 'Subversive', 'Unintelligible'. All these words applied to artists mean: 'You are getting warm, you are getting dangerous, you are approaching that everflowing fountain of passion, incandescent with intelligence, at the centre of the maze—the soul of man'.

\*　　\*　　\*

We come up once more against the truth that although it is perfectly clear to many artists, philosophers, men of religion, how we must act to be saved from modern means of self-destruction it is almost impossible for them to convince other people. The particular note of the mid-century is hopelessness, and the artists who reflect the feeling of their time have to struggle against this desperate indifference, not in the public only, but in themselves. The robust and elderly, with a pre-1914 intellectual formation, are able to do this; very few others can and the young are perhaps the weakest of all. There is a kind of galloping demoralization of the West which is affecting everybody. America cannot save us, for it is more demoralized than anywhere; it is unlikely that Russia, beneath the veneer, is any better; French humanism or English gentility may preserve a few pockets but they cannot inspire us, because the truly modern world to which we all shut our eyes is engulfing us too fast and brings with it a complete negation of the aesthetic values of the past. The great artists of the past, despite the love lavished on them by scholars and aesthetes, are becoming more and more remote and unfamiliar. They are not replaced by others because we are moving into a world of non-art. One has only to compare the world of the long sea voyage: of sunsets and leisure and of settling down to the complete works of so-and-so with the still mildly aesthetic world of the train and then with the completely incurious existence of the air-passenger with his reassuring leaflet issued by the company, his meals wrapped up in cellophane in a cardboard box and his copy of *Time* in case the sleeping pill doesn't work. This unseeing, unreading traveller is a symbol of the new public. Poetry for this civilization may well cease to exist for no one, except a few professors, will possess the necessary ear to follow its subtleties. Reading aloud is almost extinct and the poet who wrestles with his subtle tone-effects secures his victories for himself alone. The hopeless are the irresponsible, the irresponsible are the lazy: we must accustom ourselves to a reading public which is both too slothful and too restless to read until a

sense of values is restored to it. The position of one or two
eminent poets like Mr. Eliot and Dr. Sitwell, eminent partly
because they have become tribal medicine men and not because
their poems are yet as understood and appreciated as they
could be, must not blind us to the years of neglect they suffered
or to the terrible plight of many younger poets who, with all
their talent, are reduced to poverty and drudgery because their
music cannot reach the public ear, waxy with digests, loud-
speakers, mikes and cinema organs. Meanwhile, with literature
rapidly becoming a lost cause, editors of newspapers with large
circulations still call for books to be withdrawn on grounds of
obscenity. The demon of sex, whether normal or abnormal,
must at all costs be kept away from the bedside where the
average Englishman (and his womenfolk) frightened of love,
aggressive to art, exhausted by war, soaked in black tea and
watery beer, shuffles his tobacco-stained fingers round the
*News of the World*. There is a famous Dr. Sullivan in America,
author of a system of his own [*Horizon* No. 79], who greets his
new internes at the Mental Hospital where he works, with the
words: 'There is one thing I wish you to remember while you
work under me. In the present state of society the patient is
right and you are wrong.'

*May–June* 1949

## HAIL AND FAREWELL—I

THE next issue of *Horizon* will be a special number to com-
memorate the tenth year of our existence, after which the
magazine will close down for a year and reopen, if conditions
improve, in an invigorated form for Christmas 1950. There
are various reasons for this course. Some are technical—for
instance we have to quit our premises in Bedford Square at
the end of this year and those who have enjoyed offices in
Bedford Square require immense energy to seek them anywhere

else. Others are economic, for example, the cost of printing *Horizon* has risen steadily since the war while the circulation remains static. We have no way of recovering this expense since the public would not pay more than half a crown for *Horizon*, nor can we afford a large campaign to make people buy it. For the last three years we have watched a slow fall in the English sales of *Horizon*, fewer subscribers, more returns, increasing apathy. A traveller whom we sent round the big towns of the North was able to sell but one subscription in a year; a university town like Cambridge has imported only a dozen copies a month since the magazine started. It is the continual increase of the demand for *Horizon* in America which has saved us from drastic action for some years. A decade of our lives is quite enough to devote to a lost cause such as the pursuit and marketing of quality in contemporary writing. In the end, despite all the good will in the world, the public gets the magazines it deserves. London, of course, is a particularly disheartening centre from which to operate, one seldom comes across the people who read *Horizon* with pleasure, but is continually reminded of that sterile, embittered, traditional literary society which has killed so many finer things than a review of literature and art.

Another major problem is the discovery of material. It is fashionable to exclaim that *Horizon* was much better in the war 'when it really stood for something', and that it has gone off since. In fact the opposite is true. The war numbers contained a great deal of uneven reporting which would not have been accepted now, but there was very little to do in the blackout but read, and people enjoyed it. It is this appetite which has gone off, not *Horizon*. But a higher standard of editing has coincided with a falling off of material. Many of our considerable literary talents have grown unwilling to write except for dollars, or have become psychologically impotent or grown so immersed in less uncertain forms of livelihood as to be unproductive. Broadcasts or lectures may be offered, original literary contributions seldom or never. The constant prodding of these elusive celebrities causes one in the end to dislike oneself. If we study the Index to *Horizon* we can even see at what point various well-known writers ceased to appear and so obtain an insight into that decay of hope in the West which is the major psychological factor in the post-war world. In normal times the slow desiccation of middle-aged writers would be balanced by the emergence of younger ones, but in the world of cold war and conscription this has not proved to be the case. We have found many good, new, young short-story writers in America but hardly any here, nor have the poets or essayists come forward. Some day these will emerge. 'Nothing is certain, only the certain spring', as Binyon wrote in these pages—but we may not be here to greet them.

This inability to discover new writers led us on to the next factor in our decision. The temporary staleness of the editor. To be an editor and also a writer is even more difficult than to be a publisher or a journalist and write oneself. An editor frays away his true personality in the banalities of good mixing, he washes his mind in other people's bath-water, he sacrifices his inner voice to his engagement book. Those of us who wish to survive middle age must all walk the plank. In the country of the one-eyed, only the blind man has a chance to be king.

By suspending *Horizon* for a year we give the Editor and his Assistant a chance to become themselves and to write. If they cannot avail themselves of this opportunity they will return to editing and accept their destiny. We also give the public a breather in which to view *Horizon's* ten-year effort in a truer perspective, so that if we reappear, better geared to contemporary events, with a closer focus on the passing scene, we may receive an unexpected welcome. A thousand more subscribers or two thousand more regular readers or a dozen brilliant and fertile young writers or a generous backing from some unexpected well-wisher—all these might have saved us but they could not, perhaps, have made a great difference to the fatigue of the mind, the disabusedness with the contemporary world, the increasing antipathy to creeds and governments, the disgust with the post-war set-up with which we oppose our ever-sleeping antagonist, the British reading public.

'The second best's a gay goodnight and quickly turn away.' The swan-song of little magazines is always the same and we croak nothing now that was not said by Mr. Eliot in his farewell to the *Criterion* in 1939, and so we will now recommend to our readers an outstanding new poem of Auden and the excellent matter to be found in this and in our forthcoming Christmas number before retiring into the long-desired shade, to the satisfaction of the envious, the distress of our friends and the indifference of all but that one in every hundred and fifty thousand who constitute our world public.

# HAIL AND FAREWELL—II

WE have called this number of *Horizon* a 'special' number because it is longer than usual, but as it is in no other way out of the ordinary it might be interesting to take it to pieces and analyse them so as to explain to the reader for once exactly how a number comes to be put together. At first we hoped to have a double number, in order to print every manuscript which we had accepted, but the printers were unable to comply. Let us examine what remains. 'Flight to Italy' by Day Lewis is the second part of a long poem which has recently been broadcast. The first part has appeared in *The Listener*. The poet attempts to translate into a casual easy-seeming free-flowing verse narrative a particularly unpoetical experience, the flight from

London to Rome. In our view the poem is a triumphant success; the whole unreal paraphernalia of flight becomes absorbed into the medium and even that unreality of the spirit which makes commercial flying so ignominious, that absence of any feeling except genteel apprehension quickening some times into panic or euphoria, is poetically conveyed. Ten years ago we printed Cecil Day Lewis's *Fourth Georgic*, and with his friend Auden, whose poems appeared in the first and last but one number, he represents the continuity of the magazine. Four other favourite poets were personally asked for a contribution to this number; two of these did not reply, one was under contract to give all his poetry to an American humorous journal, the fourth had just taken a vow to publish no more poetry for ten years, so we register this one success out of five as fairly typical of the present-day problem of obtaining material. There is also the 'poetry drawer', which fills up at the rate of about eighty poems a week and is emptied by the editor, sometimes assisted by a visiting poet who has dropped in for tea. Here are poets whose names and typewriters are as well known to us after years of rejecting as if they were household words: one uses green paper, another mauve ink, another, we notice, has gone to the country, a Glasgow bard moved to town. They are an extraordinarily English phenomenon, these hundreds of amateur poets; in the end one rejects them by texture, smell, paperweave—heartlessly—because within a month they all will be back. Occasionally something good or almost good comes into the drawer, but we have noticed that poems which we publish in this way are seldom followed up.

The poems by Octavio Paz, who lives in Mexico City, were handed to Peter Watson by Henri Hell in Paris and come to us by those winged seed-ways by which many a new talent in foreign countries has reached us. We have published all too little in Spanish and it is a pleasure to air these fragments of delicate loneliness.

For the main article we had to choose between Blanchot's Sade and a brilliant essay on Proust by Mlle Claude-Edmonde Magny. Blanchot's criticism is known to our readers through his *Constant* (No. 116); Mlle Magny's is not. But whereas we have had one article on Proust and many other references (there are three new books out on him at present) we have never had anything on Sade who is still comparatively unknown in England and the essay by Blanchot is outstanding. So with regretful hesitation (and perhaps because it is less fatiguing to translate from the print than crabbed long-hand) we made our choice. It must be remembered that Blanchot's article appeared in *Les Temps Modernes* after a wave of new interest and new approaches to Sade while here we have had no book on him since Geoffrey Gorer's. Last of more than a hundred appreciations of living painters and sculptors, the article on Francis Bacon deals with the outstanding exhibition of the month, while that on the music of Dallapiccola adds a bright new name to the atonal musicians, Schoenberg, Berg and Webern on whom we have published articles by René Leibowitz. James Lord's short story is one of the first to be printed by a young American writer and continues the line of honourable craftsmen with strong feelings like Truman Capote, Paul Bowles, Eudora Welty, Paul Goodman and Donald Windham whom we have helped to disseminate in this country and their own. The notes on English character by Geoffrey Gorer bring into the fold another writer whose work we would have been glad to present before.

At this point a superficial analysis could cease: music, painting, literature, poetry, fiction and the general article: the mixture is familiar to our readers—and they might also notice that without any self-conscious polyglot attitude a Mexican, an Italian, a Rumanian, an American and a Frenchman share the honours with three English writers. But let us probe the contents further. The early issues of *Horizon* were tentative and eclectic; they were apt to combine the better Georgian writers with the official school of the Thirties. The war isolated the Georgians and scattered the Thirties group. We then moved on to a more definite war footing, fulfilling a double purpose—that of conserving the essential features of the heritage of Western humanism in time of danger and that of bringing out the young war writers and the particular kind of serious reporting that grew up round the war. Alun Lewis, William Sansom, Tom Harrisson, Maclaren Ross, Arturo Barea, were newcomers of this period, and poets like W. R. Rogers and Laurie Lee. Towards the end of the war the impact of the clandestine literature of the French Resistance movement tended almost to swamp us together with our effort to bring the conclusions of modern psychology into line with the creative arts. From being a kind of exchange where the writer in uniform sent in his records of new experience to receive in return nostalgic fragments of the *douceur de vivre* or new estimates of James Joyce and Virginia Woolf, we became a display window for Sartre and Camus and the French writers so ably interpreted for us by John Russell, Philip Toynbee and other young critics. Here we were in peril of becoming an advertisement for international fashions of the mind. We began to withdraw into the insolent tower of our anarcho-perfectionism, only to settle down with a new list towards America, and our double American number (October 1947) was probably the solidest of all the editorial attempts to convey a present atmosphere with truthful alertness. But we have always believed that the real vocation of this magazine was to feel its way to what is, in the best sense of the word, contemporary, to print what many years hence will be recognized as alive and original and to draw away from the nostalgic or inflated, to abandon the role of custodian for that of innovating interpreter, and we feel that in the last four years we have at last begun to understand what the Forties (as opposed to the

Thirties or Twenties) are really about. The 'Inscrutable Forties' we had first called them, and the results of our scrutiny are not pleasant. Let us take some examples from this number.

Thus 'The Boy Who Wrote NO' writes his 'No' explicitly against banking, commerce, the law, the church and the family, he is a mute and lonely rebel, and his punishment for his five No's is the worst society can devise. But these five No's set a cord vibrating. This year another *Horizon* author, Paul Bowles, produced a first and first-rate novel, *The Sheltering Sky*,[1] in which a dying man who exemplifies the helplessness and lucidity of our age, packs all his delirious wisdom into the same brief cry: '*No, no, no, no, no,' he said. It was all he had the strength to say. But even if he had been able to say more, still he would have said only: 'No, no, no, no.*' Bowles's characters, three hard-drinking, haunted expatriates lost against a Saharan background, carry the loneliness and isolation of human beings, even those whose ties are closest, a stage further than any other contemporary, but always with some wild and bracing enchantment in their discovery. And the loudest and most interminable 'No' in literature—No to God, No to Nature, No to Man—is perhaps that which the Marquis de Sade boomed from his prisons. The rules which he caused the Duc de Blangis to lay down for his women were a prophecy of all reigns of terror: 'Il sera peu d'excès sans doute où nous ne nous portions; qu'aucun ne vous répugne, prêtez-vous sans sourciller, et opposez à tout la patience, la soumission et le courage. Si malheureusement quelqu'une d'entre vous succombe à l'intempérie de nos passions qu'elle prenne bravement son parti; nous ne sommes pas dans le monde pour toujours exister, et ce qui peut arriver de plus heureux à une femme c'est de mourir jeune.'

This study in misunderstood genius leads us easily on to Bacon's horror-fretted canvases and to Dallapiccola's Songs

[1] John Lehmann. 10s. 6d.

for Prisoners, to the criticism made of him 'a few, a very few musicians, have an intense awareness, heightened by their intellect, of the tragedy within our time—of the religious struggle which is carried on to the last drop of blood—between the spiritual ideal of liberty and the tyrannous brutality of matter and its inexorable determinism'.

One can perceive the inner trend of the Forties as maintaining this desperate struggle of the modern movement, the struggle between man, betrayed by science, bereft of religion, deserted by the pleasant imaginings of humanism, and the blind fate of which he is now so expertly conscious that if we were to close this last Comment with the suggestion that every one who is reading it now may in ten years' time, or even five, look back to this moment as the happiest in their lives, there would be few who would gainsay us. 'Nothing dreadful is ever done with, no bad thing gets any better; you can't be too serious.' This is the message of the Forties from which, alas, there seems no escape, for it is closing time in the gardens of the West and from now on an artist will be judged only by the resonance of his solitude or the quality of his despair.

*November–December* 1949

# REPUTATIONS

SINCE the days of Homer one of the major consolations of the literary life has been the belief in reputations—in those verdicts of posterity which right the injustice of fashion and, expressed in tangible form by the law of copyright, protect in modern times the author's widow and immediate family. 'Not all of me shall die', 'Non omnis moriar.' 'On me lira vers 1880.' 'To a poet a thousand years hence', the cry of Horace, Stendhal, Flecker is reiterated.

It is also a symptom of our mental inertia in face of change that, while all of us have been presented with evidence that we live in an age of revolution, we have never considered an onslaught on established authority or the sanctity of private property as applying to literary fame. Fifty years of revolutionary art-movements have not made us aware how much of the past we unconsciously destroy in our quest for the supreme aesthetic sensation—the awareness of contemporary genius. It is as if Samson, hurling down the pillars of the temple, assumed that the candelabra, the ornamented festoons and creepers attached to them, would remain on high of their own accord.

In fact, there has been a silent upheaval in our attitude to literature. The reader is disappearing; discriminating enjoyment of the written word is on the way out. War disguises this because war, by depriving people of other entertainment, forces them to read: wars also encourage so-called 'escapist' reading which takes the mind off present horrors. Trollope became a best-seller in the last war. I doubt if he will remain one. Wars also create a too hasty enthusiasm for contemporary work; those who don't read Trollope become infatuated with Aragon or Richard Hillary. As we are generally at war the war-values which cause literary judgement to be distorted by hope, nostalgia, patriotism or sentimentality seem more permanent than they need be. But what is really happening?

People don't like buying books any more; they don't enjoy
reading poetry; they won't subscribe to magazines; they
economize on literature; they economize less, however, on
smoking or television or watching sport or gardening or beer
or buying a car. The poets feel the chill first, they are in the
front line; the conception of the 'great poet' is rooted in
European humanism, yet it seems conceivable that it may die
out. And what appears to happen is that there is room for
only one poet at a time. Yeats is dead, long live Eliot! But
Yeats's writing is uneven; how we have secretly groaned in the
company of Michael Robartes, Maud Gonne, Lady Gregory,
the Pollexfens, 'Butlers far back', Maeve, Grania, Cuchulain!
If we read Yeats aloud we are conscious of much affectation
and considerable flatness; it is sad how few of his poems are
magical from beginning to end, and yet he was the greatest
poet of his time. One of the most important elements in the
greatness of a writer, however, is uniqueness of vision. This
very uniqueness requires a special effort from the reader who
will make it for some writers, but not for others; hence an
element of capriciousness is introduced. I will take this trouble
for Eliot but not for Pound, for Joyce but not for Rilke, and
so on. Without this uniqueness a writer has not much chance
of survival: with it he may or may not endure; that depends on
whether the critics will make his obscurities seem worth while.

Because we learn to read before we learn anything else, we
attach great prestige to the written word and we do not notice
that the book as an art-form may have entered into its decadence: the golden age of the book drew to its close in the
second half of the eighteenth century and the first half of the
nineteenth. It was then beautiful in itself and without rival
either as an entertainment or as a moulder of opinion. Reading
and reading aloud were the pastimes of every family. Consider
the lives of Voltaire and Shaw, consider their effectiveness as
propagandists. Surely Voltaire was the luckier in that literature

then afforded his talent a more powerful medium? He is Shaw doubled with the Chaplin who made 'The Great Dictator' and the Priestley of the 1940 postscripts. If we assume that the art of 'readership' is in decline we can understand why a gifted writer like Cocteau becomes a man of the cinema—not for financial gain so much as to discover an atmosphere of enthusiasm in which he can expand. How many people appreciated the fine points of style of Graham Greene's *Heart of the Matter*, his bleak handling of tropical richness in the opening pages, his use of the sentimental 'old school tie' theme to increase the atmosphere of subtle treachery and moral degradation, as compared with the multitudes who revelled in the film clichés of *The Third Man*—the inevitable sewer-chase, the cat and shoe trick, the Chaplinesque ending or that mumbling tune, the 'Lambeth Walk' of post-war neurosis? In America, where a non-commercial cinema does not exist, the prestige of painting has outstripped that of writing—it is 'smarter' to be associated with art than with books: there are more art-students than budding writers.

'How many books do we read in a week? How many of those are re-readings? How many were written: 1. More than thirty years ago? 2. More than a hundred?' If one could get replies to such a questionnaire and compare them with those dating back to the early part of the century, the decay in 'readership' would be sensational. I doubt whether very many people now read more than one book a week, and I believe that book to be always a new one that, once finished, is never reopened. The spectacle of a writer driven by his own high standard to torture himself with polishing, with weeding out s's and 'its' and 'buts' and 'almost' and 'only' for readers who will no longer read him aloud, and who remain therefore completely tone-deaf, is one of the commonest, saddest and bravest of the twentieth century. The American conception of literature, the production of the right book at the right moment which then becomes a best-seller for several months, after which it dies and is forgotten, making room for others, is taking firm hold in this country. It is the natural consequence of the high cost of book-production which necessitates large editions. This conception does very little harm to the reputations of best-selling novelists—if Evelyn Waugh, Elizabeth Bowen or Rosamond Lehmann make a lot of money every two or three years, they certainly deserve it, and the body of their work continues to receive attention from the critics. But the system is unfair to many a lesser-known writer or novelist, who misses the colossal first prize and receives no other.

There are, in fact, three kinds of literary reputation. The classic—the author and his work are accepted as part of our education. He is lectured about, set for examinations, taught at schools and universities: (2) the *avant-garde*; while not necessarily admitted to academic circles, the author is revered by other writers, is of interest to the young, receives attention in the intellectual magazines: (3) the popular; the public go on buying his books.

Now it is the last reputation which is the most uncertain after death. Think of all the once-popular novelists who are found in the library lists, Maurice Hewlett, Hall Caine, Rafael Sabatini, Baroness Orczy, William J. Locke, Phillips Oppenheim, W. B. Maxwell, Hugh Walpole, Elinor Glyn. 'How swiftly it fades, the dew on the garlic leaf.' Consider the uneasy sleep of Bennett and Galsworthy, colossi of their time. Alive, they had all the qualities necessary for success, but posterity will never find them quite interesting enough. They were too doggy. Too much genial sniffing and tail-wagging went into their books, too much frisking round the reader, too much desire to please, too much money, too much leisure. They lacked first-rate minds and a feeling for perfection.

When we examine a page from the *Forsyte Saga* it will be found that only the satire has any sting to it: a row about

money, a will, a law-suit, an old man's death agony; these live
—but the love scenes, the lyrical ruminations, passages which
begin with remarks like 'By the cigars they smoke and the
composers they love, ye shall know the texture of men's souls'
(which far outnumber the others), are completely insipid.
Popularity is not enough. It is Hardy and Henry James, who
required from the reader an effort which their popular contemporaries were afraid to demand, that have now outstripped
them, or the silent self-effacing monk of—

> Margaret, are you grieving
> Over golden grove unleaving?

When we draw nearer to the present we can observe the
process in action. We can watch *The Waste Land* from being
*avant-garde* become a classic, or *The Cocktail Party* turn popular. Evelyn Waugh writes a long short story *Helena*. According
to one intellectual critic, Raymond Mortimer, this is a little
masterpiece, the best thing he has done; in the view of another,
Henry Reed, it is but one more proof of the absurdity of con-
sidering him as a serious writer. Which estimate will influence
posterity? A review, any publisher will tell us, cannot decide
the fate of a book: but a long critical article can certainly decide
the future of an author. Critics have lately come to the rescue
of Firbank and Scott Fitzgerald. Will they prove as indulgent
to Huxley or Hemingway? Judging by his success here and in
America, Maugham would seem (after Boswell) the outstanding prose writer of today. How will posterity interpret that?

Now it is clear that many successful writers possess a certain
spell-binding quality which is sometimes called a narrative
gift, sometimes readability, sometimes charm or suspense or
style, but which is in fact the materialization of an author's
personality through what he writes. In some cases—Kipling's,
for example—the personality is unpleasant, in others—
Maugham's, for instance, likable. Now Maugham has seldom

written a memorable sentence and Kipling a great many which
are excruciating, yet their personalities dominate the reader
and ensure respect and consideration for their owners. After
death there seems to be a certain shrinking of the literary personality, a little of the illusion goes, perhaps because when we
read a book we like to think of the author as a person whom we
may possibly meet and who might help us. Arnold Bennett's
steady six thousand a year made his journals more interesting
in his lifetime than now—and the living may even get very
impatient with the dead in their cardboard containers if they
blow too much in our faces. What is happening in Evelyn
Waugh's case is that his forcible personality is now manifesting
itself more and more through his work and beginning to
dominate his public. Under its spell the separate components
are united as by the patter in a conjuring trick. Mortimer
accepts the trick, while Reed isolates a paragraph to show how
fatuous is the dialogue. But when we are under a spell we do
not notice a weakness in dialogue. Extracts from books used
as examples by hostile critics usually appear worse than they
are because the continuous buzz of the author's personality is
missing.

Who then is right? Mr. J. Isaacs, who seems to think readability a blemish, gave six omniscient talks on contemporary
literature in the Third Programme without mentioning Evelyn
Waugh, while on Leo Myers, Sidney Schiff and Elias Canetti
he lavished praise. Which way will posterity jump? What will
they think of *Brideshead Revisited* or *The Cocktail Party*? If I
were in a position to advise a writer who was so ambitious as to
desire recognition both in his lifetime and after, I would say:

'Your posthumous reputation must depend on the critics.
Write always with those critics in mind. Set posterity a puzzle.
The living dislike puzzles: the unborn worship them. Henry
James's mysterious accident, Rimbaud's flight, Proust's sex
life, the meaning of *Finnegans Wake* . . . give them a mystery.

Secondly, contrive if possible to get a book written about you while still alive. It won't be a very good one at this early stage but it will establish a tradition and there is an air of distinction about an author whose biography is in circulation. Thirdly, encourage the young men who write theses for American universities to take you seriously. No one can earn their living by their pen unless they are chosen at least once by the American book of the month club, but the thesis will pay off in the long run. Sir Hugh Walpole, who handled his American audience with such unfailing charm, lectured everywhere, but failed to get lectured about. Lastly, keep your contemporary success within bounds. The unborn will derive no satisfaction from understanding you unless you appear misunderstood. A comic writer must at heart be a melancholiac; a tragic one, a clown. To know how far to go in making a fortune out of the public without antagonizing posterity is perhaps the nicest exercise of judgement of which a writer is capable. Don't write for a country or a class. Countries disappear, even the solid bourgeoisie can suddenly melt away. Beware of journalism; don't say everything about yourself; don't gather up the scraps from your own table too thoroughly; leave a little of your conversation to be reported by others; give your opinion of your contemporaries by word of mouth rather than in print. However large and loving your household, always appear lonely. "And is there one who understands me?" (*Finnegans Wake*).

'Above all, beware of the films: a portrait can be called a good or bad likeness and can, if the painter be carefully chosen, attach you to the future, but to appear personally in a film is to deprive posterity of all speculation, of its right to model you in its own image. And when a novel or a story is made into a film, it may destroy the book for many readers and indeed reveal conspicuous weaknesses in it, especially in characterization ... You must face an unpleasant thought, that perhaps in the eyes of posterity it is a devouring passion for language and truth which is most desirable. They may prefer Joyce to Shaw or Hopkins to Kipling; D. H. Lawrence and Virginia Woolf to Galsworthy and Arnold Bennett.'

At a glance, I would say that the reputations of most of the writers famous between 1900 and 1930 will dwindle: Shaw, Wells, Bennett, Galsworthy, Belloc, Chesterton—they were splendid all-rounders who lacked the supreme aesthetic gift of verbal imagination. I think that this may prove the case for many of my contemporaries, but, even as Yeats and Hopkins were the exceptions then, so are poets like Eliot and Dylan Thomas today. The first line of a poem by Dylan Thomas, 'A grief ago', seems to me to extend the limits of language and feeling. The clear thinking and fresh writing of Shaw, so admirable in its time and so original, will surely date, like self-satisfaction, when history folds up her telescope. As Sainte-Beuve said, we must write as if those who are going to read us will belong to a civilization more delicate and subtle than any we know.

But of course we cannot tell what form the civilization of the future will take. We must behave as if those who come after us will continue to demand entertainment from the written word and inspiration from the past, and not treat us as an object lesson in decadence. We must live as if our threatened ethical values will prevail, we must write as if the tragic human misfit, so lovable, discriminating and impatient, will remain our eternal audience and the reading and re-reading of old books continue, where all other improvements glut the eye, as the absorbing recreation of an understanding élite.

1950

# LOGAN PEARSALL SMITH

## I

LOGAN PEARSALL SMITH died in the early morning of
Saturday, 2 March 1946, in his eighty-first year. As a young man
he had known Whitman and Matthew Arnold; his contemporaries at Harvard were Berenson and Santayana; at Oxford
he was a favourite of Jowett; in middle-age he was the friend
of Henry James and Robert Bridges, of Edmund Gosse and
George Moore. In the last months he was particularly interested in young writers—John Russell, Stuart Preston, John
and James Pope-Hennessy, Hugh Trevor-Roper and Veronica
Wedgwood—in Edith Sitwell's poetry also, and the literary
prospects of Sir Kenneth Clark. The day before he died he
rang up a friend to demand the fullest information about
George Orwell, whose *Animal Farm* had just captivated him.
'Who is he? What is he like?' 'I'll tell you all about him at tea
tomorrow,' replied the friend, and the voice that sixty years
before had been asking the same question about Walter Pater
protested: 'No. Tell me now.' I mention this to show how
impossible it is in a few words to convey anything of that immense magical continuity of being which is the attribute of
great age. Pearsall Smith was not just an extraordinarily rich
and complicated personality, he was that personality receding
back through generations, he was 'Logan' a name consistently
conveying the same highly concentrated and specialized flavour
to people long since dead who remembered the eighteenth
century, to their children, and to their grandchildren now
middle-aged, and to the very young. This Logan-note sounded
like the ring of a fine glass through all his mutations of personality: it was his own unique resonance—a perpetual warm
ironical appreciation of life heightened by a never-failing
passion for the best in literature and the human heart. This

quality of mind owed something to the discrepancies of his character. The big, rather callow young American, brought up in an atmosphere of religious revival—his parents were successful evangelists—against a background of puritanism and the family business, deliberately chose for himself the sceptical Epicurean philosophy of Horace and Montaigne and the dedicated literary life of Flaubert and Henry James, yet, while he settled happily into them, his native puritanism and no little of his native worldliness were constantly breaking through. Some of the aggression which might have been employed in making money went into the elaborate teasing of his friends, while a relic of puritanism made him censorious of the ways we earned our living—yet it also contributed to his moral force and gave to his serene sunny philosophy that energy which Epicureanism often lacks and which chiefly distinguishes the true artist from the man of taste. In his old age a mysterious rhythm of elation and depression gained increasing hold on him; in his 'up' periods he joked and talked and went out and rearranged those elaborate sagas about his friends which were his contribution to the study of the nature of personality; in his 'down' ones he would groan ironically about the fate of the world and read, read, read—absorbing and digesting his chosen author like a python, extracting his inner nature from the verbiage, sifting all the facts and theories and appreciations of him which other critics had compiled, confiding one or two precious tit-bits, the very marrow and pope's nose of his subject, into little black note-books whence they would be disinterred to provide an astonishing epithet or a disintegrating adverb. Then during the between-stage when the bell-note of his glass rang out with its clearest and most seductive music, he would write some long essay in which the gleanings of his dark winter hibernation were set down in those long shining sentences where intelligence and feeling and scholarship and strange bleak flashes fetched from his spiritual underworld were integrated into that peculiarly radiant prose, so limpid and seeming-artless, so penetrating in insight, so warm in texture, which constituted his own secret weapon against chaos and time. Two weeks before his death, a friend asked him half-jokingly if he had discovered any meaning in life. 'Yes,' he replied, 'there is a meaning, at least, for me, there is one thing that matters—to set a chime of words tinkling in the minds of a few fastidious people.' 'And the State, Logan,' the friend went on, 'the Family, the International Situation, Russia, India?' Propped up on his pillows he waved all this away with his hand, 'A chime of words,' he repeated, 'a few discriminating people'.

Well, Flaubert said, in almost that language, that nothing in this world is worth doing except the turning of a perfect sentence and Logan Pearsall Smith was well aware that he was working out his destiny as surely as the almond tree blossomed along the terrace or the great planes by his 'bench of desolation' in the Hospital garden put out their summer shade. Let us consider how much he succeeded.

In the earlier part of his life his friends were chiefly scholar-artists, and came from academic circles; later on he preferred artist-scholars, and became himself more purely creative—and there were always some poor lame ducks of literary journalists whose complicated backslidings he would patiently take in hand. After beginning with some poems and short stories the scholar-artist spent years preparing his *Life of Sir Henry Wotton*. In 1918 the artist-scholar appeared with *Trivia* and *More Trivia* which won him a small, but choice and enduring reputation; the scholar-artist then took over with anthologies of Donne's and Jeremy Taylor's sermons (both of whose virtues he was largely responsible for re-discovering), of English prose and of English aphorisms, and with an anthology of Santayana (the philosopher whose doctrine of essences most appealed to him and whose work gave him a certain platonic

fervour of belief, an idealism which went far beyond his epicurean temperament), and with his books on the English
language. For Pearsall Smith was a word-addict who, like
Valéry, worshipped the *honneur des hommes*, *Saint Langage*,
and he wrote about words in *Words and Idioms* and *The English
Language* with the same learned and infectious passion with
which they always served him. One might complete his
scholarly works by mentioning his exquisite *On Re-reading
Shakespeare*, his Milton and his book of essays *Reperusals*
where is distilled, in essays on Montaigne, Sainte-Beuve,
Madame de Sévigné, and other favourites, some of the finest
essence of his mind.

The artist returned with two more books; his autobiography
*Unforgotten Years*, which won him fame, where he had always
maintained a fine reputation, in America, and with his
*Aphorisms* which are among the most perfect of their kind, and
where all his conflicting qualities—his loves and his hates, his
affections and severities—are resolved into a marmoreal wisdom. Finally an exquisitely revised edition of *All Trivia* and
the *Aphorisms* appeared just before his death.

One likes to think that he had this last satisfaction and that
we also shall enjoy it, but what a poor benefit it is! How dis-
mally do an author's most individual writings fail to compen-
sate for the human being we have lost! For though we may
still perceive *him* through his phrase, what has happened to his
perception of us? Just as it seemed that Logan could never
have lived anywhere except in St. Leonard's Terrace, looked
after for thirty-five years with perfect consideration by his
sister, waited on so intelligently by his devoted servant,
Hammond, giving out, through all the especially malignant
bombings of Chelsea, from his windowless, battered home his
untiring and courageous enthusiasm, rediscovering Ruskin
and Bossuet, applying to his friends that loving creative
curiosity, finding subjects for them, planning how they could

fulfil themselves—so it is impossible not to imagine him still living there, in his high study which looked over the Wren gates, 'with cloudy trophies hung' to the Hospital that symbolized that seventeenth century which he had loved so well and helped so much to elucidate, the England of Shakespeare, Milton, Donne, Taylor, and Wotton, for whose sake he had become a British subject. To us who knew him in those war years Logan Pearsall Smith personified an indispensable quality in civilization. Civilization will not lose by his death for it has his books, but his friends will all feel less civilized. Who will care now how we turn out, or warn us when we decline, or advise us how to surpass ourselves? This is the real burden of mortality; a human spirit shines out for so long that it becomes encrusted with memories, the oracle of wisdom for a whole tribe, a fountain of humorous affection. 'And yet, as with Tolstoy and with Proust, all is slowly changing beneath the unimaginable lapse of time, until suddenly the unimaginable happens; the shears of destiny snap together, the sun goes out, the curtain of darkness falls.' And round us, not about him, the shades gather.

1946

## II

A LESSON FOR THE MASTER. *Recollections of Logan Pearsall Smith by Robert Gathorne-Hardy. Constable, 18s.*

This is a most extraordinary book. It takes the reader immediately into a very strange world, a vanished society, a world in which people of independent means devoted their lives to art, living near together in creamy Georgian houses and going abroad at the same time to the same places. Chelsea was its centre—leafy, well-to-do, fig-ripening Chelsea, from Carlyle Mansions to Ebury Street, where luncheon would last till five o'clock. Moore, James, Augustine Birrell were the giants, but during the twenties their mantle fell on Logan Pearsall Smith.

Logan (it is impossible to call him anything else), because he was generous, because he lived for literature and because he had a little more money than his simple *bon-bourgeois* way of living required, conceived the idea of adopting and endowing a spiritual heir, 'a perpetual apprentice' Mr. Gathorne-Hardy calls him, and of imparting to his young secretary, companion, and eventual successor, the innermost mysteries of his art. It was a beautiful notion, medieval in its simplicity, and we are at once reminded of some early Italian painting of master and pupil, the one all wisdom and patience, the other compact of humility and zeal. And yet, since a lot of travelling was involved, an oriental flavour must be introduced; the wandering holy man and his disciple went visiting shrines—Montaigne's library tower, Madame de Sévigné's château, Miss Austen's Mansfield Park—and acquiring merit and spiritual freedom as they go. But this leaves out the scholarship, the erudition and the whimsical bantering of this precious correspondence with its bibliographical allusions and erotic undertones, its extraordinary remoteness from life as we know it, its wholly admirable preoccupation with the craftsmanship of letters. In fact there is but one word for the picture which emerges: Chinese. It is the portrait of a Chinese sage, old, bald, angry and ironical, but infinitely delicate and wise, with his devoted dapper disciple sharing his enthusiasms and discoveries, his wanderings and homecomings, his allegiances and betrayals. The first spiritual heir to be tried out (1926–9) proved something of a disappointment and left to get married, an abnormal condition which Logan always regarded as fatal to any enduring concentration of talent. Mr. Gathorne-Hardy was made of sterner stuff. He occupied his post as perpetual apprentice for some sixteen years and these years he takes us through in detail in this fascinating book. Let us deal with the faults first and get rid of them quickly: the author has learnt certain tricks of style from his master which sometimes grate, too many epithets seem to be in inverted commas, his adjectives are inclined to show off, certain effects of simplicity appear self-conscious, and the egotism of the author in regard to his own productions and his war experiences might have been curbed with advantage to the construction of the book. And, worst of all, this is a book with a grievance. For Mr. Gathorne-Hardy was ultimately dismissed and the long and wonderful friendship between the elderly and the younger man became clouded with the storms and thunder of Lear's heath. In Logan's eightieth year a new successor was found. To explain this intermittence of the heart Mr. Gathorne-Hardy adopts a thesis. Logan (who all his life had suffered from a hereditary tendency to manic depression) contracted pneumonia in Iceland which caused him to go mad. This madness persisted in latent form together with a deep resentment against Mr. Gathorne-Hardy for having witnessed the humiliating abdication of reason. In the last year of his life it broke out again and caused him to quarrel with his disciple and also with his sister. These quarrels are narrated at great length. How much of this is accurate? A friend remembers Logan pressing the *Psychology of Insanity* on him many years ago and explaining that there was no real borderline between sanity and madness and that many of us might be mad without knowing it. The manic-depressive psychosis is one of the hardest to certify, since the extent to which mania, i.e., madness, differs from mere euphoria can be assessed only by the manic patient's danger to society. Eccentric, ego-crazy, spoilt, insufferable, Logan often was. All his friends groaned their way through his manic phases to be rewarded by the exquisite thoughtful devotion, the never-failing warmth and charm of his more usual mood. The hurricane died down and the scented trade-winds of his irony and culture and sincerity blew for weeks through St. Leonard's Terrace. But even at the very end of his life no doctor or lawyer who attended on him was prepared to say he was mad, though his behaviour was in the extreme cruel and wayward. Except for Mr. Gathorne-Hardy's account of what the Icelandic doctor told him we are presented with no professional evidence. The manic-depressive cycles ran their course, the depressive phases perhaps lasting longer, the manic ones bringing more aggression and less elation than formerly and the loss of memory and wild hallucinations of advanced age, with some blood-poisoning, all helping to confuse the issue. An old and sick man one would say, but not a mad one. There exist perfectly lucid letters up to within a day or two of his death and there were also moments when the crisis of hatred and malice which he seemed to be going through (Mr. Gathorne-Hardy's theory of diabolic possession seems at times more plausible than his medical one) would abate and the natural character-climate of wisdom and love reappear. After all what position in a life-span of eighty years do the last two or three occupy? Would any of us demand more than a footnote for our 'last and seventh age of Saturn' and not tremble at a full biography of them? 'We are all ruins,' Logan used to say of the group of enchanting people in which he moved, 'Meeting us now you can have no idea of what we were really like.'

It might seem from this account that *Recollections* is an unkind book. This is not the case, there is something happy and golden about the author's temperament which frees his indictment from all malice; his truthfulness, that is to say his determination to tell the truth as he sees it, applies a styptic to the wounds he gives. In the last analysis this is a lover's quarrel —for the two friends were jealous and possessive—and the book is a kind of upside down *De Profundis* in which the young author, with much of Wilde's generous goodness, reproaches the adolescent wickedness of his elderly mentor. Mr. Gathorne-Hardy would rather prove Logan mad than admit that he was fickle and that he might have got bored with him (as he did with his predecessor). But in fact some such conclusion was inevitable because of the dichotomy in Logan's character. Logan was a self-made humanist, a Chinese Epicurus, a Prospero, a Montaigne but he grafted this Latin personality on to a fanatically Puritan stock. His two selves constantly betrayed each other, his college-garden ripe-peach personality encouraged his secretary to live modestly in a country cottage and cultivate his muse but the more he obeyed and sought the *fallentis semita vitae* the more outraged became the underlying Puritan with his raw cult of hard work and success, his loathing of failure and poverty; his ambivalence was complete. Logan's attitude to his apprentice's social status is a case in point for he regarded the English upper class both as the reward of all endeavour and the source of all corruptions. Like all such divided people who possess time, vitality and unlimited curiosity Logan devoured his friends, he ran through them, treating each as a possible cure—for his desire for self-contradictory perfection, and one's friendship with him (after the honeymoon was over), did not really begin till one had been thoroughly dropped—when we would be rediscovered and this time allowances made; our faults now being regarded as an intrinsic and valuable part. The tragedy of the relationship here described is that it was not based on friendship alone but on mutual services and so could not be so easily left to the ebb and flow of Logan's affectivity: the secretary had still to report to his captain on the bridge at stormy moments when all who could find an excuse had deserted. There remains enough material in Logan for several more biographies, his London friends could have compiled an account contemporaneous with this one which would never overlap. But never will there be another which conveys with so much intensity of detail such an extraordinary picture of a remarkable human being. The strange spell-binding quality of Logan's talk which unwrapped itself round his listeners and echoed in their ears for months afterwards like a Balinese gong 'with its peculiar curve and break and flow, its own phrasing and rhythm' is constantly brought out, his crackling jokes, his endearing travelling habits, his grace of heart, his exquisite sympathy, his high sense of honour in friendship (worthy of a noble character in Henry James), all these come out in the conversations and polished affectionate correspondence which illuminate the many years of this singularly happy relationship, from the moment when Logan meets the young author working in a bookshop and finds a spiritual double ('milver' was the word he coined for it) who shared his own passionate interest in the then little-known Jeremy Taylor. 'What a lucky meeting ours was' he wrote ten years later. 'The luckiest thing that ever happened to me' and he certainly would not have altered his opinion after reading this book—for mental anguish and a sense of injustice have extended the author's powers and driven him out of the garden of Epicurus into the jungles of the human heart: the rancour without which this book could not have been conceived falls away as the case is stated and the enormous amount of good is then found to outweigh the bad: after all, it is Death, disease, the human fate which are to blame—not their victim.

> La maladie et la mort font des cendres
> De tout le feu qui pour nous flamboya.

1950

# FAREWELL TO SURREALISM

## I

LOOKING back upon Surrealism—for, although the movement is still active in Paris under its vigorous leader, the momentum decreases, the fissions multiply—we cannot fail to become more and more impressed by the spectacle of what was without question the greatest artistic commotion of the twentieth century and one of the few enlargements of sensibility in the last thirty years which stand to the credit of humanity.

There is a tendency to discuss Surrealism and Cubism as if one proceeds out of the other, but in fact there is no similarity. Cubism was a way of painting which a group of painters imposed on themselves, Surrealism a philosophy of life put forward by a band of poets. The first was essentially a method of breaking up the object and putting it together again according to concepts of pictorial structure, a phase of the greatest importance in the development of such painters as Picasso, Braque, Marcoussis and Gris, but affecting literature only through Apollinaire, and life hardly at all. The second was the attempt of a highly organized group to change life altogether, to make a new kind of man. *Le surréalisme n'est pas une école littéraire ou critique. C'est un état d'esprit. A notre époque, seule l'imagination peut rendre aux hommes menacés le sentiment d'êtres libres.* ('Surrealism is neither a literary school nor a method of criticism. It is a state of mind. In our time, only the imagination can give back to mankind in peril the idea of liberty'—Invitation to the International Surrealist Exhibition in Amsterdam.) So in discussing Surrealism it is necessary to forget terms like Cubist, Fauve, Abstract, Post-Impressionist—which belong to painting, as Symbolist belongs to poetry—and to think of Surrealism as a new interpretation of life, as the name of one of the last and fiercest explosions in our human consciousness which has been detonating since Heraclitus and Galileo. This last combustion, whose effects we are still experiencing, was brought about by a few young poets dreaming of what man ought to be. As Aragon wrote, *It's a question of arriving at a new declaration of the rights of man.*

## II

Why a group? 'Here's the essential thing. A group is the beginning of everything. The isolated individual can do nothing, reach nowhere. A properly directed group can do a great deal and has a good chance of getting results which one man would never be in a position to obtain. You don't realize your own situation. You are all in prison. All you want, if you are in your right mind, is to escape. But how can we escape? We must break through the walls, dig a tunnel. One man can accomplish nothing. But suppose there are ten or twenty and that they all take their turn; by combining together they can finish the tunnel and escape. Besides, no one can escape from the prison without the help of those who have got out already.' (Gurdjiev, quoted by Ouspensky, quoted by the Surrealists.)

## III

In the beginning was the word. The word was 'Dada'. The darkest moments of European wars are strangely propitious to new movements in art. There is an awareness of absolutes, a closing-in on the self; like those pine cones which germinate only in forest fires, the rarest talents are liberated by the deepest despair. Zürich, Swiss capital of German humanism, was the scene in 1916–17 of a strange incubation. Here, while the battle of Verdun was raging, James Joyce was quietly working on *Ulysses*, here collected the war-weary and war-desperate, displaced neutrals or refugees from conscription like the German war-poet Hugo Ball, who opened

in 1916 the *Cabaret Voltaire*. In it congregated Richard
Huelsenbeck, another German poet in exile; Jean Arp, Alsatian
poet, sculptor and painter; Tristan Tzara, a young Rumanian
poet. The fear of extinction which dominated the group led
to a concerted attempt to render ridiculous the powers which
were destroying the world they knew. Choosing the word
'Dada' haphazard from a dictionary (according to the legend),
they baptized their revolt against futility in terms of futility.

The movement had no positive quality but an exhibitionism
of the Absurd; being against 'art' (*Art is rubbish*, wrote
Jacques Vaché in 1918), its only medium was nonsense—the
use of nonsense in public to discredit all forms of sense. This
nihilism suited the angry despair of German intellectuals in
defeat, and Dada groups soon formed in Berlin, Hanover and
Cologne, contributing Baader, Baargeld, Kurt Schwitters,
Max Ernst and many others. Meanwhile a similar trend had
come into the open in New York where Marcel Duchamp from
Paris, Picabia from Barcelona and Man Ray, in their prophetic
discontent, had published the review 291. After the war all these
bands converged on Paris. The greater the ability, the deeper
the disgustability—only thus can we explain the presence of
such pure artists as Ernst, Arp and Schwitters or the three
painters from America in this troupe of destructive harlequins.

In Paris, Tzara and Baargeld, with their sublime Dadaist
effrontery, immediately triumphed; art and life were rejected
as impostures equally vile. The first to rally round the invaders
from the East was a handful of very young poets, just released
from their War service: André Breton, a medical student, and
Louis Aragon, a law student, Paul Eluard, Philippe Soupault,
Benjamin Péret. (Breton himself had been greatly influenced
by an isolated and undeclared Dadaist, Jacques Vaché, who
had just committed suicide.) In 1919 this disillusioned group
had founded the magazine *Littérature*, in 1920 Breton and
Soupault collaborated in *Les Champs Magnétiques* and Max

Ernst gave an exhibition in Paris of his first *collages*, with Breton's introduction. All sought inspiration in three isolated and unfortunate geniuses of the nineteenth century, poets with a contempt for humanity and a deep hatred of 'literature'; Lautréamont, Rimbaud and Jarry. Both the Dadaists and the young French band, however, revered the poet of the *avant-garde* and interpreter of Cubism whose death was so recent, Guillaume Apollinaire.

At first the combination seemed to work smoothly, giving birth to books, magazines, pictures and, above all, to scandal-making public meetings, until towards the end of 1921 a quarrel of capital importance broke out between Breton and Tzara. Breton was fundamentally a poet who wished to facilitate the germination of new beauty from those lofty arts which the necessary whirlwind of Dada had uprooted. Tzara was the destructive showman. 'The true Dadaist is against Dada'— this terrible and logical axiom of Tzara would in the end render all action impossible. The absurd cannot engender even absurdity without some order creeping in. In Dada the pendulum of European vitality had reached the extreme point of its arc, the impetus of defeat and despair had exhausted itself, and now, even as Communism was replacing nihilism, capitalism beginning its recovery, Mussolini marching on Rome, insulin and the tomb of Tutankhamen being discovered, so Breton's party won. Dada abdicated and Surrealism was born.

## IV

Surrealism—out of respect to Apollinaire the word was borrowed from his last play-title—means the reality which lies beyond what we call real. As a former medical student who had treated the shell-shocked, Breton was familiar with Freud and, after the revelation of automatic writing which occasioned his first book with Soupault, it was clear to him that the reality beyond reality (Nerval's 'supernaturalism') was the subconscious mind, the universal truth that underlies all poetry, all imagery, all desire and which Lautréamont and Rimbaud had drawn on inexhaustibly, the truth in reach of all that reason is bribed to deny. The German Dada movement, however, was inclined to Bolshevism and was as susceptible to Marx as were the Surrealists to Freud. The revolutionary element in Surrealism was therefore two-fold: it was a revolt of the psyche, against the authority of reason; it was also an appeal to reason to liberate man from his oppressors—family, church, fatherland, boss. It embraced both Freud and Hegel, the promenade which the iron pot in the fable forces on the uneasy earthenware vessel had already begun.

The early years of the group, before the inner tensions became intolerable, can only be described as magical. The youthful Surrealists possessed talent, courage and charm: they had also experienced a revelation, a glimpse of a dream-dazzled world: 'The marvellous is alway beautiful, anything that is marvellous is beautiful; indeed nothing but the marvellous is beautiful,' wrote Breton. They lived only for these mystic glimpses and for each other; while the group held together, and while it was strong enough to pulverize its enemies, excommunication was a kind of torture. Meeting in large cafés on Montmartre or in the now-demolished Passage de l'Opéra, drinking Mandarin-curaçaos, whiling the afternoons away applauding at films in the wrong places, they would pass the evening in conversation, composition, confession or love, being driven on by an apostolic intoxication of liberty. To a conventional young Englishman they represented the very arcana of Paris, the spirit of insurrection arising from its most sacred flaking quarters, the dark and shabby corners which they loved—the Buttes Chaumont, Musée Grévin, Rue de la Lune—alight with their revolutionary intelligence and gaiety. I remember seeing them all one summer evening in the fun fair of Luna Park, in the blue suits and white knitted ties they affected, gathering like a band of gibbons around 'La Femme Tronc', a legless, armless wonder with a charming face who was seated on a marble pedestal, signing her photographs for them with a pen held in her teeth. The brotherhood seemed to have long given up all recognized means of livelihood and to exist only for the ecstasy of the mystical experience—'eager to discover the formula and the place'.

## V

In this early period the poets dominated the scene. Breton, Aragon, Eluard, Péret, Desnos, Char, Soupault and Crevel—they formed a central committee. Ernst, Miró, Tanguy, Arp, Man Ray, Picabia, were honoured associates but not framers of policy. Books like Breton's *Nadja* or Aragon's *Paysan de Paris* or the poems of Eluard and Péret with their exaltation of wonder and hatred of humanism appeared the supreme expression of the movement. But the painters were steadily gaining in authority. They could reach a wider public and, by the nature of their work, they were less involved in political purges. They were allowed to make a reasonable income from their pictures in a manner which was not permitted to those who sought a living from their articles. As Breton wrote: 'Surrealism requires from its participators that they should observe the utmost purity of mind and life . . . and is less ready than ever to accept departures from this purity which are justified by the obscure and revolting pretext that "one must live".'

The dissensions within the movement sprang from three causes: the attempted Freud-Marx synthesis, the Dada legacy and the economic problem. Although automatic writing had been accepted as the principal literary method of Surrealism, as the secret weapon by which reason was to be overthrown and the poetry of super-reality placed within reach of all, the new vision had certain inconveniences: it became impossible to earn a living by one's books and thus some of the weaker vessels were driven into journalism, for which they were publicly excommunicated. Nor was it a weapon of much efficacy in the class struggle and one or two persistent dreamers like the sleepy Desnos and the gifted Artaud, were viciously expelled as apolitical. As under Dada, the revolution came first and words were only to be used 'to wring the neck of literature'.

While a team of scientific researchers can devote themselves quietly to their pursuit, the Surrealists had inherited from Dada a taste for public manifestation. The group-spirit evolved according to the laws which govern groups: manifestos, excommunications, public penitences, secret betrayals; it was avid for notoriety and sensation and to miss a meeting was to court disaster. The Surrealists were too dynamic to consider the overthrowing of reason by the unconscious as separable from the destruction of bourgeois capitalism (the society which reason had created), they refused to be called parlour revolutionaries whose activities were merely aesthetic, and therefore they handed themselves over to the Communist Party as Marxist shock troops to be employed as it thought best. The automatic writing of the poets was frequently combined with a vicious polemical style, with 'humour' (in the sense of a macabre, cannibal sadistic gaiety) as the common factor of both. *Un Cadavre*, a pamphlet deriding the obsequies of Anatole France (1924), is the first of the 'jokes in bad taste' with which the group achieved notoriety in the name of integrity. The swing to and from Communism left several Surrealists behind when Breton—unable to accept the disciplines of a party-line—veered back towards Trotskyism and the formation of an independent aesthetic and revolutionary movement.

Around 1931, the widely advertised defection of Aragon to the Communists and the entry into film-making of Dali altered the balance of power. The visual arts and the exhibitions connected with them began to attract far more attention to the movement than Breton's search for his precise political position or the spread of automatic writing as 'the communism of genius'. Dali's eventual marriage to Gala, ex-wife of the poet Eluard, seemed a symbolic consecration of the new emphasis.

## VI

The master of Surrealist painting was Max Ernst. This great self-taught artist, with his bold eclectic imagination, passed effortlessly from Dada in Cologne into the Freudian Surrealist pantheon. The doctrines of Breton seemed especially created for him. His *collages*, arrangements of cut-out nineteenth-century illustrations to provoke disquieting, ironical and erotic suggestions were, like so much Surrealist art, essentially literary. They adapted the fantastic children's world of half a century before to the sophisticated wonder-seeker. *La femme cent têtes*, 1929, and *Rêve d'une petite fille*, 1930, are somewhat monotonous, but the *Semaine de Bonté* or, rather, the 'Seven Elements' as it was subtitled, is one of the masterpieces of the movement, a reassembling of lion-headed or bird-faced supermen and their passionate consorts with their adventures 'by flood and field' into a sequence new, beautiful and disturbing —a tragic-strip from the Minotaur's nursery. The romantic nineteenth century was the epoch wherein the Surrealists felt most at home, and Germany the place; in the master from Cologne they possessed a magician who could create around some familiar feature, like the Paris statue of the 'Lion de Belfort', a new mythology of poetry, bloodshed, unrest and nostalgia.

The three great forerunners of Surrealist painting stood in a very different relation. Chirico, whose early work presents a closed world of the imagination, already perfect and passing away, a dream of urban apprehension, a haunted inner city of

squares and statues, of freight trains and grief-stricken colon-
nades in the last second before the explosion, this once most
Surrealist of all painters, before the fact, had begun to trick
and evade, copying ineffectually his old paintings (according
to Breton) and falsifying the dates. He had seen the vision but
was unworthy and soon was drifting into the paranoiac false
classicism of Mussolini. Chagall remained a little too Oriental:
his imagination was like a peasant's fairy-story, marvellous,
certainly, but without the tragic intelligence of the Surrealists.
Picasso, though for a time thoroughly Surrealist, had also been
undeniably Cubist and would soon become—what else? This
giant fish, after reflecting a moment's glory on the Surrealist
anglers, would break the net. It was not painters who were
Surrealist for whom they were looking, but Surrealists who
were painters.

Two more Simon Pures were found in Tanguy and Miró.
Tanguy's world was another closed private garden, an allot-
ment of poisonous plants from remoter planets, landscapes of
which it would be impossible to say that life doesn't exist in
them or to prove that it does. Like many Surrealists, he was
obsessed by perspective and, somewhat constricted in his
handling of paint, original only in the content of his dream.
His world is static, as if he had secret access to an inexhaustible
supply of Mars salad and Venus weed. Miró, unlike the others,
is essentially a pattern-maker, an artist in whom an exquisite
gaiety seems to be always pouring out in an ever-changing
kaleidoscope of shape and colour; he combines the impeccable
taste of abstract painters with an irrepressible Catalan warmth
and audacity. His pottery is the most beautiful of Surrealist
'objects', his bird-happy colours, the yellows and blues of
serenity, pervade all his work.

Arp, the Dadaist wood-cutter, though for long associated
with the Surrealist movement, has strong affinities with abstract art. The group's most typical sculptor is rather the

earlier Giacometti, whose imagination supplied a note of austerity welcome amid the Surrealist flamboyance. His archaic personages are so etiolated by internal conflict as to seem more or less than human; his constructions appear heroic embodiments of frustration, the desire for perfection contrives to bring all his work to a ferocious standstill. His counterpart in painting is undoubtedly Masson, another rugged militant of the arts who has tried to interpret nature with a deep intuition of her violence; through the insect world, whose cruelty is too extreme to leave room for fear or hate, through the giant body whose mountain udders and pubic forests we mortals inhabit, to the cloudy clash of planetary wear-and-tear which we dimly envisage.

## VII

In Masson and Giacometti, Surrealism has discovered two of its most original artists with a revolutionary attitude to their mediums. It is they who supply it with some of the emotional discipline and intellectual tension which were the glory of Cubism and which are lacking in the fretful doodling or weary Pre-Raphaelism of many Surrealist painters. On the other side: perspective-haunted, oil-bound, conservative, even academic in their treatment, though startling in their choice of subject-matter and bold in imagination, are such typical Surrealist painters as Dali, Magritte, Delvaux, Pierre Roy and Leonor Fini.

Magritte, a very early Surrealist, remains a completely literary painter who startles us by the force and universality of his dream symbols, but who gives us little pictorial quality. With Dali we reach the core of the problem: Dali and Aragon, the two geniuses of the movement, were also its two evil geniuses, the right and left deviationists, the one leading on towards salons and *succès de scandale*, Hollywood and shiny-papered fashion magazines; the other into Marxist polemic 'the boring pamphlet and the public meeting', until each reached his perspective goal, an interview with the Pope, and the editorship of a Communist daily. Dali and his fellow-Spaniard, Bunuel, were responsible for two famous Surrealist films, *L'Age d'Or* (in which Max Ernst appeared) and *Un chien Andalou*. Man Ray, whose photography can raise the dead, also contributed *Les Mystères du Château de Dé*, a film built round the ultra-modern villa of the Vicomte de Noailles above Hyères, for this family were the Medici and chief patrons of the movement at the end of the golden age.

In the silent film Surrealism had found an almost perfect medium; Man Ray, the painter and photographer who 'drew in light', as Picasso described his work, made three films of increasing lyrical quality before the crisis of the *Age d'Or*; Dali's *Andalusian Dog*, in spite of some superfluous sadism, has a crystalline intensity that reveals unexplored regions of pure cinema; it becomes something far more moving than even the scenario leads one to expect. *The Golden Age* is less concentrated and suffers from an awareness of the new talking films, which the Surrealists didn't have the funds to produce. It contains more shocking material; erotic, blasphemous or anti-social (i.e. kicking the blind) than any picture ever made, but in spite of being a dithyrambic ode to physical passion, it is too disjointed and amateurish to qualify as great. It is a collection of incidents based on the theme of the world well lost for love, orchestrated by the Marquis de Sade. After the scandal which it caused, the cinematic expression of Dali's celebrated paranoia was compelled to filter down through the Marx brothers, reappearing in a much-watered form in his famous Hollywood dream-sequence for *Spellbound*.

The Surrealist object was also removed by Dali from the region of pure sculpture where Giacometti and Arp were confining it and took on a more ephemeral form, as in the lady's bust enlivened with ants and a necklace of corn-cobs, with Millet's *Angelus* on a loaf of bread as an inkstand-headdress, which appeared, increasingly mildewed, at several international exhibitions before the famous fur tea-set of Mereth Oppenheim took away the spotlight.

Although in theory the Surrealist object was in reach of anyone who chose to put it together, even as poetry was available to all who could hold a pen when half-asleep, it was still the painters who produced the best: the fur-lined tea-set, for instance, is not ridiculous but alarming, for there is something more horrible than one would expect about such an association, tea and cup having a deeply buried Freudian content which the fur brings up to the surface. Dali's red satin sofa, shaped like two closed lips is another uneasy-chair. The suggestiveness of so much Surrealist art, based on liberating the unconscious, takes effect only on the repressed and so it is among the guilty, puritanical and bottled-up society of Anglo-Saxony that these luxurious objects find new victims. The ascendancy of what Breton called Dali's 'master impulse', in 1931–6, brings Surrealism nearer to the big money and the fashionable crowd. Dali's genius, so dazzling in conception, so reactionary in technique, so original yet so meretricious, is baffling even now. His most recent exhibition in Paris contains some spectacular draftsmanship, painting which seems like a triumph of colour photography, and evidence of that inflation of the ego which brings this academic psychopath from the cove of Cadaqués near to Chirico, who signs his recent pictures 'Pintor Maximus'—a conjuror dazzled by his own skill.

## VIII

The later thirties were the period of success abroad and dissension within. International exhibitions flourished and Surrealism was launched in Prague, London, New York and

Teneriffe, but in 1935 the charming René Crevel, *le plus beau des surréalistes*, and also their most intelligible prose-writer, killed himself, *dégoûté de tout*; Breton's political position grew closer to Trotsky's; manifestos multiply; and the frog-march along the razor's edge perceptibly quickens. The war caught the Surrealists without a clear policy; their hatred of 1914–18 had brought them together, their bewilderment in 1939 now led to their dispersal. They remained for a while in Vichy France designing their Tarot pack of cards, and then gradually sought asylum in Mexico or the United States. Hating Hitler, they were threatened by Pétain; international, they detested a nationalist war; artists, they were also pacifists; revolutionaries, they yet lacked a political organization. When Jean Cocteau (the counterfeit Surrealist and private enemy of the movement) was told by a young poet that he was joining the Resistance, he replied: 'You are making a mistake; life is too serious for that' —which may be described as the Surrealists' final attitude.

Their arrival in America may be likened in its consequences to that of the Byzantine scholars in Italy after the fall of Constantinople. From that moment 'the Surrealists' were disbanded but Surrealism began to sow itself spontaneously. Dali in Hollywood, Breton and Masson in New York, Péret in Mexico, Ernst in Arizona, were its wandering apostles—the inevitable luxury magazine, a gelded *Minotaur*, appeared as *Triple V*; the Daliesque objects spread to fun-fairs and shop-windows; *Dyn*, edited by Paalen, appeared in Mexico City; Wilfredo Lam, Matta and Gorky and the Caribbean poet Aimé Césaire were acclaimed by Breton. When the exiles returned to Paris, where reason had been re-enthroned by Sartre, they had left behind what was worst in Surrealism—a flourishing commercial formula beloved of window-dressers or a façade for rich complex lightweights, for few, alas, were the disciples who had understood the astonishing galaxy of ideas which Breton had all his life so harmoniously assembled and

so passionately, if obscurely, expounded—his home-made
revolution: '*Changez la vie!*'

## IX

For we cannot bid farewell to Surrealism without a formal
tribute to its founder. This much-loved, much-hated and
therefore enigmatic figure, has accomplished far more than
Apollinaire; he has formed and led his group of writers and
artists instead of merely interpreting them; his distinguished
bull-like appearance, as of a serious Oscar Wilde, with some
of Wilde's dignity and benevolence and none of his vulgarity,
reflects a strange mixture of qualities, the ability to lead, inspire,
deceive and threaten, to criticize and create, to love and command both jealous rivals and the envious young. His own
writing, with its seventeenth-century fulness, at its best in
*Nadja* (that hymn to Hazard) or in the valuable art criticism
of *Les Pas Perdus* rather than when married to the welling,
inexhaustible fountain of Eluard's poetry, achieves (as in his
description of the peak of Teneriffe) an extraordinary vigour.
Condemned by the logic of the times to lead his flock along
the *arête* between militant Marxism and introverted lunacy,
this reason-hating intellectual brought safely over as many as
he could. Besides Eluard, Aragon, Péret, Crevel, Hugnet and
Gracq, one must admire his influence on many ex-Surrealists,
such as Paulhan, Pongé, Prévert, Queneau and Leiris, who are
well known today. His passion for art not only gave painters
the feeling that their ideas were important, but inclined him
towards those who were truly original rather than to the fashionable antiquarians, while he was quick to discover the Surrealist
content of much primitive and popular art.

Without the Surrealist movement, 'surrealism' might still
have come into being; the unconscious would have found other
aesthetic interpreters, but under Breton's guidance the synthesis between Freud and Marx was attempted many years in

advance, as a parachuted battalion can attack an objective weeks ahead of schedule. A share of the faults of totalitarian leaders was not lacking, but seldom has one man's intellectual honesty, courage and passion for beauty enriched us more. Always with the Surrealists, in spite of their lapses into vulgar mystification, spiteful pettiness, or Freudian cliché, one is conscious of the dedicated life; of the whole conception of *bourgeois* living being utterly rejected for the sake of a mystical idea—*le merveilleux*: 'Neither a school nor a clique, much more than an attitude, Surrealism is, in the most complete and aggressive sense of the term, an adventure', proclaims a manifesto of May 1951, an adventure which has not recoiled from madness and suicide in the search for inspiration, for the vision which is not always compatible with art, which may destroy art and literature and sometimes life itself. If Surrealism is to perish, it will be because the world we live in renders ineffectual the private rebellion of the individual and because the symbols and battle-cries of the Unconscious—Sade, Ubu, Maldoror, Oedipus—awake no answering revolt in a generation which finds its predicament too serious even for Surrealism!

They were, perhaps, the last Romantics. Despite the shapeless obscurity of so much of their writing, despite their rejection of the advances made by Impressionism, Fauvism and Cubism for 'the rehabilitation of academic art under a new literary disguise' (as the critic Clement Greenberg has written), the world of literature and art would be—and, in fact, is— the flatter and feebler without them. They have restored to man, love-child of fatality and chance, his belief in a destiny; they have given woman back her pride and her magic; they have handed the imagery of the unconscious over to poetry and returned freedom of subject to painting, imprisoned by its own rules. To the question 'What does that picture represent?' the Surrealists make answer: 'The person who did it'.

1951

# BORDEAUX–DORDOGNE

## BORDEAUX

BORDEAUX, the fourth city of France, and once, after London, York and Winchester, of England, is no place for the sightseer; it is a climate, a rest-cure, a state of mind whose principal charm is that there is nothing to see. The Palais Gallien is the dimmest of Roman ruins, the cathedral just gets by, the churches, gates and towers, except for a collection of mummified human remains, are quite without interest, while the architecture of the eighteenth century, for which it is famous, is so discreet or so damaged that one is hardly conscious of the golden age except as an atmosphere.

A great yellow river crossed by a long and lovely red-brick bridge (1810) sweeps in a semi-circle past lines of dignified *quais*. The focal point of these *quais* is the Place de la Bourse, which resembled a corner of the Place Vendôme, until a British bomb fell on it. Then comes the Quinconces, an enormous open square which is either very dull and empty or enclosed for a noisy industrial fair, and the picturesque docks. A little way into the town from the river is the true heart of the city, the holy place which is in the form of an equilateral triangle from whose apex a circle is suspended.

Contemplate this circle within the triangle for a few moments. For a stay of inside a week it should not be necessary to leave this area; it contains all that one could wish for, and those who demand more and break the magic bounds will, it is rumoured, nearly all meet with misfortune.

The sides of the triangle are three streets laid out by the Marquis de Tourny, *intendant* or governor of Bordeaux in the reign of Louis XV. At point A is the Place Gambetta, a charming and unspoilt two-storied square of the period, with a magnolia garden in the centre. From A to B is the Cours de

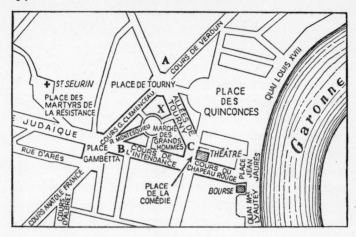

l'Intendance, the principal shopping street. At point B is the
Place de la Comédie, with its theatre, the most beautiful building of the city (1773–80) and one of the loveliest theatres in the
world in the purest classic of Louis Seize. Opposite is the
Café de Bordeaux, the pleasantest in the town (restaurant
ruined by fluorescent lighting), where one should sit in the
evening to enjoy the green sunset.

From B to C runs a wide esplanade or narrow piazza, the
pleasure promenade of the Allées de Tourny (1744), delicious
in the evenings when the theatre is floodlit. At point C is the
circular Place de Tourny, somewhat spoilt but including a
charming bar and night-club (when not too crowded), the
Palm Beach, whose salons, with their 'Empire' *boiseries*, over-
look the Allées de Tourny, and round off the evening. (As it
is forbidden to serve food after midnight, a wild night-out in
Bordeaux will usually end with a visit to a speakeasy where
*soupe à l'oignon* is consumed in the strictest secrecy.) From C
to A is the Cours Georges Clemenceau which completes the
design of the Marquis de Tourny for a shopping street, a
promenade, and a boulevard.

Now for X, the magic circle, the holy of holies. This is the Marché des Grands Hommes, a covered market approached by four little streets, the Rues Montesquieu, Voltaire, Montaigne, Buffon, which are a perpetual feast for the eye. Here in the market, surrounded by great names, is the evidence of the delicious soil, sea, and climate of Bordeaux, often sultry in summer, sometimes raw and humid in winter, but as near perfection as a temperate maritime climate can be: *ver longum, brumaeque breves*. It is southern England removed to the furthest point south at which it would remain both green and industrious. (Mean monthly temperatures of over seventy in summer or below forty in winter bespeak a different climate. Bordeaux—a drier, harsher version of Biarritz—is our own south coast but riper.)

Pyramids of Dublin Bay prawns, lobsters, *langoustes*, cod, sole and skate vie in the market with more unusual fish: lamprey, sturgeon, huge red *chapons* and enormous shad. Salt-marsh mutton, butter, cheese, ortolans and *palombes* from the Landes lead us on to the fruit and vegetable section, as fine as anywhere in the world; nectarines and muscat grapes in autumn, melons of all kinds in summer; asparagus, wild strawberries, cherries, peaches, gourds—and, in savoury stacks, the colour of Havana cigars, the *cêpes bordelaises*, glorious fungi like giant Bath buns which, when fried in oil with garlic, form the perfect link between Pauillac lamb and Gruyère cheese while a dynasty of clarets is being accommodated.

The line joining point A to the circle is the Rue Montesquieu, and here is the Hôtel Montré, which still preserves the atmosphere and Empire furniture of the great days of the European coaching inn. Henry James might well be in room 19, with its red and gold salon, writing a story about the uneasy American family next door. Opposite is the Chapon Fin. *Reverentia!*

This restaurant has the best wine list in existence for those who consider claret superior to Burgundy and brandy preferable to *alcools blancs*. It has a light, dry Château Olivier which is a perfect white wine for the fish; afterwards we can matriculate at will among the older bottles, half-bottles and magnums before we finish up with a tawny but flawless Yquem and an historic *fine maison*. The food is delectable in its simplicity; a plate of *haricots verts* is a meal in itself; eggs, fish, meat and fruit are all impeccable.

The restaurant is built in the grotto style which was fashionable in Bordeaux around 1900, and which is found in fish-stalls along the *quais* and in the amazing *art nouveau* gardens on the road to Macau. It is large, cool, quiet and comfortable and seats the full French cabinet in times of crisis. M. Sicart has managed it for fifty years, and the old wine-waiter, as expert as anyone in these matters can hope to be, has presided for nearly as long. The hotel is very pleasant, the rooms somewhat noisy. At the other end of the triangle, on the Allées de Tourny, is Dubern's, the rival establishment, a luxury grocery and wine-merchant whose window display is a combination of the best from the market with caviare and *foie gras* as seen at Fortnum's before the last war. Upstairs are two or three small panelled rooms in which excellent meals are served. The fashion is now to prefer this restaurant to the Chapon Fin; it is indeed a serious rival, but the one is unique, sole survivor from the age of Foyot and Voisin's, the other an engaging upstart.

Within the triangle in a sombre little square there is also the church of Notre-Dame, in the Jesuit style of the end of the seventeenth century, and a feeble museum of antiquities. There is a good bookshop in the Place Gambetta and an *antiquaire* in the Place de Tourny.

After two days in Bordeaux one becomes conscious of a liver: at best we are sluggish and irritable, at worst bilious and

racked with headache. This silent critic of our pleasures will
have to be placated. Exercise must be taken, luncheons cut
down. We were able to begin by a visit to this year's admirable
Goya exhibition, testimony to the vision of Bordeaux's vigorous young Mayor and member of Parliament, M. Chaban-
Delmas, ex-general of the Resistance and international Rugby
player, then on to the public garden, another creation of M. de
Tourny, full of lovely southern trees and romantic charm. A
longer walk may be taken to the town hall, cathedral and
picture gallery, and back via the *quais* and bridge. The river is
always soothing, and little boats take one over to Lormont,
where the country begins, and there is usually a breeze. Just
off the Place de Tourny is the terminal bus station, and here
buses radiate in all directions: an ideal regime, we found, is
to take a bus every morning and return to dine at the Chapon
Fin, Dubern's or the Château Trompette every night. Here
are some of the most pleasant excursions:

1. South-east down the Garonne to Labrède, where the
Château of Montesquieu can be visited, a moated castle in
which the noble author's mid-eighteenth century study and bed-
room are preserved intact. From Langon one can go south to the
Sauternes country, to Bazas with its unrestored cathedral and
then seek out the chain of churches and castles associated
with the *bordelais* Pope, Clement VII (fl. 1300). Cadillac, St.
Macaire and La Réole are interesting places along the river,
before vines give place to tobacco as we approach Agen.

2. Due east, along the Dordogne, stands Libourne, with its
reminders of the English occupation, and St. Emilion, a
sparkling southern hill-village full of Romanesque churches
and crypts, the best antiquarian value of the whole neighbour-
hood, and Vélines whence Montaigne's château can be visited,
with the painted tower where this most modern of all ancient
writers had his library. An evening autorail goes right up the

Dordogne to Bergerac, Souillac and eventually the mountains of Aurillac. The Dordogne is a far more beautiful river than the Garonne, despite the latter's villages and vineyards, but becomes spectacular only above Lalinde, at a considerable distance from our base.

3. North up the estuary of the Gironde, here a noble stream like the Mississippi at New Orleans, lie Bourg and Blaye, both charming places, and Jonzac, Pons and Saintes which are remarkable indeed: silver Romanesque cities, far more southern than anywhere between Bordeaux and Biarritz, and unpolluted by the general stream of tourist traffic. It is a country, towards Angoulême, of bright limestone hills and precious twelfth-century churches. Royan, on the coast, was almost blown to pieces in the last war, but Talmont, a white village islanded on the estuary, repays a visit.

4. North-west to the claret country. The journey to the vineyards of the Médoc is indispensable, but if several vineyards are to be visited it must be undertaken by car, and introductions provided by a wine-merchant will be necessary.

We shall take as an example a visit to Mouton, one of the best-managed and most welcoming of vineyards, whose wines, relatively heavy for the Médoc, have a certain bull-like grace and solidity. '*Ça fait très Mouton*,' as they say of some particularly noble specimen.

As a region, the Médoc illustrates all the subtlety of the Bordeaux climate. Until the seventeenth century it was unreclaimed marsh, and compared to the great names of Saint Emilion, whose wines were prized by Ausonius, its châteaux seem absurdly *nouveau riche*. The vine-ripening belt is a narrow strip running north-northwest; on one side lie the salt marshes and the brown estuary, on the other the sandy Landes with their commons and pine-forest. Between the sand and the mud runs the magic vein of stony soil. The flints, the light earth, the rainy spring, the hot blue summer and the lingering autumn have all contributed to this perfection of the grape: fruit of sunny sea-wind radiance, of Dutch polders silver-gilt by the warmth of the Midi. To understand the Médoc is to begin to love Bordeaux, to which it forms a companion-piece.

Flat, bright, dusty—subject to sudden storms and lowering clouds which as suddenly clear—the plain, between the tidal water and the dark belt of forest, is peppered with sacred names: Latour, Lafite, Margaux, Cantenac; each vineyard marked out by an army of knotted green bushes whose powdery clusters dangle among the pebbles, whose wine gives out the most delicate of civilized aromas; fragrant, light and cavernous as myrtle-berries from an Etruscan tomb, the incomparable *bouquet du vieux Médoc*, offspring of sunshine and hard work, parent of warmth, wit, and understanding.

The châteaux are strung out irregularly along the strip. Two at all costs must be seen, Beychevelle and Margaux. They are the loveliest of the region, the one Louis Quinze (1753), the other Louis Seize. As befits the age of Adam, Margaux is the statelier pile, while Beychevelle is lower and more rambling, with a garden pavilion to each wing and fine wrought-iron gates. Classical perfection or rococo charm? We must examine both from as near at hand as impertinence will take us and then forever take our stand. Other enchanting neighbours are Issan, with its moat, the British-owned Léoville-Barton, with its cypress, and the eighteenth-century tower of Château Latour, stoniest of all vineyards, most perfect of all wines.

Mouton seems more like a pleasant English villa—until we enter the group of low buildings across the courtyard. The first room, which one might call an ante-chapel, contains old prints, decanters, documents and statues likely to induce a mood of reverence: vestry would be a better term for it, the robing-room of Bacchus. Great doors silently open and we look across an enormous low nave with the heraldic sheep of

Mouton emblazoned on the far wall over the pew-like rows of
silent barrels in which the new wine rests for three years, before being bottled, numbered, labelled and sent out to the
world on its goodwill mission.

We walk down the nave to its far end, rinse our mouths with
the sharp new wine and, lighting our pious candles, descend
to the crypt. Here stand the enormous vats in which the newly
pressed wine ferments before being stored in barrels, each vat
as big as a Nissen hut, with the temperature-chart and case-
history of its tumultuous inmate pinned up outside. Here also
is an electric wind-machine which will dry grapes gathered in
wet weather; and at the end of the crypt, in greater darkness,
heavy iron doors which lead to the catacombs, the long dry cellars
where the bottles themselves mature in their cobwebby cages.

A vista of shiny black disks recedes before us, the bottled vin-
tages of the last few years, then come the years we covet most, the
*reserve de Monsieur le Baron* and lastly the 'museum' of rare and
ancient wines from this and neighbouring properties, where
fabulous bottles, too precious to drink, may peacefully end
their days like kings in the Escurial. ' *Ça fait très Mouton.*'

At last we must climb back from catacombs to crypt, crypt
to cathedral, cathedral to vestry to visit the winepresses themselves, where the grapes are poured in by the pickers, then
sifted and trodden by labourers with wooden rakes and
paddles who shuffle round to the music of a fiddle. M. Marjory,
the enchanting manager, will imitate the motions for us as a
special favour. This age-old sifting of the grape and pressing
of the wine (before it flows into the huge vats below) is per-
formed by human hands, or rather feet, and wooden imple-
ments. More complicated modern machinery has been tried
and found wanting, and the process illustrates the archaic and
dedicated life of the great vineyards, where quantity is sacrificed to quality and where the munificent owners sometimes
prefer to carry on the business at a loss rather than lower the

standard or destroy the tradition to suit the declining taste and coarsening palate of our frantic epoch.

It is always hard to keep awake at Mouton; the sea-air, the sun, the wines (decanted and served again from their own bottles) and the simple but outrageous perfection of the cooking—*risotto aux truffes, gigot de pré salé*—deal one knock-out blow after another—or I would recommend a prolonged stay in the district to all painters and writers. But the region is anti-art and the villages lack the Romanesque beauties and pastoral surroundings of those across the estuary. Tennis, hospitality and big business occupy the claret-kings, with their American cars and English nicknames, and there are few walks and fewer books in the artificial landscape. Fleecy clouds drift across the high blue sky, slow carts with spraying machines pass between the squat regiments of vines, 'ole man liver' rumbles a warning against *galanteries vinicoles*; it is time to go.

South-west of Bordeaux lies its principal pleasure-ground, the Basin of Arcachon, an inland sea like a glorified Poole Harbour, ideal for yachting, safe for children, famous for oysters, cool in summer, mild in winter, surrounded by undulating pine-forests with a back-cloth of arbutus. A mile or two down the coast, where the Basin joins the Atlantic, stretch the beaches of Le Moulleau and Le Pyla, each with an hotel, and beyond them the Dune de Pilat, the highest in Europe.

The view from this dune is one of the loveliest that I know. The white sand runs for several miles in a steep hog's back; on one side it descends to the Atlantic in a long deserted beach, on the other to the pine forest which extends without a break or a building to the limit of the horizon. To the north the violet waters of the Basin and its sea-channel wind before us. The woods come right down to the argent shore and hardly a villa is to be seen, only the curving sand and the green pine-trees. It might be some vast inlet of the Carolinas as viewed by the first explorers.

It will have taken us about ten days to visit Arcachon, the Médoc, the Sauternes, the lower Dordogne and the Gironde, returning to Bordeaux, if we choose, every evening. After ten days the traveller may have seen enough and may even depart complaining that Guyenne is not nearly so interesting as Provence or the Pays Basque. But he will never be cured of it. Months later, generally at the beginning of March or by the middle of September, the bridges across the Dordogne at Libourne or Saint André de Cubzac will rise before his inner eye. If he is in Spain the image of the old wine waiter at the Chapon Fin, with his brown face and twinkling eye, will appear in a dream, he will just distinguish the words '*Prenez le Dix-huit, c'est plus léger*' before awaking to his sultry flagon of Rioja or Valdepeñas. If he be in the mountains he will suddenly envisage the delicious flatness of *Entre deux mers*, the land of the two rivers, he will remember the rose-red arches of Napoleon's bridge stemming the yellow eddies, the sober *quais* with their *mascarons*—carved faces, all different—above each doorway. If we are in the South of France it will be the waters of Arcachon we covet, cool and tidal, its unspoilt beaches and the nights without mosquitoes, the south-west wind—and if we are in London it will be something of them all, with the limestone greys of Saint Emilion, the tall magnolias of the public garden, the evening patina of the Place de la Comédie and the pale clear sunshine of the Médoc.

For when we say there is nothing to see at Bordeaux we mean that there is everything to feel, if we would enjoy the sensuous atmosphere of this Bristol three hundred and fifty miles south, an atmosphere witty, inquiring, earthy, a little complacent and provincial, the climate of eighteenth-century philosophers like Montesquieu, of its wise mayor who gave Shakespeare the idea for *The Tempest*, Michel de Montaigne, or of its last Roman Governor whose vineyard at Saint Emilion is still famous as Château Ausone and who celebrated in one

of his most charming poems the air of his native city, that
green and yellow harmony of the South West, the climate of
humanism. 1951

## THE DORDOGNE

THE Dordogne is exactly 300 miles long, which puts it into
the second rank among French rivers; no town of any size,
except Bergerac, lies on its banks; it does not even reach the
sea. Yet year by year it grows in prestige and when people say
they are going to the Dordogne (and they never say they are
going to the Garonne or the Seine or the Loire) they mean
something which the words do not express and which is intelligible only to those who have already taken the cure—for that
is what the visit is.

What is the essential quality of this 'Dordogne'? It means
a certain climate, a certain relationship between man and
nature, a special blend of landscape and architecture, which,
taken together, form a complete and self-dependent little
world somehow different in time from our own and exercising
an extraordinarily soothing effect on all who stay there more
than a week. The climate is peculiar to the south-western
slopes of the Massif Central which are influenced by the
Atlantic. The winters are not very cold, the springs and
autumns are dry and sunny, the summers wet and thundery.
The plateaux are bleak but the long river valleys, Dordogne,
Lot, Vézère, Isle, are soft and balmy. Mediterranean ever-
greens bloom on the cliffs of Les Eyzies while the Basins of
Brive, of Beaulieu and Souillac enjoy the same climate as Pau.
Early vegetables and delicious fruit thrive round Brive. The
plateaux are covered with oak copses, rich in truffles; in the
valleys maize, walnuts, tobacco, vines spread out. The vegetation is northern; the air and light are of the south. Oxen are
in general use and if we replace the cypress by the poplar

we receive an impression of Tuscany which accounts for the epithet 'Vergilian' which is sometimes applied.

Each river has certain characteristics: the Lot is wild and lonely, the Vézère seems consecrated to prehistory, the Isle, which passes through Périgueux, is quiet and placid. The Dordogne alone combines a noble grace and austerity with a civilized overtone of feudal castles and Romanesque churches. If one were to sum up its appeal, especially to English visitors, one would be tempted to ascribe it to a quality of remembered childhood. If we go for a walk anywhere along the Dordogne we find everything is English—the flowers, the trees, the fields, the hedges—but multiplied to a vast size and enriched by the southern light with a kind of radiance. Things look as when we first saw them and recall by their luxuriance the indelible sensation of the turf round Corfe Castle or the heather at Oban when for the first time we apprehended them with wonder. Summer showers pelt down but never create a sensation of darkness: the vast landscape stretches out in its lowering greens broken by the white cliffs along the river, the brown of a castle—and suddenly the sun reappears. The turf is warm and springy, steam rises from the wild quinces along the hedges, the enormous blackberries glisten, the lemon-yellow walnut-trees or dazzling chestnuts shake themselves, the geese go back into single file, the rainbow forms across the Cirque de Montvalent; the deluge is over.

The villages are among the most beautiful in the world: the pointed roofs are covered with round grey tiles, the walls are of unhewn stones, there is a profusion of small towers and dove-cotes, of rough stone steps leading up to lofts, and tall vines cover every door. The castles of the Dordogne are on a gigantic scale but every village boasts a small manor or *gentil-hommière* (they are graded according to whether they have four towers or two towers or one) which fits perfectly into the landscape, like the little Romanesque church with its carved porch and ruined cloister. These small manors seem the ideal retreat for the present time and it is a pleasant day-dream to search for one's favourite—Autoire, St. Sozy, Salignac, Terregaie or the magnificent Latreyne.

The Dordogne rises high in the Puy de Sancy and for many miles remains a mountain river flowing through sombre gorges and newly made lakes. From Argentat to Beaulieu there is a road along it for twenty-five kilometres; this stretch is very little known and most beautiful. At Beaulieu civilization begins, there is a good hotel and a wonderful Romanesque church and portico. Five miles further on, near Bretenoux, is the first of the enormous castles, a triangular block of red masonry with a stupendous view and a series of rooms 'restored' by a retired tenor from the Paris opera. Two miles south is the most beautiful of all the Renaissance buildings of the Dordogne, the Château de Montal, which M. Fenaille almost put back into its original state, recovering its carved chimney-pieces and dormers from all over the world. Only the South Kensington museum has refused to disgorge its *lucarne*. The frieze in the courtyard with the old family motto for the son who never came back from the war in Italy, '*Plus d'espoir*', is exquisite. From here a road runs up through the lovely village of Autoire to the Causse, the scrubby plateau which conceals the *bondieuseries* of Rocamadour and the preposterous Gouffre de Padirac with its chilly underground river. The Causse de Gramat with its snakes and pot-holes forms a southern rampart to the ravishing valley of the Dordogne which now enters its most beautiful reaches. There is a road along the left bank to Carennac where the hotel is part of an old monastery in which Fénelon wrote some of his *Télémaque*, making golden apples of the quinces on 'Calypso's Island' below in the river. Carennac is the sunniest and loveliest of all the Dordogne villages. The road continues through the walnut orchards over high ground and one can walk to the edge of the cliffs which

overhang the river and look down on the landscape of Claude
and Poussin. After Floirac we cross over and take a cobbled
lane which runs from Gluges, with its underground church,
to Creysse. We are now in the Cirque de Montvalent, an
amphitheatre of rock through which the river meanders; the
road goes under the cliff through woodland with endless
glimpses of broken water and sandy beaches. Creysse, by its
variegated stone-colours and its church, is a water-bound
rival to Carennac. From here one can go straight to Souillac
or else follow the river by Meyronne and Lacave and the
Louis XIII Château de Latreyne, rising out of the water, to
Pinsac and Souillac.

Souillac is the capital of the upper Dordogne; it is on the
main line from north to south, possesses a first-class hotel and
two good cafés. The church has a statue of Isaiah which is one
of the most graceful, even dandified triumphs of the Romanesque. Souillac is the only small town of the region to make an
appeal to the mind. The *Syndicat d'Initiative* is in the charge
of M. Pierre Betz who edits from Souillac his art magazine *Le
Point*. M. Couderc's hotel used to be a favourite of writers and
painters (though now swamped by charabancs in the high
season) and many Paris intellectuals, who made the district
their headquarters during the Resistance, return for holidays.
Souillac is the best centre from which to explore the region,
not only of the Dordogne, but of the surrounding Causses.
Martel with its towers is the most interesting of the neighbouring towns and a few miles to the north, in the direction of
Brive and Tulle, is an area of hill and forest, the Massif de
Meyssac, which has an appeal of its own. The soil is red
sandstone, the bracing uplands are covered with heather and
enormous chestnuts, the villages unspoilt, the views superb.
The rich earth has none of the gloomy aridity of the Causses,
and Collonges, where the vines make arbours of every rose-
red house, is full of those bargains in masonry which tempt one

to settle. Brive is worth a visit, if only for its admirable train services; there are expresses to Bordeaux, Paris, Barcelona, Milan, and it has a good bookshop. In the last two years new hotels have been opened south of Souillac in two old country-houses set in wild country and enormous parks, one near Gramat and one outside Cahors. Both these can be reached from Souillac by the main line and may help those travellers who wish to get away from the bustle of Souillac in summer where the hotels have never recovered from '*l'article*'—as they call an enthusiastic description of their beauties which appeared simultaneously in the French and American *Vogue*.

Below Souillac the Dordogne becomes more public and for the rest of its course is kept company by the railway. As the hills dwindle and the valley widens, the castles grow more and more magnificent until we reach a stretch between Domme and Beynac which can compare in beauty and interest with the Rhine and the Loire. Domme is one of those rectangular thirteenth-century *bastides* which shows the English influence of the Hundred Years' War; it is built on a cliff some 500 feet above the river and enjoys one of the most beautiful prospects in the world. Below, on the river-level, is the village of La Roque-Gageac which some consider to be the loveliest in France. At Beynac, a little lower down, is a good inn and two of the finest castles on the river. The Château de Beynac, of the thirteenth, fourteenth and sixteenth centuries, is restored and sumptuously kept up. The view from its ramparts, if we can gain admission, embraces another château, Fayrac. Across the Dordogne is the ruined stronghold of Castelnaud whose construction was completed by the English, who added the dungeon. Many of the Dordogne castles are difficult of access but the ruins of Castelnaud are like some English feudal beauty-spot; the wild thyme and valerian grow over the walls and the pomegranate flowers in the courtyard. Even without its view it is one of the most romantic corners on the whole river and its white battlements and crumbling arches are for ever safe from the rich owner in Paris and the careful restorer.

The centre for this part is Sarlat, a pleasant sleepy little town renowned for its truffles and its medieval architecture. Here lives the bookseller made famous as a symbol of French culture by Henry Miller in his *Colossus of Maroussi*. The Vézère enters the Dordogne near Le Bugue and the combined rivers flow through the Périgord Noir with its sandy tracks and pinewoods to Bergerac and prosperity; but from Sarlat a road cuts across to the Vézère at Les Eyzies. The prehistoric cave-drawings are disappointing after the new discoveries higher up at Montignac, but the situation is more beautiful and there is a particular charm about the nineteenth-century civilization which grew up round the caves; the wistaria-hung hotels, with their comfortable sitting-rooms, have something of the atmosphere of Olympia and Delphi. There is no space to go into the mysteries of prehistory, we can only say that the warm sheltered valley with its low bluffs and easily tunnelled rock must have had some special appeal for a vanished race of artists and hunters. The caves at Lascaux, near Montignac, are one of the wonders of the world. The recently discovered paintings have a scope and freshness that make one proud to belong to a species which so many thousand years ago was able to create this pictorial magic. Lascaux is the Parthenon of prehistory: the valley of the Vézère is the foundation of humanism, a landscape where the work of man is like a mineral flower on the tunnelled rock, as exciting and beautiful as the stalagmites and stalactites of Lacave and Padirac are monotonous and unfriendly. To all who have not quite given up hope for mankind this is holy ground. So accomplished are the paintings of this race which was suddenly to vanish, so peculiar are the sites chosen for them, that one wonders if the valley of the Vézère was not a site specially allotted to an élite, like the castles where Hitler perfected his future *gauleiters*. If the paintings, as many think, formed part of magical rites which conferred on the huntsmen particular powers over animals, their inaccessibility might itself have been a test of prowess.

The people of the Dordogne are nearly all peasants, they do not emigrate like the Auvergnats but remain on the land; they are sober, honest and hard-working nor have they yet been much affected by the spread of tourism or by contact with the foreigner. The whole region was one of the fairest provinces of the old feudalism of the Languedoc and contact with the north has not benefited it. The English or rather the Anglo-Normans brought the ravages of the Hundred Years' War whose vestiges remain in ruined castles and regular bastides; the Albigensian Crusade enabled the northern French to sack all the treasures of the castles where troubadours and courts of love had flourished. There is little architecture of the Renaissance, of the seventeenth and eighteenth centuries; great families like the Turennes and Noailles moved north and built elsewhere. The whole of this 'other château country' would have fallen into decay were it not for a movement back to the great castles with their wonderful outlooks which arose among the rich world of nineteenth-century Paris in search of summer enchantment. It is to Parisians that we owe the saving of so many fine buildings, like Bretenoux and Montal. If exchange restrictions are ever lifted, there remain any amount of delicious, if ramshackle, small houses to be acquired for a thousand pounds or two where writers, painters, retired people or refugees from our climate can enjoy a warmer version of English rural life in fertile surroundings. The cost of living is much lower here than in the south of France, the Pays Basque or the coastal regions. Everything grows here and ripens but the cooking is apt to be monotonous. There are all the dishes with truffles as an ingredient, but one gets tired of goose and chicken, and the spectacular *lièvre à la royale* is hard to come by. Sea-food is sadly lacking and one must remember that the

higher Dordogne, under the patronage of Fénelon, whose
château is midway between Sarlat and Souillac, is, apart from
the valley, an austere and infertile region, very different from
the lower river, with its *primeurs* and vineyards, its shad and
salmon, whose presiding genius is Montaigne.

The most interesting city of the department is certainly
Périgueux, which adds Byzantinism and Roman remains to
the riches of the province. It has a château-country of its own
to the north, with Brantôme and Bourdeilles, in the delicious
valley of the Dronne, as members by courtesy of the Dordogne
fraternity. But somehow it is to Beynac, Souillac or Les
Eyzies that one is constantly returning, the evening autorail
from Bordeaux or the *rapide* from Paris deposit one at the high
station of Souillac and soon we are wandering under the planes
in the main street, inspecting the two rival cafés and M.
Couderc's tables opposite, surrounded by geraniums and
oleanders in tubs. One English novelist has left, we hear with
relief. Some Americans have arrived *depuis l'article*; it is not
too hot and not too cold, there is still some of the old *eau de vie
de prunes*, not too sweet, tomorrow we shall walk along the
river, not too far, there is a one-towered farm to let at Meyronne, not too dear. 'How shall I find words to describe my
pleasure in this countryside,' wrote Delacroix a hundred years
ago, from the Château de Croze. 'It is a mixture of all the
sensations that are lovely and pleasant to our hearts and
imaginations.'

# THE ELEGIAC TEMPERAMENT

ONE of the unsolved mysteries of poetry is the life-cycle of its various forms. In our time we have seen the sonnet and the iambic blank verse line totter and possibly fall: the last century watched the heroic couplet get into difficulties and suddenly fade away. Two facts seem to have some bearing on what happens. A great poet can exhaust the possibilities of the metre which he chooses; one age may find one metre appropriate to it which a succeeding age will reject. The blank verse iambic and the sonnet belong to all periods, but Milton, Keats, Wordsworth, Tennyson, may be said to have pre-empted them from less talented aspirants; the heroic couplet is a metre suited to the temper of the eighteenth century only to be rejected by the nineteenth.

But the lifetime of such metres has been but three or four hundred years, a mere fraction of the life of the hexameter from Homer to Claudian or of the elegiac couplet, longest-lived of them all. Sixteen hundred years divide the Greek couplet of Mimnermus from Cometas and the same huge span links the first Latin elegiacs of Catullus with the spate of his imitators in the Italian renaissance. The hexameter may well be the 'stateliest measure ever moulded by the lips of man'; the couplet has proved the more enduring. Often have I fancied, though this kind of statement can never possibly be proved, that the rise and fall of the elegiac couplet bears some relation to the waves breaking on the Greek islands with the retreating backwash that follows. 'The surge and thunder of the Odyssey' has been celebrated—what of the less positive assertion and milder withdrawal of the Mediterranean sea? It is not impossible that listening to this eternal susurrus awoke in these island peoples an instinctive poetry of flux and reflux expressed in the alternation of the long and sonorous with the short and melodious line. *Litore sic tacito sonitus rarescit harenae*—'so on the quiet shore does the sound of the wave-swept sand grow fainter'. Certainly a preponderating quantity of all elegiac poetry has been about the sea. The cruel and calm rhythms of the great mother, so vivid in the many Greek epigrams on seafaring, on headland shrines and drowned sailors, provide an immense stock of metaphor even where the subjects are largely pastoral or amorous in content.

I believe that the elegiac metre is unique in this, that alone of all verse forms it has produced a certain character-type. When we compare the true masters of elegiac poetry, leaving out those who employed the form only for epigrams, we find distinct resemblances between Theognis and Mimnermus in Greek, Tibullus, Propertius and Ovid in Latin, or Meleager, the Syro-Greek who immediately preceded them. All these poets consider physical love as the particular end of their existence and the majority have proclaimed their creed defiantly. Literary fame comes a close second, a fame which is achieved through a mixture of love and learning. All in addition suffer from profound melancholy and nostalgia. Many profess an inclination for the simple pastoral life (and an aversion to the military) though generally they spend their time in Rome. They are unhappy in their love affairs and invite deception and infidelities for which they blame the cupidity of their often ill-chosen mistresses, rather than admit their own inconstancy. They are addicted to alcohol and to rich patrons, while showing unexpected flashes of malice, envy and cynical understanding. All are terrified of old age, prone to self-pity, obsessed by death, and apt to die young. They are in fact poets whose character is inferior to their talent and this, perhaps, is what keeps them out of the first rank with Horace, Catullus and Vergil, or the Greek tragedians.

They are *poètes maudits*, dandies ingrown into their pose, and if thus committed to the second rank, then their genius and their air of modernity, with perhaps that vein of stoicism which was never far from the surface in the ancient world, keep them very high in it. As long as people will wish to hear about love and the pleasures of the country, and while young lovers 'long to talk with some old lover's ghost', and while the old keep an ear for music and a warm corner for grace, then these boasters will retain exactly the immortality to which, living, they laid claim. We all know the charming lines that a late Victorian addressed to Mimnermus in Church; I do not know how familiar it is that Sainte-Beuve put Tibullus in a sacred position among writers and that his ideal of happiness was to read Tibullus with a young girl in the country. And there was another French critic—or was it the same one?—who remarked that 'every elegiac spirit is a scoundrel'.

When we come to the situation of the Latin elegiac poet a complication appears. The Greek elegiast formed part of an accepted tradition, his Roman successor had to borrow the metre, transpose it into Latin and make it popular; he had also to borrow Greek mythology and make that his own, and he had even to justify to Roman eyes the somewhat discreditable stance of the elegiac amorist. This inclined him to be self-conscious and to appear somewhat of a pedant, flattering Caesar or giving a mythology lesson when he should have remained in wistful wanton mood. Erudition, the literary vice which a rich culture imposes on its poor relations, mars all the Latin elegiasts, including, alas, Catullus. In fact the tragedy of Latin poetry is the onus of its debt to Greece; it is as if no English poetry could survive except that which derived from the French. I do not think we are enough aware of the super-human and exhausting effort which the Roman poets made to create a native poetry out of Greek idiom and mythology. Only two hundred years separate the extreme limits of good Latin poetry between the birth of Lucretius and the death of

Martial, while the golden age, the age of Catullus, Vergil, Horace, Tibullus, Propertius, Ovid, is compressed into one life-time between about 60 B.C., when Catullus was twenty-four, to Ovid's banishment in A.D. 8. In that time, especially in the ten years at the centre of it, all Greek culture was absorbed and regurgitated. The masterpieces of Latin poetry made their appearance—and the rot set in. The Latin ode almost vanishes with Horace; the magnificent tapestry of the Vergilian hexameter, the smooth narrative brilliance of Ovid's, the grace and *brio* and sadness of the elegiasts make their hail and farewell.

The appearance of Tibullus on this stage was of the briefest. He was an impoverished young squire whose life was largely passed in the little court of Messalla, a Roman nobleman whom he loyally followed on one military expedition; he died aged about thirty-five in 19 B.C., the same year as Vergil. He was of a gentle, lovable disposition, handsome and careful of his appearance. He certainly won the esteem and friendship of Ovid, and probably of Horace. He loved two women: the first called Delia (her real name was Plania) and who was apparently married, but unfaithful both to her husband and to him; and the second Nemesis, who was probably a courtesan. The secret of his appeal is that he was a quietist, like our own poet Collins. There is in him an exquisite taste, a sincerity, a freshness, which avoids the traps his successors fell into—one might compare him with Watteau as opposed to Pater or Lancret, with Propertius as Boucher, Ovid as Fragonard or Greuze, but such comparisons are waste of breath. Mackail dismisses him in a terrible sentence—'He stands easily at the head of Latin poets of the second order. In delicacy, in refinement, in grace of rhythm and diction, he cannot easily be surpassed; he only wants the final and incommunicable touch of genius which separates really great artists from the rest of the world.' His poetry has a strange gaiety, a colloquial simplicity, yet it is also melancholy and affecting. Those four lovely lines to Delia:

> *te spectem, suprema mihi cum venerit hora,*
> *te teneam moriens deficiente manu.*
> *flebis et arsuro positum me, Delia, lecto,*
> *tristibus et lacrimis oscula mixta dabis*

> May I behold you when my last hour comes, and dying, clutch you with my failing hand. You will weep, Delia, and when they lay me on my funeral pyre you will give me kisses mixed with tears

echoed round the ancient world (Ovid quotes a line in his memorial poem) like a stanza from Gray's elegy. But there was another side to Tibullus: a passion for the simple rites of the peasant's religion; for spring festivals and harvest-homes. In this way he is like our own Herrick and Marvell.

Propertius was born somewhere about 50 B.C. at Assisi; it is nice to think that he may have had some Etruscan blood. (He mentions their 'ruined hearths' with feeling.) He was destined for the Bar but deserted it for poetry. He was tall, pale, thin, delicate, vain of his appearance. Today we should perhaps call him a masochist, he boasted that his vice was to be perpetually in love. That was the whole pattern of his life, his only function, and he revelled in his terrible subservience to the body of his beautiful mistress. No other wars for him. The one deep passion of his life was for a courtesan called Cynthia. Her real name was Hestia; she was tall and fair, with long hands and a lovely walk.

> *fulva coma est, longaeque manus et maxima toto*
> *corpore . . .*

He constantly refers to her as *docta puella*, a learned girl, and tells how in a low voice she would recite his verses or dance, play and sing for him. She was violent in temper, jealous, revengeful, unforgiving, fond of money, unfaithful (though perhaps not more than he was), and died in great misery. They had several long quarrels and we are inevitably reminded of the relationship between Jeanne Duval and Baudelaire. Seen at this distance they appear as a lonely and ill-starred couple of life-long lovers and combatants, and yet for all their tale of shared death-beds, Cynthia was as far from Propertius as Delia from Tibullus when the end came. When he was a very young man Propertius published his first book, *Cynthia*; the first two lines are a revelation:

> *Cynthia prima suis miserum me cepit ocellis*
> *contactum nullis ante cupidinibus.*

Cynthia to my great undoing first ensnared me with her eyes— though no other passion had ever touched me.

His whole genius as a poet, his cast of mind as a lover, flowers in one marvellous poem:

> *Scribant de te alii, vel sis ignota licebit.*
>   *ludet, qui sterili semina ponit humo.*
> *omnia, crede mihi, tecum uno munera lecto*
>   *auferet extremi funeris atra dies.*
> *et tua transibit contemnens ossa viator,*
>   *nec dicet, cinis hic docta puella fuit.*

Let others write of you or let you be forgotten, let him praise you who will plant seeds in a sterile soil. Believe me every gift of yours is consumed on a narrow bed when the black day comes and the traveller who spurns your bones as he goes on his way will never cry 'this dust was once a learned girl'.

Propertius is quite unlike any other Roman author who has gone before. He is tempestuous, oriental as his master Meleager, and like his other master, Callimachus, often intolerably erudite and brilliant. He burst on the world at the age of twenty-one with a complete mastery of the Greek elegiac metre, and he gave to his Latin a glassy and metallic radiance that had never been seen before. The critics called it *Blanditia*, enchantment, and found it irresistible. Consider this ravishing and so Greek texture, drugged with lovely names, compact of learning and lubricity—it is the beginning of his third poem. This is Butler's translation:

> Like as the maid of Cnossus lay swooning on the desert strand whilst the bark of Thesus sped swiftly away, or as Andromeda, child of Cepheus, sank into her first sleep, freed at last from her hard couch of rock, or as the Thracian maenad, no less foredone by the unending dance, lies sunk in slumber on the grassy banks of Apidanus, even so, meseemed, did Cynthia breathe the spirit of gentle rest, her head propped on faltering hands, when I came dragging home my reeling feet, drunken with deep draughts of wine, and the slaves were shaking their dying torches in the gloom of night far-spent.

> *Qualis Thesea jacuit cedente carina*
>     *languida desertis Gnosia litoribus:*
> *qualis et accubuit primo Cepheia somno*
>     *libera jam duris cotibus Andromede:*
> *nec minus assiduis Edonis fessa choreis*
>     *qualis in herboso concidit Apidano:*
> *talis visa mihi mollem spirare quietem*
>     *Cynthia, non certis nixa caput manibus,*
> *ebria cum multo traherem vestigia Baccho,*
>     *et quaterent sera nocte facem pueri.*

The reading of this first book of Propertius is an outstanding literary experience. One is altogether enraptured by this strange gusty music, by the glimpses of Greek mythology, of drunken quarrels and heavenly reconciliations, of the moon gliding across the window over Cynthia's bed, of her basking among the sun-bathers on the beach at Baiae, of a group of week-end guests, wine-glass in hand watching the fast skiffs and slow barges drift under the woods along the Tiber, of Propertius battering in vain at the locked door of her whom he called his mother and sister, his only home and parent, while the little cold breeze of early dawn blows across him as he lies outside; a moment he will often recall with feeling. Among his loveliest lines are those which describe the pool of the nymphs where Hylas was sucked under.

> At last the children of Orithyia, Pandion's daughter, retired discomforted, and Hylas, alas! went upon his way, went to be the wood-nymphs' victim.

> Here beneath the peak of Arganthus' mount lay the well of Pege, the watery haunt so dear to Bithynia's nymphs, o'er which from lonely trees there hung dewy apples that owed naught to the hand of man, and round about in a water-meadow sprang snowy lilies mingled with purple poppies.

> *Iam Pandioniae cessit genus Orithyiae:*
> *a dolor! ibat Hylas, ibat Hamadryasin.*
> *hic erat Arganthi Pege sub vertice montis*
> *grata domus Nymphis umida Thyniasin,*
> *quam supra nullae pendebant debita curae*
> *roscida desertis poma sub arboribus*
> *et circum irriguo surgebant lilia prato*
> *candida purpureis mixta papaveribus.*

The remaining three books of Propertius, though stored with fine things, lack the magical impetus of the first.

His last poem, a magnificent ode of consolation to his friend Paullus, was put into the mouth of his wife who had just died and shows that Propertius was learning to feel and live for others—he had burst his bonds and thrown off his stifling neurotic obsession with lust and glory. In the poem the dead wife asks her husband to look after the children, to hide his grief from them, while they in turn must not mention her in front of their new stepmother, if he remarries, nor do anything which may upset his old age if he stays single. Enough for him must be the nights he wears out with his memories of her—*sat tibi sint noctes quas de me, Paulle, fatiges*—the dreams in which she seems to confront him again. And when he talks to her image, he must breathe every word as though to one *responsurae*, who 'was about to reply'.

On this query we leave him, on this doubt about human survival which was all that the Roman world permitted itself in the rare moments when it went beyond a flat negation. He himself died, probably of consumption, in 15 B.C., aged thirty-five, and prematurely grey, he tells us, and old. He left a splendid posterity—this antique Baudelaire—yet one cannot read him without a sense of despair, not on his personal account (he writes too well for that) but from the appalling gloom and emptiness of the late pagan world. What an intolerable ennui surrounded them when once they lost their religion, when the shining deities, Zeus and Apollo, Pan and Dionysos, Artemis and Athena, Orpheus and Hermes became empty symbols; how quickly youth passed, and how little consolation to those whose temperament was extravagant were the Stoic's grim courage or the Epicurean's frugal caution! Only the worship of the Emperor, the germ of totalitarianism, remained open to them, or the private religion of the Mistress, the sacred *egoisme à deux*, with its tears, sighs, scenes and ecstasies, its multiplication of deceit and its dread of old age. All poets who have made a trial of it have ultimately found sexual passion liberating as a means only, not as an end. *Sunt apud infernos tot milia formosarum.* 'So many thousands of beautiful girls have gone to the grave.' A great love is a great doom, an unconscious method of self-destruction and the foreboding, as of *Tristan* or *Pelléas*, which haunts the couplet is no accident.

> *Sic nobis, qui nunc magnum speramus amantes, forsitan includet crastina fata dies.*

\*            \*            \*

Propertius, for all his learning and passion, is condemned to the monotony of his own limited personality, a monotony which is precisely that expressed by the elegiac metre. He was a weary and precocious adolescent in a tired world—for I think it is beyond doubt that the unlimited indulgence in promiscuous sexual intercourse from the earliest age had a more deleterious effect on the constitution of the pagan body than wealth or luxury or wars, and thus assisted the insidious progress of oriental religions. The Romans of the Empire, through physical excesses, were stunting the growth of the spirit. A change had to come. There is a line from a poem long attributed to Tibullus which was scrawled on the plaster of a house in Pompeii as the molten pellets were raining down. I do not believe this referred to a mortal Delia any more than Valéry's

> *Tes pas, enfants de mon silence . . .*
> *Tu mihi curarum requies, tu nocte vel atra*
>   *lumen . . .*

> Thou art the repose of my troubles; even in night's darkness thou art my light.

1948.